LOEB CLASSICAL LIBRARY
FOUNDED BY JAMES LOEB 1911

EDITED BY
JEFFREY HENDERSON

FLORUS

LCL 231

FLORUS

EPITOME OF ROMAN HISTORY

WITH AN ENGLISH TRANSLATION BY

EDWARD SEYMOUR FORSTER

HARVARD UNIVERSITY PRESS
CAMBRIDGE, MASSACHUSETTS
LONDON, ENGLAND

First published (with Cornelius Nepos) 1929
This separate edition 1984

ISBN 978-0-674-99254-2

Printed on acid-free paper and bound by
The Maple-Vail Book Manufacturing Group

CONTENTS

INTRODUCTION

The Author

Remarkably little is known of the author of the *Epitome*; even his correct name is quite uncertain. Most recent editors give him the name of L. Annaeus Florus, which is found in the title of the work in the *Codex Palatinus* 894, rejecting the name Julius Florus, which occurs in the title of the *Codex Bambergensis*, on the grounds that the absence of any *praenomen* is suspicious and that the name Julius may well be due to a corruption.[1] It is not impossible, however, that none of the titles given in the MSS. are correct, and that the author of the *Epitome* is identical with the P. Annius Florus who was a poet and a friend of Hadrian (Spartianus, *Hadr.* 16) and author of the Dialogue *Vergilius orator an poeta*, part of the introduction of which has been preserved in a MS. at Brussels and is appended to the editions of Halm and Rossbach. He may have been a relative of Seneca, Lucan and Pomponius Mela. The Brussels fragment gives us some biographical detail about its author. He was born, we are told, in Africa and as a boy took part at Rome under Domitian in the Capitoline Competition, but was unsuccessful owing to favouritism; in disgust at

[1] See Rossbach in the Teubner text, pp. xliii.

his failure, he travelled abroad for a time, eventually settling down at Tarraco in Spain and adopting the profession of letters. He must subsequently have migrated to in Rome in the principate of Hadrian.

The *Epitome* itself contains no internal evidence about the life of its author except as to the date at which he composed the work. He states (I. Introd., 8) that a period of not much less than two hundred years had elapsed since Caesar Augustus (*a Caesare Augusto in saeculum nostrum haud multo minus anni ducenti*). It is difficult to decide how to interpret the words *a Caesare Augusto*. It would perhaps be most natural to take 27 B.C., the date of the foundation of the Principate, as the *floruit* of Augustus, in which case the composition of the *Epitome* would fall in the Principate of Marcus Aurelius. If, on the other hand, we may take the birth of Augustus in 63 B.C. as the beginning of the period of two hundred years, the date of the composition will fall in the second half of the Principate of Hadrian, a date which is consistent with the identification of the author as the literary friend of Hadrian.

The Work

The *Epitome* is an abridgment of Roman History with special reference to the wars waged by the Roman people from the foundation of the city down to the age of Augustus. In the MSS. it is described as an epitome of Livy, and no doubt owes much to that author, who is sometimes quoted *verbatim*, but Livy is by no means the only source, and Florus frequently makes statements which are at variance with those of Livy. The works of Sallust and

Caesar were certainly employed by the epitomist, and there are reminiscences of Vergil and Lucan. There is reason to suppose the *Histories* of the elder Seneca were also used as a source. It is probable that Florus imitated the division of the history of Rome into four ages—infancy, youth, manhood and old age—from this writer, who, according to Lactantius (*Inst. Div.* VII, 15, 4), employed this division.

The work was deliberately planned as a panegyric of the Roman people, and interprets events, wherever it is possible, in a sense favourable to the Romans. The author is strikingly free of any political bias, except that in the Civil War he appears to side with Julius Caesar rather than with Pompeius.

The Bamberg MS. adopts a division, which has been followed by most editors, into two books, the first dealing with the growth and establishment of the empire, and the second with its decline, the Gracchan age forming the line of division.

Though not ineffective as giving a general sketch of Roman History, the work is inaccurate in detail and full of inconsistencies and errors both chronological and geographical. The author possesses a certain literary gift, often, however, marred by a strong tendency to rhetoric, which, though occasionally felicitous, more frequently shows itself in fantastic exaggeration and empty bombast. The author's love of brevity too often leads to obscurity, and the constant insertion of exclamatory remarks and the poverty of vocabulary are irritating characteristics.

The *Epitome* once enjoyed—perhaps owing to its rhetorical character—a considerable popularity and

was widely used as a school-book as late as the end of the seventeenth century. The Elzevir Press alone published six editions between the years 1638 and 1674.

The Text

It is now generally recognized that the best MS. of Florus is the *Codex Bambergensis* E III 22 (*B*), which dates from the beginning of the ninth century. Its importance was first pointed out by Seebode in 1821, but Otto Jahn was the first editor to make full use of it in the Teubner edition of 1852. It has also been collated by Halm and Rossbach. It is written on parchment and contains also the *History* of Dares Phrygius and the *Breviarium* of Festus.

The *Codex Bambergensis* ends abruptly at *profundo,* ten words before the end of II, 33, and the preceding passage beginning at *recreatus,* twenty-six words before the end of II, 32, is written in rather darker ink by a later hand (B^1), which also added several omitted passages (I, Introduction 1, *Populus* to 3, *videantur;* II, 1, 1, *seditionum* to 2, *gentium;* II, 29, *sarmatae* to *pacem;* II, 30, 34, *tres legiones* to 36, *patronos;* II, 31, *Haec* to *victoria fuit*, and inserted the headings and lists of chapters, besides making minor corrections throughout the text. It seems certain that B^1 had the same original before him, adding passages where *B* had been unable to decipher the MS., and making corrections where *B* had erred; his readings, therefore, are to be regarded as worthy of every consideration. Another hand (B^2) made a smaller number of less

important corrections in the eleventh or twelfth century.

The *Codex Bambergensis* stands in a class by itself; the other existing MSS. belong to one family. The oldest of these is the *Codex Palatinus Latinus* 894 (*N*), formerly in the Library of the Monastery of St. Nazarius at Lorsch, and therefore often known as the Codex Nazarianus. It is written on parchment and dates from the end of the ninth century. It has corrections, no doubt taken from the same archetype, by the same hand that wrote the original, and by a later hand of the twelfth century which sometimes emends small errors but more often introduces corrupt readings. It has been collated by Jahn (in a somewhat summary manner), by Wölflinn and by Rossbach

The third MS. of first-rate importance is the *Codex Leidensis Vossianus* 14 (*L*), written on parchment in a fine hand of the eleventh century. It is closely related to *N*, but contains too many discrepancies to be derived directly from it.

Other MSS. of the same class are:—

The *Codex Palatinus Heidelbergensis* 1568 (*Palat.*) of the eleventh century;

The *Codex Harleianus* 2620 (*Harl.*), in the British Museum, of the thirteenth century;

The *Codex Monacensis* 6392 (*Monac.*) of the eleventh century;

The *Codex Parisinus* 5802 (*Paris.* 5802), which is known to have been used by Petrarch, and the *Codex Parisinus* 7701 (*Paris.* 7701), both of the twelfth century.

The *Codex Leidensis Vossianus* 77 (*Voss.*); and

The *Codex Vratislaviensis Rehdigeranus* R78 (*Rehd.*), of the fifteenth century but containing some excellent corrections.

Another important authority for the text of Florus is the work of the historian *Jordanes* (I), a Goth, who in the middle of the sixth century wrote a work entitled *De summa temporum vel origine actibusque gentis Romanorum,* in which he made extensive use of Florus; he copies him, with a few omissions and alterations, for the period down to the Macedonian wars (Florus, I, 1–28), and again for the Parthian war (I, 46), the war against Antony and Cleopatra (II, 21), and the wars of Augustus (II, 22–27). Although the MS. of Florus which Jordanes used was much older than *B,* it was closely allied to it and has many faults in common with it, and only occasionally provides a better reading. Jordanes is a somewhat uncertain guide: he himself confesses that he was *agrammaticus,* and he sometimes misunderstands his authorities; but where he confirms the reading of *B,* as he often does, his testimony is of great value. His work has been preserved in several MSS., of which the *Codex Heidelbergensis* and the *Codex Pollingensis* are the most important.

For the text of the present edition *B* is taken as the basis, and the *apparatus criticus* aims at giving the authority, whether of an MS. or of an editor, for any important variations from the readings of *B* which have been inserted in the text. In order not to overburden the *apparatus criticus,* where the reading of *B* has been adopted, none of the variants which may be presented by the other MSS. are

usually mentioned, and small corrections of orthography have not been noted. Readers who require a complete *apparatus criticus* should consult the edition of Rossbach.

Bibliography

The following are the principal editions of Florus:—

Editio Princeps, without date or place (Paris, *circa* 1470).

Addus: Venice, 1521.
E. Vinetus: Poitiers, 1554.
C. Salmasius: Heidelberg, 1609.
J. Freinsheim: Strassburg, 1632.
J. G. Graevius: Utrecht, 1680.
C. A. Duker: Leyden, 1722.
G. Seebode: Leipzig, 1821.
O. Jahn: Leipzig, 1852.
C. Halm: Leipzig, 1854.
O. Rossbach: Leipzig, 1896.

Florus has been translated into English by J. Davies (1670; a version which was re-issued in 1672 with corrections by Casaubon), and by J. S. Watson in Bohn's Classical Library.

I wish to express my warmest thanks to my colleague, Professor W. C. Summers, Firth Professor of Latin in the University of Sheffield, who kindly read through the translation in MS. His suggestions have enabled me to make improvements on practically every page of the book.

Edw. S. Forster.

BIBLIOGRAPHICAL ADDENDUM (1984)

Editions

E. Malcovati, Rome 1938, 1972[2]

Budé: *Oeuvres*, P. Jal, Paris 1967

Utet: *Epitome e frammenti*, J. G. Deangeli, Turin 1969

See also the Loeb *Minor Latin Poets* (1934) 421–435 (volume two of new edition)

Studies

S. Lilledahl, *Florusstudien*, Lund 1928

E. Malcovati, 'Studi su Floro,' *Athenaeum* 15 (1937) 69ff, 289ff; 16 (1938) 46ff

P. Jal, 'Nature et signification politique de l'ouvrage de Florus,' *REL* 43 (1965) 358–383

L. Bessone, 'Di alcuni errori di Floro,' *RFIC* 106 (1978) 421–431

L. Bessone, 'Ideologia e datazione dell'Epitome di Floro,' *GFF* 2 (1979) 33–57

Lexicon

M. L. Fele, Hildersheim 1975

M. L. Fele, 'Additamenta' (poetical fragments), *AFMC* II (1977–8) 87–142

LUCIUS ANNAEUS FLORUS

L. ANNAEI FLORI

EPITOMAE DE TITO LIVIO BELLORVM OMNIVM ANNORVM DCC LIBRI II

Capita Libri I[1]

[1] Epithoma Iuli Flori de Tito Liuio · bellorum omnium · annorum septingentorum · libri · N · duo · feliciter *B*: L · Annei · Flori · epitoma de Tito Liuio · incipit liber primus · lege feliciter *N*: Incjpit liber primus epitomarum Annei Flori · detitoliuio *L*.

LUCIUS ANNAEUS FLORUS

THE TWO BOOKS OF THE EPITOME, EXTRACTED FROM TITUS LIVIUS, OF ALL THE WARS OF SEVEN HUNDRED YEARS

The Chapters of Book I

I. A Romvlo Tempora Regvm Septem

Populus Romanus a rege Romulo in Caesarem Augustum septingentos per annos tantum operum pace belloque gessit, ut, si quis magnitudinem imperii cum annis conferat, aetatem ultra putet.
2 Ita late per orbem terrarum arma circumtulit, ut qui res illius legunt non unius populi, sed generis humani facta condiscant. Tot in laboribus periculisque iactatus est, ut ad constituendum eius im-

I. The Period of the Seven Kings, beginning with Romulus

The Roman people during the seven hundred years, from the time of King Romulus down to that of Caesar Augustus, achieved so much in peace and war that, if a man were to compare the greatness of their empire with its years, he would consider its size as out of all proportion to its age. So widely have they extended their arms throughout the world, that those who read of their exploits are learning the history, not of a single people, but of the human race. By so many toils and dangers

perium contendisse Virtus et Fortuna videantur.
3 Qua re cum, si quid aliud, hoc quoque operae pretium sit cognoscere, tamen quia ipsa sibi obstat magnitudo rerumque diversitas aciem intentionis abrumpit, faciam quod solent, qui terrarum situs pingunt: in brevi quasi tabella totam eius imaginem amplectar, non nihil, ut spero, ad admirationem principis populi conlaturus, si pariter atque insemel universam magnitudinem eius ostendero.

4 Si quis ergo populum Romanum quasi unum hominem consideret totamque eius aetatem percenseat, ut coeperit utque adoleverit, ut quasi ad quandam iuventae frugem pervenerit, ut postea velut consenuerit, quattuor gradus processusque
5 eius inveniet. Prima aetas[1] sub regibus fuit prope per annos quadringentos, quibus circum urbem ipsam cum finitimis luctatus est. Haec erit eius infantia.
6 Sequens a Bruto Collatinoque consulibus in Appium Claudium Quintum Fulvium consules centum quinquaginta annis patet, quibus Italiam subegit. Hoc fuit tempus viris armis incitatissimum, ideoque
7 quis adulescentiam dixerit. Deinceps ad Caesarem Augustum centum et quinquaginta anni, quibus totum orbem pacavit. Hic iam ipsa iuventus imperii
8 et quasi robusta maturitas. A Caesare Augusto in

[1] gradus—aetas *NL*: quattuor gradibus romae aetas *B*.

---

[1] *i.e.* as geographers represent the world in a map.

[2] This number is clearly wrong, since Brutus and Collatinus were Consuls in 509 B.C., Appius Claudius and Quintus Fulvius in 212 B.C.

have they been buffeted that Valour and Fortune seem to have competed to establish the Roman empire. So, as the history of Rome is especially worthy of study, yet because the very vastness of the subject is a hindrance to the knowledge of it, and the diversity of its topics distracts the keenness of the attention, I intend to follow the example of those who describe the geography of the earth, and include a complete representation of my subject as it were in a small picture.[1] I shall thus, I hope, contribute something to the admiration in which this illustrious people is held by displaying their greatness all at once in a single view.

If anyone were to contemplate the Roman people as he would a single individual and review its whole life, how it began, how it grew up, how it arrived at what may be called the maturity of its manhood, and how it subsequently as it were reached old age, he will find that it went through four stages of progress. The first period, when it was under the rule of kings, lasted for nearly four hundred years, during which it struggled against its neighbours in the immediate vicinity of the capital. This period will be its infancy. Its next period extends from the consulship of Brutus and Collatinus to that of Appius Claudius and Quintus Fulvius, a space of one hundred and fifty years,[2] during which the Roman people subjugated Italy. It was an age of extreme activities for its soldiers and their arms, and may therefore be called its youth. The next period is the hundred and fifty years down to the time of Augustus Caesar, during which it spread peace throughout the world. This was the manhood and, as it were, the robust maturity of the empire. From the time of Caesar

saeculum nostrum haud multo minus anni ducenti, quibus inertia Caesarum quasi consenuit atque decoxit, nisi quod sub Traiano principe movit lacertos et praeter spem omnium senectus imperii quasi reddita iuventute reviruit.

1 Primus ille et urbis et imperii conditor Romulus
2 fuit, Marte genitus et Rhea Silvia. Hoc de se
sacerdos gravida confessa est, nec mox fama dubi-
tavit, cum Amulli regis imperio iactatus in pro-
fluentem cum Remo fratre non potuit extingui.
3 Si quidem et Tiberinus amnem repressit, et relictis
catulis lupa secuta vagitum uber admovit infantibus
matremque egit. Sic repertos apud arborem Fau-
stulus regii gregis pastor tulit in casam atque
4 educavit. Alba tum erat Latio caput, Iuli opus;
nam Lavinium patris Aeneae contempserat. Ab his
Amullius iam septima subole regnabat, fratre pulso
5 Numitore, cuius ex filia Romulus. Igitur statim
prima iuventutis face patruum ab arce deturbat,
avum reponit. Ipse fluminis amator et montium,
apud quos erat educatus, moenia novae urbis agi-
6 tabat. Gemini erant; uter auspicaretur et regeret,

[1] See Introduction, p. x.

Augustus down to our own age there has been a period of not much less than two hundred years,[1] during which, owing to the inactivity of the emperors, the Roman people, as it were, grew old and lost its potency, save that under the rule of Trajan it again stirred its arms and, contrary to general expectation, again renewed its vigour with youth as it were restored.

1. The first founder both of the city and of the empire was Romulus, the son of Mars and Rhea Silvia. That Mars was his father the priestess confessed when she was pregnant, and presently common report no longer doubted it when, by order of King Amulius, Romulus was thrown with his brother Remus into the river: but his life could not be destroyed; for not only did the Tiber stay its stream, but a she-wolf left her young to follow the infants' cries, offered them her udder and played the part of mother to them. Finding them in these circumstances under a tree, Faustulus, the shepherd of the royal flock, took them to his cottage and brought them up. Alba was at that time the chief city of Latium, having been built by Iulus; for he had disdained Lavinium, the city of his father Aeneas. Amulius, of the seventh generation from Aeneas and Iulus, was reigning, having driven out his brother Numitor, whose daughter was mother of Romulus. Romulus, therefore, in the first ardour of youth, expelled his uncle from the citadel and restored his grandfather. He himself, being a lover of the river and mountains amongst which he had been brought up, conceived the idea of building a new city. As he and Remus were twins, they resolved to call in the help of the gods to decide which of them should

adhibere placuit deos. Remus montem Aventinum,
hic Palatinum occupat. Prius ille sex vulturios,
7 hic postea, sed duodecim videt. Sic victor augurio
urbem excitat, plenus spei bellatricem fore; id
8 adsuetae sanguine et praeda aves pollicebantur. Ad
tutelam novae urbis sufficere vallum videbatur, cuius
dum angustias Remus increpat saltu, dubium[1] an
iussu fratris, occisus est: prima certe victima fuit
munitionemque urbis novae sanguine suo consecravit.

Imaginem urbis magis quam urbem fecerat; in-
9 colae deerant. Erat in proximo lucus; hunc asylum
facit, et statim mira vis hominum; Latini Tuscique
pastores, quidam etiam transmarini, Phryges qui sub
Aenea, Arcades qui sub Evandro duce influxerant.
ita ex variis quasi elementis congregavit corpus
10 unum, populumque Romanum ipse fecit rex.[2] Erat
unius aetatis populus virorum. Itaque matrimonia
a finitimis petita, quia non inpetrabantur, manu
capta sunt. Simulatis quippe ludis equestribus virgines, quae ad spectaculum venerant, praedae fuere:
et haec statim causa bellorum. Pulsi fugatique
11 Veientes. Caeninensium captum ac direptum est

[1] increpat saltu dubium *NL*: increpat saltu transiluit dubium *B*.

[2] rex *Iordanis cod. Rehd.* : res *BINL*.

inaugurate the city and rule there. Remus took his stand on the Aventine, Romulus on the Palatine hill. Remus first observed six vultures, Romulus was after him in time but saw twelve. Being thus victorious in augury, he began to build the city, full of hope that it would prove warlike; for the birds, accustomed to blood and prey, seemed to indicate this. It was thought that a rampart was enough for the protection of the new city. In derision of its small size Remus leaped over it and was put to death for doing so, whether by his brother's order or not is uncertain; at any rate he was the first victim and hallowed the fortification of the new city with his blood.

Romulus had brought into being the idea of a city rather than an actual city; for inhabitants were lacking. There was in the neighbourhood a grove, and this he made a place of refuge; and immediately an extraordinary number of men flocked thither—Latin and Tuscan shepherds, and even men from across the sea, Phrygians who had entered the country under Aeneas, and Arcadians who had come with Evander. Thus he gathered together a single body consisting of various ingredients and, as king, himself created the Roman people. But a population consisting solely of men could only last for a single lifetime; wives were, therefore, demanded from the neighbouring peoples and, when they were refused, were seized by force. For, a pretence being made of holding horse-races, the maidens who had come to look on were carried off. This immediately gave rise to wars. The Veientines were defeated and put to flight; the city of Caenina was captured and plundered. Moreover, Romulus with his own

oppidum. Spolia insuper opima de rege Agrone
12 Feretrio Iovi manibus suis rex reportavit. Sabinis
proditae portae per virginem Tarpeiam. Haec do-
lose [1] pretium rei quae gerebant in sinistris peti-
verat, dubium clipeos an armillas; illi, ut et fidem
13 solverent et ulciscerentur, clipeis obruere. Ita
admissis intra moenia hostibus, atrox in ipso foro
pugna, adeo ut Romulus Iovem oraret, foedam
suorum fugam sisteret; hinc templum et Stator
14 Iuppiter. Tandem furentibus intervenere raptae
laceris comis. Sic pax facta cum Tatio foedusque
percussum, secutaque res mira dictu, ut relictis
sedibus suis novam in urbem hostes demigrarent
et cum generis suis avitas opes pro dote sociarent.
15 Auctis brevi viribus, hunc rex sapientissimus statum
rei publicae inposuit: iuventus divisa per tribus in
equis et armis ad subita belli excubaret, consilium
rei publicae penes senes esset, qui ex auctoritate
16 patres, ob aetatem senatus vocabantur.[2] His ita
ordinatis repente, cum contionem haberet ante
urbem aput Caprae paludem, e conspectu ablatus
17 est. Discerptum aliqui a senatu putant ob asperius

[1] haec dolose *Rossbachius*: non dolo sed puella *B I*: nec dolos sed puella *N*.
[2] vocabantur: vocabatur *B I*.

---

[1] Jupiter as the "Striker" of his enemies.
[2] The King of the Sabines.
[3] *i.e.* men between the ages of twenty and forty.
[4] *Senatus* from *senes*, "old men."

hands bore to Jupiter Feretrius[1] the "spoils of honour" won from their king Agron. To the Sabines the gates of Rome were betrayed by the maiden Tarpeia. She had craftily demanded as the reward of her act the objects which they carried on their left arms—it is doubtful whether the words meant their shields or their bracelets; they, in order both to fulfil their promise and to take vengeance upon her, overwhelmed her with their shields. The enemy having been thus admitted within the walls, so fierce a battle took place in the very forum that Romulus prayed to Jupiter to stay the disgraceful flight of his men; in commemoration of this a temple was erected and Jupiter received the title of "the Stayer of flight." At last the women who had been carried off, with their hairs dishevelled, interposed between the furious combatants. Thus peace was made and a treaty concluded with Tatius[2]; and a wonderful event followed, namely, that the enemy left their homes and migrated to the new city and, by way of dowering their daughters, shared their ancestral wealth with their sons-in-law. Their strength rapidly growing, the king very wisely imposed the following new organization upon the State: the young men[3] were divided into tribes and were to keep watch with arms and horses against any unexpected attack, while the policy of the State was to be in the hands of the old men, who were called "fathers" from the authority which they exercised, and from their age "the senate."[4] After making these arrangements, Romulus was suddenly borne away from human sight while he was holding an assembly near the lake of the She-goat. Some think he was torn to pieces by the Senate because

ingenium; sed oborta tempestas solisque defectio
18 consecrationis speciem praebuere. Cui mox Iulius
Proculus fidem fecit, visum a se Romulum adfirmans
augustiore forma quam fuisset; mandare praeterea
ut se pro numine acciperent; Quirinum in caelo
vocari; placitum dis ut gentium Roma poteretur.

2 Succedit Romulo Numa Pompilius, quem Curibus
Sabinis agentem ultro petiverunt ob inclitam viri
2 religionem. Ille sacra et caerimonias omnemque
cultum deorum inmortalium docuit, ille pontifices,
augures, Salios ceteraque sacerdotia, annumque in
3 duodecim menses, fastos dies nefastosque discripsit,[1]
ille ancilia atque Palladium, secreta quaedam im-
perii pignora, Ianumque geminum, fidem pacis ac
belli, in primis focum Vestae virginibus colendum
dedit, ut ad simulacrum caelestium siderum custos
imperii flamma vigilaret: haec omnia quasi monitu
4 deae Egeriae, quo magis barbari acciperent. Eo
denique ferocem populum redegit, ut, quod vi et
iniuria occuparat imperium, religione atque iustitia
gubernaret.

3 Excipit Pompilium Numam Tullus Hostilius, cui

[1] discripsit *NI*: descripsit *BL*.

---

[1] Priests of Mars.

[2] The sacred shields were said to have fallen from heaven, and were in the charge of the Salii in the Temple of Mars; the Palladium, an image of Pallas (Minerva), was reputed to have been saved at the sack of Troy.

of his excessive harshness; but a storm which arose and an eclipse of the sun created the impression that he had been deified. This belief was strengthened when Julius Proculus declared that Romulus had appeared to him in a form more majestic than he had possessed in his lifetime, and also commanded that they should regard him as a deity, and declared that his name in heaven was Quirinus, and that it was the will of the gods that Rome should rule over the world.

2. The successor of Romulus was Numa Pompilius, whom, while he was living at Cures in the territory of the Sabines, the Romans of their own accord invited to become king owing to the fame of his piety. He instructed them in sacred rites and ceremonies and all the worship of the immortal gods; he established pontiffs, augurs, the Salii,[1] and the other priesthoods; he divided the year into twelve months and appointed the days upon which the courts could and could not meet; he gave them the sacred shields and the Palladium,[2] the mystic tokens of empire, and the double-faced Janus, the symbol of peace and war; above all he handed over the care of the hearth of Vesta to the Vestal Virgins, that the flame, imitating the heavenly stars, might keep guardian watch over the empire. All these arrangements he attributed to the advice of the goddess Egeria, so that his barbarous subjects might accept them with greater willingness. In a word, he induced a fierce people to rule with piety and justice an empire which they had acquired by violence and injustice.

3. Numa Pompilius was succeeded by Tullus Hostilius, to whom the kingship was voluntarily

in honorem virtutis regnum ultro datum. Hic omnem militarem disciplinam artemque bellandi
2 condidit. Itaque mirum in modum exercitata[1] iuventute provocare ausus Albanos, gravem et diu
3 principem populum. Sed cum pari robore frequentibus proeliis utrique comminuerentur, misso in compendium bello, Horatiis Curiatiisque, trigeminis hinc atque inde fratribus, utriusque populi fata
4 permissa sunt. Anceps et pulchra contentio exituque ipso mirabilis. Tribus quippe illinc volneratis, hinc duobus occisis, qui supererat Horatius addito ad virtutem dolo, ut distraheret hostem, simulat fugam singulosque, prout sequi poterant, adortus exuperat.
5 Sic—rarum alias decus—unius manu parta victoria est, quam ille mox parricidio foedavit. Flentem spolia circa se sponsi quidem, sed hostis, sororem viderat. Hunc tam inmaturum amorem virginis
6 ultus est ferro. Citavere leges nefas, sed abstulit virtus parricidium,[2] et facinus infra gloriam fuit.

Nec diu in fide[3] Albanus. Nam Fidenate bello missi[4] in auxilium ex foedere medii inter duos
7 expectavere fortunam. Sed rex callidus ubi inclinare socios ad hostem videt, tollit animos, quasi man-

[1] exercitata *Iordanis cod. Emmeranus* : exercitate *B*: exercita *N*.

[2] parricidium *Iordanis cod. Emmeranus*: parricidam *B I N L*.

[3] nec diu in fide *L I* : nec desit deinde *B*.

[4] missi *L* : misit *B N I*.

offered out of respect for his worth. It was he who founded all military discipline and the art of warfare. So when he had wondrously trained the soldiers of Rome, he ventured to challenge the Albans, an important and for a long time a leading people. But when both sides, possessed of equal strength, were becoming weakened by frequent battles, the fortunes of the two peoples were entrusted, as a method of shortening the war, to the Horatii and Curiatii, triplets of brothers on either side. It was a well-contested and noble struggle and remarkable in the manner of its end. For when three had been wounded on one side and two killed on the other, the surviving Horatius, adding craft to valour, pretended flight in order to separate his adversaries, and attacking them singly, in the order in which they were able to follow him, overcame them. In this way (an honour rarely won on any other occasion) victory was achieved by one man's hand—a hand which he soon afterwards sullied by murder. He had noticed his sister weeping because he wore the spoils of one who, though he was her betrothed, was her country's foe. The maiden's girlish affection he punished with the sword. Justice arraigned the crime, but his valour saved him from the penalty for murder, and his guilt was accounted less than the glory which he had won.

The Alban people were not long true to their allegiance. For in the war against Fidenae the contingent sent according to the treaty remained neutral and waited to see what fortune would bring. But the crafty king, when he saw that his allies were inclined to join the enemy, raised the spirit of his men by giving out that they did so by

dasset: spes inde nostris, metus hostibus. Sic fraus
8 proditorum irrita fuit. Itaque hoste victo ruptorem
foederis Mettum Fufetium religatum inter duos
currus pernicibus equis distrahit, Albamque ipsam
9 quamvis parentem, aemulam tamen diruit, cum
prius omnes opes urbis ipsumque populum Romam
transtulisset; prorsus ut consanguinea civitas non
perisse, sed in suum corpus redisse rursus videretur.

4 Ancus deinde Marcius, nepos Pompilii ex filia,
2 pari avo[1] ingenio. Igitur et muro moenia amplexus
est, et interfluentem urbi Tiberinum ponte commisit,
Ostiamque in ipso maris fluminisque confinio
coloniam posuit; iam tum videlicet praesagiens
animo futurum ut totius mundi opes et commeatus
illo velut maritimo urbis hospitio reciperentur.

5 Tarquinius postea Priscus, quamvis transmarinae
originis, regnum ultro petens[2] accepit ob industriam
atque elegantiam; quippe qui oriundus Corintho
2 Graecum ingenium Italicis artibus miscuisset. Hic
et senatus maiestatem numero ampliavit, et centuriis
tribus auxit equites[3] quatenus Attius Naevius
numerum augeri[4] prohibebat, vir summus augurio.
3 Quem rex in experimentum rogavit, fierine posset,

[1] pari avo *F. E. Koehlerus*: pravo *N*: raro *B*.
[2] petens: potens *B*.
[3] equites *add. Iahnius*.
[4] augeri *L I*: augure *B*.

---

[1] From Liv. I. 36, 2 (cp. Cic. *de rep.* 2, 36), it is clear that Tarquinius had wished to add three new centuries, but, owing to Attius' opposition, had to be content with doubling the number of knights in each century (cp. Mommsen, *Staatsrecht*, III. p. 107[3]). *Centuriis* must, therefore, be a dative, or else we must read ⟨*in*⟩*centuriis* with Sauppe.

his orders; this aroused hope in the minds of our soldiers and fear in those of the enemy. Thus the deceit of the traitors proved fruitless. So after the defeat of the enemy Tullus bound Mettus Fufetius, the violator of the treaty, between two chariots, and tore him asunder with swift horses. The city of Alba itself, the parent of Rome but also its rival, he destroyed, after first transferring all its wealth and the inhabitants themselves to Rome, in order that thus a kindred State might seem not to have perished but to have been reunited to the body to which it belonged.

4. The next king was Ancus Marcius, a grandson of Pompilius through his daughter, a man of a disposition like that of his grandfather. He both surrounded the city with a wall and built a bridge over the Tiber which flows through it. He also planted a colony at Ostia where the sea and river join, even then evidently foreseeing that it would form as it were the maritime store-house of the capital and would receive the wealth and supplies of the whole world.

5. After him Tarquinius Priscus, though sprung from a country across the seas, petitioned for the kingdom on his own account, and obtained it because of his industry and refinement; for, having been born at Corinth, he had combined the intellect of a Greek with the qualities of an Italian. He augmented the dignity of the senate by raising its numbers and increased the number of knights in the three centuries, since Attius Naevius, a man much skilled in augury, forbade the number of centuries to be increased.[1] By way of testing this man, the king asked him whether what he had

4 quod ipse mente conceperat. Ille rem expertus
augurio, posse respondit. "Atqui hoc" inquit "agitaram, an[1] cotem illam secare novacula possem";[2]
5 et augur "potes ergo," inquit, et secuit. Inde
Romanis sacer auguratus. Neque pace Tarquinius
quam bello promptior; duodecim namque Tusciae
6 populos frequentibus armis subegit. Inde fasces,
trabeae, curules, anuli, phalerae, paludamenta,
praetextae, inde quod aureo curru, quattuor equis
triumphatur, togae pictae tunicaeque palmatae,
omnia denique decora et insignia, quibus imperii
dignitas eminet,[3] sumpta sunt.

6 Servius Tullius deinceps gubernacula urbis invadit, nec obscuritas inhibuit quamvis matre serva
creatum. Nam eximiam indolem uxor Tarquinii
Tanaquil liberaliter educaverat, et clarum fore visa
2 circa caput flamma promiserat. Ergo inter Tarquinii mortem adnitente regina substitutus in locum
regis quasi in tempus, regnum dolo partum sic
3 egit industrie, ut iure adeptus videretur. Ab hoc
populus Romanus relatus in censum, digestus in
classes, decuriis atque collegiis distributus, summaque regis sollertia ita est ordinata res publica,
ut omnia patrimonii, dignitatis,[4] aetatis, artium

[1] an *om.* *BI.* [2] possem: posse *BI.*
[3] ea *ante* sumpta *add.* *B*: *del.* *Iahnius.*
[4] dignitatis: dignitas *B.*

conceived in his mind was possible of execution. He made trial by augury and replied that it was possible. "Well, but that I had thought of," replied the king, "was this, whether I could cut this whetstone with a razor." To which the augur replied, "Then you can do it"; and the king cut it. Hence augury became a sacred practice among the Romans. Tarquinius was quite as able in war as in peace; for he subdued the twelve peoples of Etruria by frequent attacks. It was from them that were derived the fasces, robes of State, official chairs, rings, horse-trappings, military cloaks, purple-bordered togas, the practice of riding in triumph in a gilded car drawn by four horses, embroidered robes and tunics adorned with palms—in fact all the ornaments and insignia which serve to emphasize the dignity of office.

6. Servius Tullius next entered upon the government of the city, nor was the obscurity of his birth (for his mother was a slave) any hindrance to his advancement. For Tanaquil, the wife of Tarquinius, had trained his extraordinary abilities by a liberal education, and had foretold his future distinction from a flame which was seen playing round his head. And so, through the efforts made by the queen when Tarquinius was on his death-bed, he was put in the king's place on the pretence of a temporary measure, and filled the position, thus obtained by craft, with so much diligence that he seemed to have acquired it by right. It was by him that the Roman people were entered on a census-roll and arranged in classes, being distributed into divisions and corporations, and by the king's extraordinary skill the State was so organized that all distinctions of inheritance, dignity, age, employ-

officiorumque discrimina in tabulas referrentur, ac sic[1] maxima civitas minimae domus diligentia contineretur.

7 Postremus fuit omnium regum Tarquinius, cui
2 cognomen Superbo ex moribus datum. Hic regnum avitum, quod a Servio tenebatur, rapere maluit quam expectare, missisque in eum percussoribus scelere partam potestatem non melius egit quam
3 adquisiverat. Nec abhorrebat moribus uxor Tullia, quae, ut virum regem salutaret, supra cruentum patrem vecta carpento consternatos equos exegit.
4 Sed ipse in senatum caedibus, in plebem verberibus, in omnis superbia, quae crudelitate gravior est bonis, grassatus, cum saevitiam domi fatigasset, tan-
5 dem in hostes conversus est. Sic valida Latio oppida capta sunt, Ardea, Ocricolum, Gabii,[2] Suessa
6 Pometia. Tum quoque cruentus in suos. Neque enim filium verberare dubitavit, ut simulanti trans-
7 fugam apud hostis hinc fides esset. Cui Gabiis, ut voluerat, recepto et per nuntios consulenti, quid fieri vellet, eminentia forte papaverum capita virgula excutiens, cum per hoc interficiendos esse principes vellet intellegi, quasi[3] superbia sileret,[4] respondit tamen. De manubiis captarum urbium
8 templum erexit. Quod cum inauguraretur, ceden-

[1] sic: si *B*.
[2] Gabii *N*: gravii *B*.
[3] quasi *Titzius*: qua *B I*: quae *N L*.
[4] sileret *Hauptius*: sic *codd.*

ment and office were committed to registers, and thus a great State was ruled with the exactitude of a small household.

7. The last of all the kings was that Tarquinius to whom the name of Superbus was given on account of his character. He preferred to seize rather than to wait for the kingdom of his grandfather which was held by Servius, and, having sent assassins to murder him, administered the power thus won by crime no more righteously than he had acquired it. His wife Tullia was of like character, and, driving in her chariot to hail her husband as king, forced her affrighted horses over the bloodstained corpse of her father. Tarquinius himself struck at the senate with executions, at the plebs by scourging them, at all by his pride, which good men think more oppressive than cruelty. When he had exhausted his brutality at home, he at last turned his attention to his enemies. Thus the powerful cities in Latium were captured, Ardea, Ocricolum, Gabii, Suessa Pometia. At the same time he was bloodthirsty towards his own family; for he did not hesitate to scourge his son, in order that, by pretending to be a deserter, he might inspire the confidence of the enemy. When his son had been welcomed at Gabii, as he had intended, and consulted him by messengers as to what action he wished to be taken, he replied, it is true, but in such a way as to give the impression that his pride forbade him to speak, by knocking off with his staff the heads of some of the poppies which happened to be taller than the rest, thus signifying that the leading men were to be put to death. He erected from the spoils of the captured cities a temple, at the consecra-

tibus ceteris dis mira res dicitur extitisse: restitere
9 Iuventas et Terminus. Placuit vatibus contumacia[1] numinum, si quidem firma omnia et aeterna pollicebantur. Sed illud horrentius, quod molientibus[2] aedem in fundamentis humanum repertum est caput, nec dubitavere cuncti monstrum pulcherrimum imperii sedem caputque terrarum promit-
10 tere. Tam diu superbiam regis populus Romanus perpessus est, donec aberat[3] libido; hanc ex liberis
11 eius inportunitatem tolerare non potuit. Quorum cum alter ornatissimae feminae Lucretiae stuprum intulisset, matrona dedecus ferro expiavit, imperium regibus abrogatum.

II. Anaceφalaeosis de Septem Regibvs

8 Haec est prima aetas populi Romani et quasi infantia, quam habuit sub regibus septem, quadam fatorum industria tam variis ingenio, ut rei publicae
2 ratio et utilitas postulabat. Nam quid Romulo ardentius? tali opus fuit, ut invaderet regnum.
3 Quid Numa religiosius? Ita res poposcit, ut ferox
4 populus deorum metu mitigaretur. Quid? ille

[1] contumacia: contumatiam *B*.
[2] molientibus: moventibus *B*.
[3] aberat: aderat *B*.

tion of which the marvel is said to have occurred that, while the other gods permitted its erection,[1] Juventas and Terminus refused to give way. The obstinacy of these deities pleased the seers, since they gave promise that the whole building would be strong and eternal. A more alarming incident was the discovery of a human head in the foundations when they were building the temple; but no one doubted that it was a most favourable omen, portending that here would be the seat of an empire and the capital of the world. The Roman people tolerated the king's pride as long as it was not accompanied by unlawful passion; but outrage of this kind on the part of his sons they could not endure, and when, after one of them had offered violence to Lucretia, a woman of the highest rank, she atoned for her dishonour by stabbing herself, the rule of the king was abolished for ever.

II. Recapitulation of the Rule of the Seven Kings

8. The period of its rule under the Seven Kings forms the first age and, as it were, the infancy of the Roman people. These kings, by a dispensation of fate, possessed just such a variety of qualities as the circumstances and advantage of the State demanded. For where could greater boldness be found than in Romulus? Such a man was needed to seize the kingship. Who was more pious than Numa? Circumstances demanded such a man in order that the temper of a barbarous people might be tamed by the fear of the gods. Again, how

[1] cp. Liv. i, 55, *cum omnium sacellorum exaugurationes admitterent aves, in Termini fano non addixere.*

militiae artifex Tullus bellatoribus viris quam necessarius, ut acueret ratione virtutem. Quid? aedificator Ancus, ut urbem colonia[1] extenderet, ponte
5 iungeret, muro tueretur. Iam vero ornamenta Tarquinii et insignia quantam principi populo addide-
6 runt ex ipso habitu dignitatem. Actus a Servio census quid effecit, nisi ut ipsa se nosset Romana
7 res publica? Postremo Superbi illius inportuna dominatio non nihil, immo vel plurimum profuit. Sic enim effectum est, ut agitatus iniuriis populus cupiditate libertatis incenderetur.[2]

III. De Mvtatione Rei Pvblicae

9 Igitur Bruto Collatinoque ducibus et auctoribus, quibus ultionem sui moriens matrona mandaverat, populus Romanus ad vindicandum libertatis ac pudicitiae decus quodam quasi instinctu deorum concitatus regem repente destituit, bona diripit, agrum Marti suo consecrat, imperium in eosdem libertatis suae vindices transfert, mutato tamen et
2 iure et nomine. Quippe ex perpetuo annuum[3] placuit, ex singulari duplex, ne potestas solitudine vel mora corrumperetur, consulesque appellavit pro

[1] colonia: coloniam *B*.
[2] incenderetur: incendetur *B*.
[3] annuum *LI*: annum *B*.

---

[1] Ostia. [2] Lucretia.
[3] Brutus and Collatinus.

necessary to a nation of warriors was Tullus, the creator of the army, that he might temper their valour by discipline! Again, how necessary was Ancus, the builder, to give the city a colony [1] to expand it, a bridge to unite it, and a wall to protect it! Further, how much did the ornaments and insignia of Tarquinius add to the dignity of a sovereign people in its very dress! What was the effect of the census carried out by Servius but that the Roman State should be made aware of its own strength? Finally, the outrageous tyranny of Tarquinius Superbus was of some, nay, of great service; for its result was that the people, exasperated by the wrongs which he inflicted upon them, were fired with a desire for liberty.

III. On the Change of Government

9. And so under the leadership and guidance of Brutus and Collatinus, to whom the dying matron [2] had entrusted the avenging of her wrong, the Roman people, as though urged by an impulse from heaven to assert the honour of insulted liberty and chastity, suddenly deposed the king, plundered his possessions, dedicated his lands to their god Mars, and transferred the rule to these same champions of their freedom,[3] with a change, however, both of powers and title. For it was resolved that it should be an annual instead of a perpetual office, and that it should be exercised by two instead of by one, lest any abuse of power should arise through its possession by a single person or for a long period of time; and these men they called consuls instead of kings, in order that they might be mindful that they

regibus, ut consulere civibus suis se[1] debere me-
3 minissent. Tantumque libertatis[2] novae gaudium
incesserat,[3] ut vix mutati status fidem caperent[4]
alterumque ex consulibus, Lucretiae maritum, tan-
tum ob nomen et genus regium fascibus abrogatis
4 urbe[5] dimitteret. Itaque substitutus Horatius Publi-
cola summo studio adnisus est ad augendam[6] liberi
populi maiestatem. Nam et fasces ei pro contione
summisit, et ius provocationis adversus ipsos dedit,
et ne specie arcis offenderet eminentis[7] aedis suas
5 in plana[8] summisit. Brutus vero favori civium
etiam domus suae clade et parricidio velificatus est.
Quippe cum studere revocandis in urbem[9] regibus
liberos suos comperisset, protraxit in forum et
contione media virgis cecidit, securi percussit, ut
plane publicus parens in locum liberorum adoptasse
sibi populum videretur.

6 Liber iam hinc populus Romanus prima adversus
exteros arma pro libertate corripuit, mox pro finibus,
deinde pro sociis, tum gloria et imperio, lacessen-
7 tibus[10] adsidue usquequaque finitimis; quippe cum
patrii soli glaeba nulla, sed statim hostile pomerium,
mediusque inter Latium atque Etruscos quasi in
quodam bivio conlocatus omnibus portis in hostem

[1] se *add. Halmius.*
[2] libertatis: libertati *B.*
[3] incesserat: incenserat *B.*
[4] caperent: caperet *B.*
[5] urbe: urbem *B I N.*
[6] augendam: augendum *B.*
[7] eminentis *N*: aeminenti *B.*
[8] plana: planas *B.*
[9] urbem: urbe *B.*
[10] imperio, lacessentibus: imperium lacescentibus *B.*

must consult the interests of their fellow-citizens. So great a delight in this new-found liberty had taken possession of the people that they could scarcely believe in their changed condition, and deprived one of the consuls, the husband of Lucretia, of the fasces and expelled him from the city because he bore the name of the royal house and was related to it. And so Horatius Publicola, who was chosen in his place, strove with the utmost zeal to promote the dignity of the newly-freed people; for he lowered the fasces before them in the public assembly and granted them the right of appeal against the decisions of himself and his colleague. He also removed his abode to the level part of the city, lest he should offend by appearing to occupy a commanding position. Brutus, on his part, courted the favour of the citizens even by the ruin and slaughter of his own family; for, having discovered that his own sons were eager to restore the kings to the city, he dragged them into the forum and, in the public assembly, beat them with rods and then beheaded them, so that he might appear in the guise of the father of the State who had adopted the people in place of his own children.

The Roman people, henceforward free, took up arms against other nations, first to secure their liberty, then to extend their bounds, afterwards in defence of their allies, and finally to win glory and empire; for they were continually harassed by their neighbours on every side, since they possessed not a clod of soil of their own, but the land immediately outside their walls belonged to enemies, and, being placed as it were at the meeting-place of two roads between Latium and Etruria, they met the enemy

8 incurreret; donec quasi contagio quodam per singulos itum est et proximis quibusque correptis totam Italiam sub se redegerunt.

IIII. Bellvm Etrvscvm Cvm Rege Porsenna

10 Pulsis urbe regibus prima pro libertate arma
corripuit. Nam Porsenna rex Etruscorum ingentibus copiis aderat et Tarquinios manu reducebat.
2 Hunc tamen, quamvis et armis et fame urgueret
occupatoque Ianiculo in ipsis urbis faucibus incubaret, sustinuit, reppulit, novissime etiam tanta
admiratione perculit, ut superior ultro cum paene
3 victis amicitiae foedera feriret. Tunc illa tria
Romani nominis[1] prodigia atque miracula, Horatius,
Mucius, Cloelia, qui nisi in annalibus forent, hodie
4 fabulae viderentur. Quippe Horatius Cocles post-
quam hostes undique instantes solus summovere
non poterat, ponte rescisso transnatat Tiberim nec
5 arma dimittit. Mucius Scaevola regem per insidias
in castris ipsius adgreditur, sed ubi frustrato circa
purpuratum eius ictu tenetur, ardentibus focis inicit
6 manum terroremque geminat dolo. "En, ut scias,"

[1] illa tria Romani nominis *Koehlerus*: illa in romani nominis *B*: illa romana *N L*.

---

[1] His mistake was due to the fact that the attendant was *pari* (*cum rege*) *fere ornatu* (Liv. II. 12, 7).

outside all their gates. Finally, spreading just as a fever spreads, they attacked their enemies one by one and, by continually fastening on the nearest of them, brought the whole of Italy under their sway.

IIII. The Etruscan War against King Porsenna

10. The first arms which the Roman people took up after the expulsion of the kings were for the defence of their liberty. For Porsenna, king of the Etruscans, arrived with a huge army and was eager to restore the Tarquinii by force. Although he pressed hard upon them both with arms and with famine and, having seized the Janiculum, held the very approach to the city, they withstood and repelled him and finally inspired him with such admiration that, in spite of his superior strength, he actually concluded a treaty of friendship with an all but conquered enemy. It was on this occasion that those three prodigies and marvels of Rome made their appearance, Horatius, Mucius and Cloelia, who, were they not recorded in our annals, would seem fabulous characters at the present day. For Horatius Cocles, finding that he could not alone drive back the enemies who threatened him on every side, after the bridge had been broken down, swam across the Tiber without abandoning his arms. Mucius Scaevola by a stratagem attempted an attack upon the king in his own camp, and when he was seized after aiming a blow by mistake at his purple-clad attendants,[1] placed his hand in a blazing fire and by a crafty device doubled the king's alarm. "Behold," he said, "and know from what sort of

inquit, "quem virum effugeris; idem trecenti iuravimus"; cum interim—inmane dictu—hic interritus,
7 ille trepidaret, tamquam manus regis arderet. Sic quidem viri; sed ne qui sexus a laude cessaret, ecce et virginum virtus. Una ex opsidibus regi datis elapsa custodiam,[1] Cloelia, per patrium flumen
8 equitabat. Et rex quidem tot tantisque virtutum territus monstris valere liberosque esse iussit. Tarquinii tamen tam diu dimicaverunt, donec Arruntem filium regis manu sua Brutus occidit superque ipsum mutuo volnere expiravit, plane quasi adulterum ad inferos usque sequeretur.

V. Bellvm Latinvm

11 Latini quoque Tarquinios adserebant aemulatione et invidia, ut populus qui foris dominabatur saltim domi serviret. Igitur omne Latium Mamilio Tusculano duce quasi in regis ultionem tollit animos.
2 Apud Regilli lacum dimicavit diu Marte vario, donec Postumius ipse dictator signum in hostis iaculatus est—novum et insigne commentum—, ut inde re-
3 peteretur.[2] Cossus equitum magister exuere frenos

[1] datis elapsa custodiam *Tollius*: data etlapsa custodiae *B*: data elapsa custodiam *L*.
[2] ut inde repeteretur *Iahnius*: ut inde ipse peteretur *B*: uti peteretur *N L*.

---

[1] Florus here by mistake substitutes the name of Cossus as master of the horse on this occasion for that of Titus

a man you have escaped; three hundred of us have sworn to attempt the same deed." Meanwhile, incredible to relate, Mucius was unafraid, but the king was startled as though his own hand were burning. So much for the valour of the men; but that neither sex might lack praise, lo and behold, maidens too showed valour. Cloelia, one of the hostages handed over to the king, escaped from her guards and swam on horseback through the river of her native city. The king, indeed, alarmed at all these prodigies of valour, bade the Romans farewell and told them to keep their freedom. The Tarquinii, however, continued the struggle until Brutus with his own hand killed Arruns, the king's son, and fell dead on his body from a wound dealt him by his foe, as though he would pursue the adulterer even to the infernal regions.

V. The Latin War

11. The Latins also supported the Tarquins in a spirit of rivalry and jealousy towards the Romans, wishing that a people which was gaining dominion abroad might at any rate be slaves at home. All Latium, therefore, under the leadership of Mamilius of Tusculum, summoned up their courage under the pretence of avenging the king. A battle was fought at Lake Regillus, for a long time with shifting fortune, until Postumius, the dictator, himself adopted the new and remarkable stratagem of hurling a standard among the enemy, in order that it might be recovered. Cossus,[1] the master of the horse,

Aebutius. A. Cornelius Cossus was master of the horse to the dictator Aemilius Mamercinus in 426 B.C.

imperavit—et hoc novum—quo acrius incurrerent.
4 Ea denique atrocitas proelii fuit, ut interfuisse
spectaculo deos fama tradiderit. Duo in candidis
equis iuvenes more siderum praetervolaverunt;
Castorem atque Pollucem nemo dubitavit. Itaque
et imperator ipse veneratus est pactusque victoriam
templa promisit et reddidit, plane quasi stipendium
commilitonibus dis.

5 Hactenus pro libertate, mox de finibus cum
isdem Latinis adsidue et sine intermissione pug-
6 natum est. Cora[1]—quis credat?—et Alsium terrori
fuerunt, Satricum atque Corniculum provinciae. De
7 Verulis et Bovillis pudet, sed triumphavimus. Tibur,
nunc suburbanum, et aestivae Praeneste deliciae
8 nuncupatis in Capitolio votis petebantur. Idem
tunc Faesulae quod Carrhae nuper, idem nemus
Aricinum quod Hercynius saltus, Fregellae quod
9 Gesoriacum,[2] Tiberis quod Euphrates. Coriolos
quoque—pro pudor—victos[3] adeo gloriae fuisse, ut
captum oppidum Gnaeus Marcius Coriolanus quasi
10 Numantiam aut Africam nomini indueret.[4] Extant
et parta de Antio spolia, quae Maenius[5] in suggestu
fori capta hostium classe suffixit—si tamen illa

[1] Cora *Rehd.*: sora *B I*: Ora *L*.
[2] Gesoriacum: gesoria; cum *N*: gersoriacum *L*: caesoriacum *B I*.
[3] victos: victus *B*.
[4] indueret: induere *B*: induceret *N*.
[5] Maenius: menius *I*: menenius *B*: moenibus *N*.

---

[1] See p. 211.

ordered the cavalry to discard their bits—another new device—in order that they might charge with greater vigour. So desperate was the fight at last that a tradition has been handed down that gods were present as spectators. Two young men on white horses sped over the battle-field like stars across the heavens; and no one doubted that they were Castor and Pollux. The Roman commander, therefore, himself prayed to them and, bargaining for victory, promised them a temple, and carried out his promise as though in payment to the gods who were his comrades in arms.

Hitherto they had fought for their freedom; they presently were at war with these same Latins, persistently and without intermission, in defence of their frontier. Cora (though it seems incredible) and Alsium were formidable: Satricum and Corniculum were provinces. Over Verulae and Bovillae, I am ashamed to say it—but we triumphed. Tibur, now a suburban retreat, and Praeneste, now a charming summer resort, were attacked after the offering of solemn vows in the Capitol. Faesulae meant the same to us then as Carrhae[1] lately meant; the Arician Wood corresponded to the Hercynian Forest,[2] Fregellae to Gesoriacum,[3] the Tiber to the Euphrates. The capture of Corioli—alas for the shame of it!—was regarded as so glorious an achievement that Gnaeus Marcius became Coriolanus, taking the city into his name, as though he had conquered Numantia or Africa. Spoils won from Antium still exist, which Maenius fixed up on the tribunal of the forum after the capture of the enemies' fleet—if it can be called a fleet,

[2] See p. 337. [3] See pp. 205, 337.

classis, nam sex fuere rostratae. Sed hic numerus
illis initiis navale bellum fuit.
11 Pervicacissimi tamen Latinorum Aequi et Volsci
12 fuere et cotidiani, ut sic dixerim, hostes. Sed hos[1]
praecipue Titus Quinctius domuit, ille dictator ab
aratro, qui obsessa et paene iam capta Manili consulis
13 castra egregia victoria recuperavit. Medium erat
tempus forte sementis, cum patricium virum innixum
aratro suo lictor in ipso opere deprehendit. Inde
in aciem profectus, victos, ne quid a rustici operis
imitatione cessaret, more pecudum sub iugum misit.
14 sic expeditione finita rediit ad boves rursus trium-
phalis agricola—fidem numinum—qua velocitate.
15 Intra quindecim dies coeptum peractumque bellum,
prorsus ut festinasse dictator ad relictum opus
videretur.

VI. Bellvm cvm Etrvscis Faliscis Veientibvs Fidenatibvs

12 Adsidui vero et anniversarii hostes ab Etruria
fuere Veientes, adeo ut extraordinariam manum
adversus eos promiserit privatumque gesserit bellum
gens una Fabiorum. Satis superque nota clades.
2 Caesi apud Cremeram trecenti, patricius exercitus;

[1] sed hos *om. B.*

for it consisted of only six beaked ships. In those primitive days, however, a fleet of that number was enough for a war at sea.

But the most persistent of the Latins were the Aequi and Volsci, who were, if I may use the phrase, the everyday enemies of Rome. These were subdued chiefly by Titus Quinctius, the dictator who was summoned from the plough and by a famous victory rescued the camp of the consul Manilius, which was beleaguered and almost captured. It happened to be the middle of the season of sowing, when the lictor found the patrician actually at work bending over his plough. Setting out thence to the battle-field, in order that he might keep up the tradition of his rustic employment, he made his conquered enemies pass like cattle under the yoke. The campaign being concluded, this farmer who had enjoyed a triumph returned to his oxen, and, ye Heavens, with what speed! For the war was begun and finished within fifteen days, so that it seemed for all the world as if the dictator had hurried back to finish the work which he had left.

VI. The War with the Etruscans, Falisci, Veientines and Fidenates

12. From the direction of Etruria the Veientines were persistent enemies who attacked each year; so much so that the single family of the Fabii undertook to form a special force and waged a private war against them. The disaster which befell them is well, all too well, known. Near Cremera three hundred of them, an army of patricians,

itaque scelerato signata[1] nomine quae proficiscentes
3 in proelium porta dimisit. Sed ea clades ingentibus
expiata victoriis, postquam per alios atque alios
robustissima capta sunt oppida, vario quidem eventu.
4 Falisci sponte se dediderunt, crematae suo igne
5 Fidenae, direpti funditus deletique Veientes. Fa-
lisci cum obsiderentur, mira est visa fides imperatoris,
nec inmerito, quod ludi magistrum, urbis proditorem,
cum his quos adduxerat pueris vinctum sibi ultro remi-
6 sisset. Eam namque vir sanctus et sapiens veram scie-
bat esse victoriam, quae salva fide et integra dignitate
7 pareretur. Fidenae quia pares non erant ferro, ad
terrorem movendum facibus armatae et discoloribus
serpentium in modum vittis furiali more proces-
serant; sed habitus ille feralis eversionis omen fuit.
8 Veî quanta res fuerit, indicat decennis obsidio. Tum
primum hiematum sub pellibus, taxata stipendio
hiberna, adactus miles sua sponte iure iurando ne
9 nisi capta urbe remearet. Spolia de Larte Tolumnio
rege ad Feretrium triumpho reportata.[2] Denique
non scalis nec inruptione, sed cuniculo et subter-
10 raneis dolis peractum urbis excidium. Ea denique

[1] itaque scelerato signata *Koehlerus*: it scel. signat *B*: et scel. signata *N*.

[2] ad Feretrium triumpho reportata *Iahnius*: afferret triumphum reportaret *B*.

were slain, and so the gate which sent them forth to the battle was branded with the name of the Evil Gate. But for this disaster atonement was made by great victories, when the strongest cities were captured under different leaders and with different results. The Falisci surrendered voluntarily; Fidenae was consumed by its own flames; Veii was thoroughly plundered and destroyed. When the Falisci were being besieged, the honourable conduct of the Roman commander was a subject of admiration, and not without reason; for he actually sent back in chains a schoolmaster who offered to betray the city, together with the boys whom he had brought with him. For, being a man of integrity and wisdom, he knew that the only true victory is that which is won with untainted honour and unimpaired dignity. The people of Fidenae, not being a match for the Romans with the sword, had armed themselves with torches and had put on vari-coloured fillets resembling serpents, in order to inspire terror, and had marched forth like furies; but their funereal attire was an omen of their overthrow. The ten years' siege which Veii sustained is an indication of its strength. It was the first occasion on which a Roman army spent the winter under tents of skin, and winter service was compensated by special pay, and the soldiers at their own suggestion were bound under an oath not to return until the city had been captured. The spoils won from Lars Tolumnius, the king, were brought back in triumph and dedicated to Jupiter Feretrius. In the end the fall of the city was brought about, not by scaling-ladders or assault, but by a mine and underground

visa est praedae magnitudo, cuius decima[1] Apollini
Pythio mitteretur, universusque populus Romanus
11 ad direptionem urbis vocaretur. Hoc tunc Veî fuere.
Nunc fuisse quis meminit? Quae reliquiae? Quod
vestigium? Laborat annalium fides, ut Veios fuisse
credamus.

VII. Bellvm Gallicvm

13 Hic sive invidia deum sive fato rapidissimus
procurrentis imperii cursus parumper Gallorum
2 Senonum incursione supprimitur. Quod tempus
populo Romano nescio utrum clade funestius fuerit,
3 an virtutis experimentis speciosius. Ea certe fuit
vis calamitatis, ut in experimentum inlatam putem
divinitus, scire volentibus inmortalibus dis, an
Romana virtus imperium orbis mereretur.

4 Galli Senones, gens natura ferox, moribus incon-
dita, ad hoc ipsa corporum mole, perinde armis
ingentibus, adeo omni genere terribilis fuit, ut plane
nata ad hominum interitum, urbium stragem vide-
5 retur. Hi quondam ab ultimis terrarum oris et
cingente omnia Oceano ingenti agmine profecti,
cum iam media vastassent, positis inter Alpes et
Padum sedibus, ne his quidem contenti per Italiam

[1] decima *Iahnius*: decumae *codd.*

stratagems. Lastly, the booty appeared so rich that a tithe of it was sent to Pythian Apollo, and the whole of the Roman people was summoned to plunder the city. Such was Veii in those days. Who now ever remembers its former existence? What remains or traces of it are left? Our trust in our annals has a difficult task to make us believe that Veii ever existed.

VII. The War with the Gauls

13. At this point, owing to the envy of the gods or a decree of fate, the rapid progress of the growing empire was checked for a while by the invasion of the Gallic Senones. Whether this period should rather be considered harmful to the Roman people through the disasters which it brought, or glorious owing to the tests which it gave of their valour, I cannot say. At any rate the force of calamity was such that I can only think that it was inflicted upon them by heaven as a test, because the immortal gods wished to know whether Roman valour deserved the empire of the world.

The Gallic Senones were a naturally wild race and quite uncivilized; moreover, by their vast stature and proportionately huge arms and all sorts of other circumstances, they inspired such terror that they seemed created for the destruction of human life and the ruin of cities. Having originally set out with a huge host from the remotest shores of earth and the all-encircling ocean, after they had laid waste all the intervening land, they settled between the Alps and the Po, and then, not content even with this territory, they began to wander through

6 vagabantur; tum Clusium urbem obsidebant. Pro
sociis ac foederatis Romanus intervenit; missi ex
more legati. Sed quod ius apud barbaros? Ferocius
7 agunt, et inde certamen. Conversis igitur a Clusio
Romamque venientibus ad Aliam flumen cum exer-
citu Fabius consul occurrit. Non temere foedior
clades; itaque hunc diem fastis Roma damnavit.
8 Fuso exercitu iam moenibus urbis propinquabant.
Erant nulla praesidia. Tum igitur sic, ut numquam
9 alias, apparuit vera illa Romana virtus. Iam primum
maiores natu, amplissimis usi honoribus, in forum
coeunt, ibi devovente pontifice dis se[1] manibus
10 consecrant, statimque in suas quisque aedes regressi,
sic ut in trabeis erant et amplissimo cultu, in curu-
libus sellis sese reposuerunt, ut, cum venisset hostis,
11 in sua quisque dignitate moreretur. Pontifices et
flamines quidquid religiosissimi in templis erat partim
in doleis defossa terra recondunt, partim inposita
12 plaustris secum Veios auferunt. Virgines simul ex
sacerdotio Vestae nudo pede fugientia sacra comi-
tantur. Tamen excepisse fugientis unus ex plebe
fertur Albinius,[2] qui depositis uxore et liberis virgines
in plaustrum recepit. Adeo tunc quoque in ultimis

[1] se *om.* *B.*
[2] Albinius *Liv.* V. 40: Atinius *B*: Albinus *L.*

Italy; finally they besieged the city of Clusium. The Romans intervened on behalf of their allies and confederates; and, according to the usual custom, ambassadors were sent to protest. But what sense of justice could be expected from barbarians? They only acted with greater ferocity, with the result that an open conflict ensued. The Senones turned away from Clusium and, as they marched upon Rome, were met by the consul Fabius with an army at the river Alia. One could not easily find a more disgraceful defeat, and so Rome has set a black mark against that day in its calendar. The Roman army having been routed, the enemy were approaching the walls of the city, and there was no garrison. It was then, as upon no other occasion, that the true Roman valour showed itself. In the first place the older men who had held the highest offices collected in the forum and there consecrated themselves to the infernal deities, the chief pontiff performing the ceremony; they then immediately returned each to his own house and, still clad in their official robes and richest attire, they seated themselves in their curule chairs, so that, when the enemy arrived, they might all die with proper dignity. The pontiffs and priests dug holes and buried some of the most sacred objects which were in the temples and carried off others with them on waggons to Veii. At the same time the virgins of the priesthood of Vesta, barefooted, accompanied the sacred objects in their flight. It is said, however, that a plebeian, Albinius, assisted the virgins in their escape, and having set down his wife and children, received them in his waggon; to such an extent, even in the utmost extremities,

religio publica privatis adfectibus antecellebat. Iu-
13 ventus vero, quam satis constat vix mille hominum fuisse, duce Manlio[1] arcem Capitolini montis insedit, obtestata ipsum quasi praesentem Iovem, ut quem ad modum ipsi ad defendendum templum concurrissent, ita ille virtutem eorum numine suo tueretur.
14 Aderant interim Galli apertamque urbem primo trepidi, ne quis subesset dolus, mox, ubi solitudinem vident, pari clamore et impetu invadunt. Patentis passim domos adeunt. Ibi sedentes in curulibus suis praetextatos senes velut deos geniosque venerati, mox eosdem, postquam esse homines liquebat, alioquin nihil respondere dignantes pari vaecordia mactant, facesque tectis iniciunt, et totam urbem
15 igni ferro manibus exaequant. Sex mensibus barbari—quis crederet?—circa montem unum pependerunt, nec diebus modo, sed noctibus quoque omnia experti; cum tamen Manlius nocte subeuntis clangore anseris excitatus a summa rupe deiecit, et ut spem hostibus demeret, quamquam in summa[2] fame, tamen ad speciem fiduciae panes ab arce iaculatus
16 est. Et stato quodam die per medias hostium custodias Fabium pontificem ab arce dimisit, qui sollemne sacrum in Quirinali monte conficeret.

[1] Manlio: Manilio *B.*
[2] rupe—summa *om. B.*

---

[1] *i.e.* tutelar deities of the place.

did the respect for religion prevail over personal affection. A band of young men, whose number is generally held to have been scarcely a thousand, under the leadership of Manlius, took up a position on the citadel of the Capitoline hill, having called upon Jupiter himself, as though he were there in very presence, to defend their valour as they themselves had met to guard his temple. Meanwhile the Gauls arrived and entered the open city, at first in alarm lest some hidden stratagem was in the background, but afterwards, when they saw no one about, with equal noise and impetuosity. They approached the houses, which were everywhere open: here they were overawed by the elders in their purple-edged robes seated in their curule chairs as though they were gods and genii; [1] but presently, when it was obvious that they were mortals, and when, besides, they disdained to answer a word, they slaughtered them all, acting with the same brutality, and hurled torches into the houses and razed the whole city to the ground with fire and sword and the labour of their hands. For six months (who could credit it?) the barbarians clung round that single hill, making every kind of attempt upon it by night as well as by day. Manlius, on his part, roused by the cries of a goose, hurled them from the top of the rock as they were climbing up at night and, in order to deprive the enemy of their hopes, though he was suffering the extremities of famine, cast down loaves of bread from the citadel so as to create the impression that he was confident. Also on the appointed day he sent Fabius the pontiff through the midst of the enemy's guards to perform a solemn sacrifice on the Quirinal

Atque ille per media hostium tela incolumis re-
ligionis auxilio redivit propitiosque deos renuntiavit.
17 Novissime cum iam obsidio sua barbaros fatigasset,
mille pondo auri recessum suum venditantes, idque
ipsum per insolentiam, cum ad iniqua pondera
addito adhuc gladio superbe "vae victis"[1] incre-
parent, subito adgressus a tergo Camillus adeo
cecidit, ut omnia incendiorum vestigia Gallici san-
18 guinis inundatione deleret. Agere gratias dis in-
mortalibus ipso tantae cladis nomine libet. Pasto-
rum casas ignis ille, et flamma paupertatem Romuli
abscondit. Incendium illud quid egit aliud, nisi ut
destinata hominum ac deorum domicilio civitas non
deleta nec obruta, sed expiata potius et lustrata
19 videatur? Igitur post adsertam a Manlio,[2] restitutam
a Camillo urbem acrius etiam vehementiusque in
finitimos resurrexit.

VIII. Bella Gallica

Ac primum omnium illam ipsam Gallicam gentem
non contentus moenibus expulisse, cum per Italiam
naufragia sua latius traherent, sic persecutus est
duce Camillo, ut hodie nulla Senonum vestigia
20 supersint. Semel apud Anienem trucidati, cum
singulari certamine Manlius aureum torquem

[1] superbe "vae victis" *Aldus* (*cf. Liv.* V. 48): insuper victis *B*: superbe victis *N L*.

[2] a manlio *L*: amillio *B*: a manilio *N*.

Hill; he returned safely, protected by the sacred character of his mission, through the enemies' weapons, and announced that the gods were propitious. Finally, when the barbarians had been worn out by their own siege-operations and were offering to depart for a payment of 1000 pounds of gold (making their offer, moreover, in an insolent manner by throwing a sword into the scale to make the weights unfair, and uttering the proud taunt "Woe to the vanquished!"), Camillus, suddenly attacking them from the rear, made such a slaughter as to wipe out all traces of the burning of the city with the deluge of Gallic blood. We are inclined to thank the gods that the destruction of the city was so complete; for they were the huts of shepherds that the fire overwhelmed, and the flames buried Romulus' poor little settlement. What other effect then did the fire produce except that the city, destined to be the abode of men and of gods, seemed not so much to have been destroyed and overthrown as to have been sanctified and purified? Thus, when the city had been saved by Manlius and restored by Camillus, the Roman people rose up again against their neighbouring foes with increased vigour and force.

VIII. Further Wars with the Gauls

First of all, not content with having driven away this particular tribe of the Gauls from the walls, Camillus followed them so closely, as they were dragging their shattered remains across Italy, that to-day no trace is left of the Senones. On one occasion a slaughter of them took place on the River Anio, during which, in single combat, Manlius took from a barbarian, among other spoils, a torque

barbaro inter spolia detraxit, unde Torquati. Ite-
rum Pomptino agro, cum in simili pugna Valerius,
insidente galeae sacra alite adiutus, tulit spolia ; et
21 inde Corvini. Nec non tamen post aliquot annos
omnis reliquias eorum in Etruria ad lacum Vadi-
monis Dolabella delevit, ne quis extaret ex ea
gente, qui[1] incensam a se Romanam urbem
gloriaretur.

VIIII. Bellvm Latinvm

14 Conversus a Gallis in Latinos Manlio Torquato
Decio Mure consulibus, semper quidem aemulatione
imperii infestos, tum vero contemptu urbis incensae,
cum ius civitatis partem imperii[2] et magistratuum[3]
poscerent, apud Capuam proeliis congredi audentes.[4]
2 Quo tempore quis cessisse hostem mirabitur? Cum
alter consulum filium suum, quia contra imperium
pugnaverat, quamvis victorem occiderit ostende-
3 ritque plus esse in imperio quam in victoria ; alter
quasi monitu deorum capite velato primam ante
aciem dis manibus se devoverit, ut in confertissima
se hostium tela iaculatus novum ad victoriam iter
sanguinis sui limite aperiret.

[1] qui *L* : quae *BIN*.
[2] partem imperii *Rossbachius* : pari imperio *BI*.
[3] magistratuum *Rossbachius* : magistratum *B*.
[4] audentes *Mommsenus* : auderent *codd.*

of gold, which gave their name to the family of the Torquati. On another occasion, in the Pomptine territory, in a similar fight Valerius, aided by a sacred bird which settled on his helmet, won spoils from the foe, and from this incident the Corvini derived their name.[1] Moreover, some years later, near the Lake of Vadimo in Etruria, Dolabella destroyed all that remained of the tribe, so that none might survive of the race to boast that he had burnt the city of Rome.

VIIII. The Latin War

14. In the consulship of Manlius Torquatus and Decius Mus,[2] the Romans turned their attention from the Gauls to the Latins, who, always their foes through rivalry of empire, at this time, in their contempt for the burnt city, demanded the rights of citizenship and a share in the government and public offices, and dared to meet them in battle at Capua. Who will wonder that on this occasion the enemy yielded, when one of the consuls put his own son to death, though he had been victorious, because he had fought against his order (thus showing that to enforce obedience was more important than victory), while the other consul, as though acting upon a warning from heaven, with veiled head devoted himself to the infernal gods in front of the army, in order that, by hurling himself where the enemy's weapons were thickest, he might open up a new path to victory along the track of his own life-blood?

[1] Corvinus from *corvus*, a crow.
[2] 340 B.C.

X. Bellvm Sabinvm

15 A Latinis adgressus est gentem Sabinorum, qui
immemores factae sub Tito Tatio adfinitatis quodam
2 contagio bellis se Latinis adiunxerant. Sed Curio
Dentato consule omnem eum tractum, qua Nar,
Anio, fontes Velini, Hadriano tenus mari igni
3 ferroque vastavit. Qua victoria tantum hominum,
tantum agrorum redactum est in potestatem, ut
in utro plus esset nec ipse posset aestimare qui
vicerat.

XI. Bellvm Samniticvm

16 Precibus deinde Campaniae motus non pro se,
2 sed eo speciosius pro sociis Samnitas invadit. Erat
foedus cum utrisque percussum, sed hoc Campani
sanctius et prius omnium suorum deditione fecerunt;
sic ergo Romanus bellum Samniticum tamquam sibi
gessit.

3 Omnium non modo Italiae, sed toto orbe
terrarum pulcherrima Campaniae plaga est. Nihil
mollius caelo: denique bis floribus vernat. Nihil
4 uberius solo: ideo Liberi Cererisque certamen
dicitur. Nihil hospitalius mari: hic illi nobiles

---

[1] See p. 13.
[2] 290 B.C.

X. The Sabine War

15. After the Latins they attacked the race of the Sabines, who, forgetful of the relationship formed under Titus Tatius,[1] had become as it were infected by the spirit of the Latins and had joined in their wars. During the consulship of Curius Dentatus,[2] the Romans laid waste with fire and sword all the tract of country which is enclosed by the Nar, the Anio and the sources of the Velinus, and bounded by the Adriatic Sea. By this conquest so large a population and so vast a territory was reduced, that even he who had won the victory could not tell which was of the greater importance.

XI. The Samnite War

16. Next, moved by the prayers of the Campanians, the Romans attacked the Samnites, not on their own behalf but, what is more honourable, on that of their allies. A treaty had been made with both nations, but that made with the Campanians was more formal and older, having been accompanied by the surrender of all their possessions. Thus the Romans entered upon war with the Samnites as though they were fighting for themselves.

The district of Campania is the fairest of all regions not only in Italy but in the whole world. Nothing can be softer than its climate: indeed it has spring and its flowers twice a year. Nowhere is the soil more fertile; for which reason it is said to have been an object of contention between Liber and Ceres. Nowhere is the coast more hospitable,

portus Caieta, Misenus, tepentes fontibus Baiae,
5 Lucrinus et Avernus, quaedam maris otia. Hic
amicti[1] vitibus montes Gaurus, Falernus, Massicus
et pulcherrimus omnium Vesuvius, Aetnaei ignis
6 imitator. Urbes ad mare Formiae, Cumae, Puteoli,
Neapolis, Herculaneum, Pompei, et ipsa caput
urbium Capua, quondam inter tres maximas[2]
7 numerata. Pro hac urbe, his regionibus populus
Romanus Samnitas invadit, gentem, si opulentiam
quaeras, aureis et argenteis armis et discolori veste
usque ad ambitum ornatam[3]; si fallaciam, saltibus
fere et montium fraude grassantem; si rabiem ac
furorem, sacratis[4] legibus humanisque hostiis in
exitium urbis agitatam; si pertinaciam, sexies rupto
8 foedere cladibusque ipsis animosiorem. Hos tamen
quinquaginta annis per Fabios ac Papirios patres
eorumque liberos ita subegit ac domuit, ita ruinas
ipsas urbium diruit, ut hodie Samnium in ipso
Samnio requiratur nec facile appareat materia
9 quattuor et viginti triumphorum. Maxime tamen
nota et inlustris apud Caudinas furculas ex hac
gente clades Veturio Postumioque consulibus
10 accepta est. Cluso per insidias intra eum saltum
exercitu, unde non posset evadere, stupens tanta

[1] amicti: amici *B.*
[2] *post* maximas *add. BINL* romam carthaginemque, *del. Hauptius.*
[3] ornatam *Iord. Cod. Bamb.*, *Heinsius*: armatam *BI.*
[4] sacratis: sacris *BI.*

---

[1] 321 B.C.

which contains the famous harbours of Caieta, Misenus, Baiae with its hot springs, and the Lucrine and Avernian Lakes where the sea seems to enjoy perpetual repose. Here are the vine-clad mountains of Gaurus, Falernus and Massicus, and Vesuvius, the fairest of them all, which rivals the fires of Etna. Towards the sea-coast lie the cities of Formiae. Cumae, Puteoli, Naples, Herculaneum and Pompeii, and Capua, queen among cities, formerly accounted among the three greatest in the world. It was on behalf of this city and these regions that the Roman people attacked the Samnites, a race which, if you would know its wealth, was clad, even to the point of ostentation, in gold and silver armour and motley-coloured raiment; if you would learn its craft, it usually attacked its foes from its defiles and the ambushes of its mountains; if you would know its rage and fury, it was hounded on by its hallowed laws and human sacrifices to destroy our city; if you would know its obstinacy, it had been exasperated by a treaty six times broken and by its very disasters. In fifty years, however, under the leadership of two generations of the Fabii and Papirii, the Romans so thoroughly subdued and conquered this people and so demolished the very ruins of their cities that to-day one looks round to see where Samnium is on Samnite territory, and it is difficult to imagine how there can have been material for twenty-four triumphs over them. Yet a most notable and signal defeat was sustained at the hands of this nation at the Caudine Forks in the consulship of Veturius and Postumius.[1] The Roman army having been entrapped by an ambush in that defile and being unable to escape, Pontius

occasione dux hostium Pontius Herennium patrem consuluit. Et ille, mitteret omnes vel occideret,
11 sapienter ut senior suaserat: hic armis exutos mittere sub iugum maluit, ut nec amici forent beneficio et post flagitium hostes magis. Itaque et consules statim magnifice voluntaria deditione turpitudinem foederis dirimunt, et ultionem flagitans miles Papirio duce—horribile dictu—strictis ensibus per ipsam viam ante pugnam furit; et in congressu arsisse omnium oculos hostis auctor fuit. Nec prius finis caedibus datus, quam iugum et hostibus et duci capto reposuerunt.

XII. Bellvm Etrvscvm Samniticvm Gallicvm

17 Hactenus populus Romanus cum singulis gentibus, mox acervatim; sic tamen quoque par omnibus fuit. Etruscorum duodecim populi, Vmbri in id tempus intacti, antiquissimus Italiae populus, Samnitium reliqui in excidium Romani nominis repente
2 coniurant. Erat terror ingens tot simul tantorumque populorum. Late per Etruriam infesta

the commander of the enemies' forces, dumbfounded at the opportunity offered to him, asked the advice of his father Herennius. The latter, with the wisdom of advanced years, had advised him either to let them all go free or else to slay them all; Pontius preferred to strip them of their arms and send them under the yoke, so that they were not made his friends by an act of kindness but rendered bitterer enemies by the affront put upon them. The result was that the consuls by a generous act of devotion immediately wiped out the disgrace of the treaty by voluntarily surrendering themselves; and the soldiers, under the leadership of Papirius, calling for vengeance, rushed furiously along (horrible to relate) with their swords drawn as they advanced before they came to blows, and, when the encounter took place, the enemy affirmed that the eyes of all the Romans blazed with fire. Nor was an end put to the slaughter until they retaliated by making the enemy and the captured general pass under the yoke.

XII. The War against the Etruscans, Samnites and Gauls

17. Hitherto the Roman people had waged war against single nations; they soon had to meet a combined attack. Yet even so they were a match for them all. Twelve tribes of the Etruscans, the Umbrians, the most ancient people in Italy and up to that time unassailed in war, and the survivors of the Samnites suddenly conspired together to destroy the very name of Rome. The simultaneous attack of so many powerful peoples caused the greatest terror. The hostile standards of four

3 quattuor agminum signa volitabant. Ciminius[1]
interim saltus in medio, ante invius plane quasi
Caledonius vel Hercynius, adeo tum terrori erat,
ut senatus consuli denuntiaret ne tantum periculi
4 ingredi auderet. Sed nihil horum terruit ducem,
quin fratre praemisso exploraret accessus. Ille per
noctem pastorali habitu speculatus omnia refert
5 tutum iter. Sic Fabius Maximus periculosissimum
bellum sine periculo explicuit. Nam subito inconditos atque palantis adgressus est captisque
superioribus iugis in subiectos suo iure detonuit.
6 Ea namque species fuit illius belli, quasi in terri-
7 genas e caelo ac nubibus tela iacerentur. Nec
incruenta tamen illa victoria. Nam oppressus in sinu vallis alter consulum Decius more patrio devotum dis manibus optulit caput, sollemnemque familiae suae consecrationem in victoriae pretium peregit.

XIII. Bellvm Tarentinvm

18 Sequitur bellum Tarentinum, unum quidem titulo et nomine, set victoria multiplex. Hoc enim Campanos, Apulos atque Lucanos et caput belli Tarentinos, id est totam Italiam, et cum iis omnibus Pyrrhum, clarissimum Graeciae regem, una

[1] Ciminius: Cyminius *Rehd. man. sec.*: geminius *BIN*.

armies fluttered far and wide through Etruria. Meanwhile the Ciminian forest, which lay between Rome and Etruria, and which was formerly as pathless as the Caledonian or the Hercynian forest, inspired such terror that the senate forbade the consul to venture to face its perils. But no such warning could frighten the general from reconnoitring a passage by sending forward his brother, who, disguised as a shepherd, by night spied out the land and brought back news of a safe route. In this way Fabius Maximus brought a most dangerous war to a close without running any danger; for he suddenly attacked the enemy as they were disordered and straggling, and having captured commanding heights, launched his thunders at his own pleasure on the enemy below—a species of warfare which resembled the hurling of weapons upon the giants from the heaven and clouds above. But it was not a bloodless victory, for one of the consuls, Decius, being surprised in the bend of a valley, following the example of his father, offered his life as a sacrifice to the gods below, and thus by performing an act of devotion, which was habitual in his family, paid the price of victory.

XIII. The Tarentine War

18. Next followed the Tarentine war, in name and title a single campaign, but manifold in its victories; for it involved as it were in a single ruin alike the Campanians, the Apulians and the Lucanians and the Tarentines, who were the original cause of it—in fact, the whole of Italy—and, besides all these, Pyrrhus, the most renowned ruler in Greece. It

veluti ruina pariter involvit, ut eodem tempore et
Italiam consummaret et transmarinos triumphos
2 auspicaretur. Tarentus, Lacedaemoniorum opus,
Calabriae quondam et Apuliae totiusque Lucaniae
caput, cum magnitudine et muris portuque nobilis,
3 tum mirabilis[1] situ. Quippe in ipsis Hadriani
maris faucibus posita in omnis terras, Histriam,
Illyricum, Epiron, Achaiam, Africam, Siciliam vela
dimittit. Inminet portui ad prospectum maris
positum theatrum, quod quidem causa miserae
4 civitati fuit omnium calamitatium. Ludos forte
celebrabat, cum adremigantes litori Romanas classes
vident, atque hostem rati emicant, sine discrimine
5 insultant. Qui enim aut unde Romani? Nec
satis. Aderat sine mora querellam ferens legatio.
Hanc quoque foede per obscenam turpemque dictu
6 contumeliam violant; et hinc bellum. Sed ap-
paratus horribilis, cum tot simul populi pro
Tarentinis consurgerent omnibusque vehementior
Pyrrhus, qui semigraecam ex Lacedaemoniis con-
ditoribus civitatem vindicaturus cum totis viribus
Epiri, Thessaliae, Macedoniae incognitisque in id
tempus elephantis mari terra, viris equis armis,
addito insuper ferarum terrore veniebat.

7 Apud Heracleam Campaniae fluviumque Lirim
Laevino consule prima pugna, quae tam atrox fuit
ut Ferentaneae turmae praefectus Obsidius, in-

[1] mirabilis *N Iahnius* : mirabili *BI.*

---

[1] 280 B.C.

thus at the same time completed the subjugation of Italy and inaugurated the triumphs of Rome beyond the sea. Tarentum, built by the Lacedaemonians, formerly the capital of Calabria, Apulia and all Lucania, is famous for its size, its walls and its harbour, and admired for its situation; for lying at the very exit of the Adriatic it sends forth its ships to all lands, to Istria, Illyricum, Epirus, Achaea, Africa and Sicily. The theatre lies immediately above the harbour in such a position as to command a view of the sea, and this was the cause of all the misfortunes which befell the unhappy city. They happened to be celebrating a festival when they saw the Roman fleet rowing towards the shore, and thinking that they were enemies, they rushed out and began to hurl indiscriminate insults at them, asking who the Romans where and whence they had come. Nor was this all; for when an embassy immediately came and lodged a complaint, they foully affronted them also by a shameful and indecent insult. The result was a declaration of war. The preparations inspired terror, so numerous were the peoples who rose in the defence of the Tarentines, of whom the most active was Pyrrhus, who came to protect a city which was half Greek through its Lacedaemonian founders, with all the forces of Epirus, Thessaly and Macedonia, and with elephants, till then unknown in Italy, threatening Rome by land and sea, with men, horses and arms and the added terror of wild beasts.

The first battle was fought in the consulship of Laevinus[1] at Heraclea in Campania, near the river Liris, and was so fierce that Obsidius, the commander of the Ferentanean squadron, charged the

vectus in regem, turbaverit coegeritque proiectis
8 insignibus proelio excedere. Actum erat, nisi
elephanti, converso in spectaculum bello, procu-
currissent, quorum cum magnitudine tum deformi-
tate et novo odore simul ac stridore consternati
equi, cum incognitas sibi beluas amplius quam
erant suspicarentur, fugam stragemque late de-
9 derunt. In Apulia deinde apud Asculum melius
dimicatum est Curio Fabricioque consulibus. Iam
quippe terror beluarum exoleverat, et Gaius
Numicius quartae legionis hastatus unius proboscide
10 abscisa mori posse beluas ostenderat. Itaque in
ipsas pila congesta sunt, et in turres vibratae faces
tota hostium agmina ardentibus ruinis operuerunt,
nec alias[1] cladi finis fuit quam nox dirimeret,
postremusque fugientium rex ipse a satellitibus
11 umero saucius in armis suis referretur. Lucaniae
suprema pugna fuit Arusinis quos vocant campis,
ducibus isdem quibus superius; sed tum tota
victoria. Exitum, quem datura virtus fuit, casus
12 dedit. Nam provectis in primam aciem rursus
elephantis, unum ex eis pullum adacti in caput
teli gravis ictus avertit; qui cum per stragem
suorum recurrens stridore quereretur, mater agnovit

[1] alias *Salmasius*: alius *codd.*: citius *Sauppius*: ante *Aldus*: prius *Mommsenus.*

---

[1] 279 B.C.

king and put him to flight, forcing him to throw away his royal insignia and leave the battle-field. All was over, had not the elephants come up and turned the battle into a wild-beast show; for the horses, frightened by their huge bulk and ugliness and also by their strange smell and trumpeting, imagining the unfamiliar monsters to be more formidable than they really were, caused panic and destruction far and wide. A second and more successful engagement took place in the consulship of Curius and Fabricius[1] at Asculum in Apulia. By this time, to be sure, the terror inspired by the monsters had passed away, and Gaius Numucius, a front-rank soldier of the fourth legion, had shown, by cutting off the trunk of one of them, that the monsters were mortal. And so javelins were concentrated against them, and torches, hurled against the towers which they carried, covered all the ranks of the enemy with flaming ruins. The slaughter was brought to an end only when night separated the armies, and the king, the last to desert the field, was himself carried away by his attendants on his own shield wounded in the shoulder. The last engagement was fought under the leaders already mentioned above on the so-called Arusine Plains in Lucania. On this occasion the Romans won a complete victory. Chance brought about a result which valour otherwise would have secured. For, when the elephants again moved forward into the front rank, a young one that happened to be among them was struck a heavy blow on the head with a spear and turned round; and when it was hurrying back through the confused mass of its fellows, trumpeting with pain, its dam recognized it and

et quasi vindicaret exiluit, tum omnia circa quasi
13 hostilia gravi mole permiscuit. Ac sic eaedem ferae, quae primam victoriam abstulerunt, secundam parem fecerunt, tertiam sine controversia tradide-
14 runt. Nec vero tantum armis et in campo, sed consiliis quoque et domi[1] cum rege Pyrrho dimicatum est. Quippe post primam victoriam intellecta vir callidus virtute Romana statim desperavit armis
15 seque ad dolos contulit. Nam interemptos cremavit, captivosque indulgenter habuit et sine pretio restituit, missisque legatis in urbem omni modo adnisus est ut facto foedere in amicitiam recipe-
16 retur. Sed et bello et pace et foris et domi omnem in partem Romana virtus tum se adprobavit, nec alia magis quam Tarentina victoria ostendit populi Romani fortitudinem, senatus sapientiam,
17 ducum magnanimitatem. Quinam illi fuerunt viri quos ab elephantis primo proelio obtritos accepimus? Omnium vulnera in pectore, quidam hostibus suis morte sua conmortui, omnium in manibus ensis, et relictae in voltibus minae, et in ipsa morte
18 ira vivebat. Quod adeo Pyrrhus miratus est ut diceret "o quam facile erat orbis imperium occupare, aut mihi Romanis militibus datis, aut me rege Romanis!" Quae autem eorum in reparando

[1] intra urbem *ante* cum *add. codd.: del. Iahnius.*

left her place to defend it, causing by her vast bulk as great a disturbance around her as if she were attacking the enemy. Thus the same beasts which deprived the Romans of their first victory and equalized the second battle, gave them undoubted victory in the third fight. And it was not only with arms and on the battle-field that the struggle with King Pyrrhus was carried on, but also by intrigue at home; for after his first victory the wily king, recognizing the valour of the Romans, immediately gave up hope of military success and had recourse to craft. For he burnt the bodies of the slain, treated his prisoners with indulgence and gave them back without ransom, and sending ambassadors to Rome strove by every device to obtain a treaty and be admitted to friendship. But in peace and war, at home and abroad, Roman valour proved its worth in every respect; and the victory in the Tarentine war, more than any other, showed the bravery of the Roman people, the wisdom of the senate and the magnanimity of the generals. For what kind of men were those who, we are told, were trampled underfoot by the elephants in the first battle? The wounds of all of them were upon their chests; some shared death with their foes, all had their swords still in their hands, a threatening mien still marked their features, and their anger yet lived even in death. So struck was Pyrrhus with admiration that he exclaimed, "How easy were it for me to win the empire of the world if I had an army of Romans, or for the Romans to win it if they had me as their king!" Again, how great must have been their promptitude in

19 exercitu festinatio? Cum Pyrrhus "video me"[1]
inquit "plane procreatum Herculis semine, cui
quasi ab angue Lernaeo tot caesa hostium capita
20 quasi de sanguine suo renascuntur." Qui autem
ille senatus fuit, cum perorante Appio Caeco pulsi
cum muneribus suis ab urbe legati interroganti regi
suo, quid de hostium sede sentirent, urbem templum
sibi visam, senatum regum esse concessum[2] confite-
21 rentur? Qui porro ipsi duces? Vel in castris, cum
medicum venale regis caput offerentem Curius
remisit, Fabricius oblatam sibi a rege imperii partem
22 repudiavit; vel in pace, cum Curius fictilia sua
Samnitico praeferret auro, Fabricius decem pondo
argenti circa Rufinum consularem virum quasi
23 luxuriam censoria gravitate damnaret. Quis ergo
miretur his moribus ea virtute militum victorem[3]
populum Romanum[4] fuisse, unoque bello Tarentino
intra quadriennium maximam partem Italiae, fortis-
simas gentes, opulentissimas urbes uberrimasque
24 regiones subegisse? Aut quid adeo fidem superet,
quam si principia belli cum exitu conferantur?
Victor primo proelio Pyrrhus, tota tremente Cam-
pania Lirim Fregellasque populatus, prope captam
urbem a Praenestina arce prospexit et a vicensimo

[1] video me *L Voss. Rehd. Palat.*: idem omne *BN*.
[2] concessum *add. Aldus, cf. Plut. Pyrrh.* 19, *Liv.* ix, 17, 14.
[3] victorem *NL*: exercitum *B*.
[4] populum romanum *NL*: populi romani *B*.

replacing their losses! For Pyrrhus said, "I plainly see that I am sprung of the seed of Hercules, when I see all these heads of foes cut off springing up again from their blood as they sprang from the Lernaean hydra." Again, what was the character of the senate? When, on the proposal of Appius Caecus, the ambassadors of Pyrrhus had been expelled from the city with their presents and the king asked them what they thought of the abode of their enemies, they confessed that the city seemed to them to be a temple and the senate an assembly of kings. Again, what kind of men were their generals? Even in the field, Curius sent back the physician who offered the head of Pyrrhus for sale, and Fabricius refused a share in his kingdom offered to him by the king; in peace, Curius preferred his earthenware vessels to Samnite gold, and Fabricius, with all the authority of the censorial office, stigmatized as a luxury the possession of Rufinus, a man of consular rank, of ten pounds of silver. Who then can wonder that with such moral principles and such military valour the Roman people were victorious, and that, in their single war against the Tarentines, they subdued, within the space of four years, the greater part of Italy, the bravest nations, the richest cities and the most fertile regions? Or what can be more incredible than the contrast presented by the beginning of the war and its conclusion? Pyrrhus victorious in the first battle, while all Campania trembled, laid waste the banks of the Liris and Fragellae, looked forth from the city of Praeneste upon a Rome which he had all but captured, and, at a distance of only about twenty miles, filled the eyes

lapide oculos trepidae civitatis fumo ac pulvere
25 inplevit. Eodem postea bis exuto castris, bis saucio
et in Graeciam suam trans mare ac terras fugato,
pax et quies et tanta de opulentissimis tot gentibus
26 spolia, ut victoriam suam Roma non caperet. Nec
enim temere ullus pulchrior in urbem aut speciosior
27 triumphus intravit. Ante hunc diem nihil praeter
pecora Vulscorum, greges Sabinorum, carpenta
Gallorum, fracta Samnitium arma vidisses: tum si
captivos aspiceres, Molossi, Thessali, Macedones,
Brittius, Apulus atque Lucanus; si pompam, aurum,
purpura, signa, tabulae Tarentinaeque deliciae.
28 Sed nihil libentius populus Romanus aspexit quam
illas, quas ita timuerat, cum turribus suis beluas,
quae non sine sensu captivitatis summissis cervicibus
victores equos sequebantur.

XIIII. Bellvm Picens[1]

19 Omnis mox Italia pacem habuit—quid enim post
Tarentum auderent?—nisi quod ultro persequi
2 socios hostium placuit. domiti ergo Picentes et
caput gentis Asculum Sempronio duce, qui tremente
inter proelium campo Tellurem deam promissa aede
placavit.

[1] Picens *N*: Pycense *B*.

of the trembling citizens with his smoke and dust. Yet afterwards, when this same king had twice had his camp captured and had been twice wounded and had been driven as a fugitive over sea and land back to his own land of Greece, peace and tranquillity ensued, and so rich a spoil was gathered from so many wealthy races that Rome could not contain the fruits of her victory. Scarcely ever did a fairer or more glorious triumph enter the city. Up to that time the only spoils which you could have seen were the cattle of the Volscians, the flocks of the Sabines, the waggons of the Gauls, the broken arms of the Samnites; now if you looked at captives, they were Molossians, Thessalians, Macedonians, Bruttians, Apulians and Lucanians; if you looked upon the procession, you saw gold, purple statues, pictures and all the luxury of Tarentum. But upon nothing did the Roman people look with greater pleasure than upon those huge beasts, which they had feared so much, with towers upon their backs, now following the horses which had vanquished them, with heads bowed low not wholly unconscious that they were prisoners.

XIIII. The Picenian War

19. Then all Italy enjoyed peace—for who could venture upon resistance after the defeat of Tarentum?—except that the Romans thought fit themselves to punish those who had been the allies of their enemies. The people of Picenum were therefore subdued and their capital Asculum was taken under the leadership of Sempronius, who, when an earthquake occurred in the midst of the battle, appeased the goddess Earth by the promise of a temple.

XV. Bellvm Sallentinvm

20 Sallentini Picentibus additi caputque regionis Brundisium inclito portu M. Atilio duce. In hoc certamine victoriae pretium templum sibi pastoria Pales ultro poposcit.

XVI. Bellvm Volsiniense

21 Postremi Italicorum in fidem venere Volsinii, opulentissimi Etruscorum, inplorantes opem adversus servos quondam suos, qui libertatem a dominis datam in ipsos erexerant translataque in se re publica dominabantur. Sed hi quoque duce Fabio Gurgite poenas dederunt.

XVII. De Seditionibvs

22 Haec est secunda aetas populi Romani et quasi adulescentia, qua maxime viruit et quodam flore virtutis exarsit ac ferbuit. Itaque inerat quaedam adhuc ex pastoribus feritas, quiddam adhuc spirabat
2 indomitum. Inde est, quod exercitus Postumium imperatorem, infitiantem quas promiserat praedas, facta in castris seditione lapidavit; quod sub Appio Claudio noluit vincere hostem, cum posset; quod

XV. The Sallentine War

20. The Sallentines and Brundusium, the capital of their country, with its famous harbour, shared the fate of the people of Picenum at the hands of the Romans under the leadership of Marcus Atilius. During this struggle Pales, the goddess of shepherds, demanded further for herself a temple as the price of victory.

XVI. The Volsinian War

21. The last of the Italians who came under the protection of Rome were the Volsinians, the richest of all the Etruscans, who asked for help against those who had formerly been their slaves and had used against their masters the liberty which the latter had granted to them, and, having shifted the power to themselves, were playing the tyrants in the State; they too were punished by the Romans under the leadership of Fabius Gurges.

XVII. Of Civil Discords

22. This period forms the second age, which may be called the youth, of the Roman people, during which it was most vigorous, and showed fire and heat in the flower of its strength. Hence there was still in it a certain spirit of ferocity inherited from shepherd ancestors, and an untamed spirit yet breathed. Hence it was that the army mutinied in camp and stoned the general Postumius, when he denied them the spoils which he had promised; that under Appius Claudius they refused to defeat the enemy when it was in their power to

duce Volerone detrectantibus plerisque militiam,
3 fracti consulis fasces. Inde clarissimos principes,
quod adversarentur voluntati suae, exulatione
multavit, ut Coriolanum colere agros iubentem—
nec minus ille ferociter iniuriam armis vindicasset,
nisi quod iam inferentem signa filium mater Veturia
4 lacrimis suis exarmavit;—ut ipsum Camillum, quod
inique inter plebem et exercitum divisisse Veientem
praedam videretur. Sed hic melior Veis[1] in capta
urbe consenuit et mox supplices de hoste Gallo
5 vindicavit. Cum senatu quoque vehementius aequo
bonoque certatum est, adeo ut relictis sedibus
solitudinem et interitum patriae suae minaretur.

23 Prima discordia ob inpotentiam feneratorum.
Quibus in terga quoque serviliter saevientibus, in
sacrum montem plebs armata secessit aegreque, nec
nisi tribunos impetrasset, Meneni Agrippae, facundi
2 et sapientis viri, auctoritate revocata est. Extat
orationis antiquae satis efficax ad concordiam fabula,
qua dissedisse quondam humanos dixit artus, quod
omnibus opere fungentibus solus venter inmunis

[1] Veis *Seebodius*: vis *B*.

do so; that when under the leadership of Volero many refused to serve, the consul's fasces were broken. Hence it was that they punished with exile their most illustrious chiefs, because they opposed their will; Coriolanus, for example, when he ordered them to till their fields (and he would have avenged his wrongs by force of arms with even greater severity, if his mother Veturia had not disarmed him by her tears when he was already advancing), and Camillus himself, because he was thought to have divided the spoils of Veii unfairly between the people and the army. Camillus, however, a truer patriot, lived to grow old in the city of Veii which he had captured, and afterwards took vengeance on behalf of those who implored his aid against the Gaulish foe. With the senate, too, there were struggles which went beyond all justice and right, since the people even left their homes and threatened their country with desolation and ruin.

23. The first dispute was due to the tyranny of the usurers. When these actually vented their fury upon their persons as though they were slaves, the common people took up arms and seceded to the Sacred Mount, and were with difficulty induced to return (and then only after their demand for a tribune had been granted) at the instance of the eloquent and wise Menenius Agrippa. The fable, quite in the old style of oratory, which was most efficacious in promoting concord, is still remembered, in which he said that the members of the human body once revolted, on the ground that, while they all performed their functions, the stomach alone lived without doing any duty, but afterwards, when they

ageret; deinde moribundos ea seiunctione redisse
in gratiam, quando sensissent quod eius opera redactis
in sanguinem cibis inrigarentur.

24 Secundam in urbe media decemviratus libido
conflavit. Allatas a Graecia leges decem principes
lecti iubente populo conscripserant, ordinataque erat
in duodecim tabulis tota iustitia, cum tamen traditos
2 fasces regio quodam furore retinebant. Ante ceteros
Appius eo insolentiae elatus est, ut ingenuam
virginem stupro destinaret, oblitus et Lucretiae et
3 regum et iuris quod ipse conposuerat. Itaque cum
oppressam iudicio filiam trahi in servitutem videret
Virginius pater, nihil cunctatus in medio foro manu
sua interfecit, admotisque signis commilitonum totam
eam dominationem obsessam armis in carcerem et
catenas ab Aventino monte detraxit.

25 Tertiam seditionem excitavit matrimoniorum
dignitas, ut plebei cum patriciis iungerentur; qui
tumultus in monte Ianiculo duce Canuleio tribuno
plebis exarsit. 26. Quartam honorum cupido, ut
2 plebei quoque magistratus crearentur. Fabius
Ambustus duarum pater alteram Sulpicio patricii

found themselves dying, owing to their separation from it, they returned to a good understanding with it, because they found that its service was to convert food into the blood which flows in them.

24. The second disagreement occurred in the very centre of the city and was caused by the lust of the Decemvirate. Ten eminent citizens had been chosen by order of the people, and had jointly drawn up a code of laws derived from Greece, and the whole system of justice had been arranged upon twelve tables; but they afterwards still retained, in the lawless spirit of the kings, the fasces which had been entrusted to them. Appius attained such a spirit of insolence beyond all the rest that he destined a free-born maiden for dishonour, forgetful of Lucretia and the kings and the code which he had himself helped to draw up. And so when Virginius, the maiden's father, saw his daughter being dragged away to slavery after an unjust sentence, without a moment's delay he slew her in the midst of the forum with his own hand and, moving up companies of his fellow-soldiers, surrounded the whole band of tyrants with an armed force and dragged them from the Aventine Hill to prison and chains.

25. The third insurrection was caused by the question of marriage-dignity, arising from the demand that plebeians should intermarry with patricians. This disturbance burst into flames on the Hill of Janiculum at the instigation of Canuleius, the tribune of the people. 26. The fourth insurrection was due to the desire for office and the demand that magistrates should be elected from among the plebeians also. Fabius Ambustus was the father of

3 sanguinis dederat, alteram plebeius Stolo sibi iunxit.
Qua[1] quodam tempore, quod lictoriae virgae sonum
ignotum penatibus suis expaverat, a sorore satis
4 insolenter inrisa, iniuriam non tulit. Itaque nanctus
tribunatum honorum et magistratuum consortium
quamvis invito senatui extorsit.

5 Verum in ipsis seditionibus principem populum
non inmerito suspexeris. Si quidem nunc libertatem,
nunc pudicitiam, tum natalium dignitatem, tum
honorum decora et insignia vindicavit, interque
haec omnia nullius acrior custos quam libertatis fuit,
6 nullaque in pretium eius potuit largitione corrumpi,
cum ut in magno et in dies maiore populo interim
7 perniciosi cives existerent. Spurium[2] largitione,
Cassium agraria lege suspectum regiae dominationis
praesenti morte multavit. Ac de Spurio quidem
supplicium pater ipsius sumpsit, hunc Quinctii
dictatoris imperio in medio foro magister equitum
8 Servilius Ahala confodit. Manlium vero Capitolii
vindicem, quia plerosque debitorum liberaverat altius
et incivilius se efferentem, ab illa ipsa quam defend-
erat arce deiecit.

[1] qua *add. Halmius.*
[2] Spurium *inseruit Salmasius.*

two daughters, one of whom he had given in marriage to Sulpicius, a man of patrician blood, while Stolo, a plebeian, had wedded the other. The wife of the latter having been the object of somewhat insolent laughter on the part of her sister because she had been alarmed by the sound of the lictor's staff (a sound which was unfamiliar to her in her own home), Stolo could not endure the affront. And so, when he obtained the tribunate, he extorted from the senate, against their will, a share in public offices and magistracies.

Even in these insurrections one may admire, not without good reason, this sovereign people, since at one time it championed liberty, at another chastity, at another the dignity of birth, at another the right to distinctions and insignia of office, and among all these things was a zealous upholder of nothing so much as of liberty, and could not be corrupted by any kind of bribery to put it up for sale, although, as was to be expected in a large and daily increasing community, dangerous citizens arose from time to time. The people punished by immediate execution Spurius and Cassius, who were suspected of aiming at the royal power, the former through his excessive largesses, the latter by his agrarian law. The punishment of Spurius was undertaken by his own father, while Cassius was stabbed in the middle of the forum at the order of Quinctius, the dictator, by Servilius Ahala, the master of the horse. Manlius too, the saviour of the Capitol, they hurled from the very citadel which he had himself defended, when he began to behave in a manner too arrogant and ill-fitting a private citizen on the strength of having set free a number of debtors.

9 Talis domi ac foris, talis pace belloque populus Romanus fretum illud adulescentiae, id est secundam imperii aetatem habuit, in qua totam inter Alpes fretumque Italiam armis subegit.

XVIII. Bellvm Pvnicvm Primvm

II, 1 Domita subactaque Italia populus Romanus prope quingentensimum annum agens, cum bona fide adolevisset, si quod est robur, si qua iuventas, tum ille vere robustus et iuvenis par[1] orbi terrarum esse
2 coepit. Ita—mirum et incredibile dictu—qui prope quingentis annis domi luctatus est—adeo difficile fuerat dare Italiae caput—his ducentis annis qui secuntur Africam, Europam, Asiam, totum denique orbem terrarum bellis victoriisque peragravit.
II, 2 Igitur victor Italiae populus Romanus cum ad fretum usque venisset, more ignis, qui obvias[2] populatus incendio silvas interveniente flumine ab-
2 rumpitur, paulisper substitit. Mox cum videret opulentissimam in proximo praedam quodam modo Italiae suae abscissam[3] et quasi revolsam, adeo cupiditate eius exarsit, ut, quatenus nec mole iungi nec pontibus posset, armis belloque iungenda et ad
3 continentem suam revocanda bello videretur. Sed

[1] et iuvenis par *Halmius*: iuvenis et par *B*.
[2] obvias *NL*: cunctas *B*.
[3] abscissam *L Halmius*: abscisam *BN*.

[1] The Straits of Messina.

Such were the Roman people at home and abroad, in peace and in war, as it passed through the stormy waters of its youth, that is to say, the second age of its empire, during which it subdued by force of arms all Italy between the Alps and the Straits.[1]

XVIII. The First Punic War

1. Italy having been subdued and conquered, the Roman people, having almost reached its five hundredth year, since it can truly be said to have reached maturity, was now robust and vigorous—if ever there is robustness, if ever vigour, in a State—and became a match for the whole world. Thus arose the wonderful and incredible phenomenon that a people, which had struggled in its own country for five hundred years (so difficult had it been to establish supremacy in Italy), during the next two hundred years overspread Africa, Europe and Asia and, finally, the whole world with its wars and victories.

2. The Romans, then, victorious over Italy, having now extended their bounds to the Straits, halted for a space, like a fire, which, having laid waste the woods that lie in its course, is held up by an intervening river. But soon, seeing in their neighbourhood a most wealthy prey which seemed somehow to have been rent away and as it were torn from their own land of Italy, they were kindled with so strong a desire for its possession that, since it could not be attached to by a mole or a bridge, they resolved that it should be reunited by arms and warfare, and thus restored to the continent to which it belonged. But lo! the fates

ecce, ultro ipsis viam pandentibus fatis, nec occasio
defuit, cum de Poenorum inpotentia foederata
Siciliae civitas Messana quereretur. Adfectabat
autem ut Romanus ita Poenus Siciliam, et eodem
tempore paribus uterque votis ac viribus imperium
4 orbis agitabat. Igitur specie quidem socios iuvandi,
re autem sollicitante praeda, quamquam territaret
novitas rei, tamen—tanta[1] in virtute fiducia est—
ille rudis, ille pastorius populus vereque terrester
ostendit nihil interesse virtutis, equis an navibus,
terra an mari dimicaretur.

5 Appio Claudio consule primum fretum ingressus
est fabulosis infame monstris aestuque violentum;
sed adeo non est exterritus, ut illam ipsam ruentis
aestus violentiam pro munere amplecteretur,[2] sta-
6 timque ac sine mora Hieronem Syracusanum tanta
celeritate devicit, ut ille ipse prius se victum quam
hostem videret fateretur.

7 Duillio[3] Cornelioque consulibus etiam mari con-
gredi ausus est. Tum quidem ipsa velocitas classis
conparatae victoriae auspicium fuit. Intra enim
sexagesimum diem quam caesa silva fuerat centum
sexaginta navium classis in anchoris stetit, ut non
arte factae, sed quodam munere deorum conversae
8 in naves atque mutatae arbores viderentur. Proelii
vero forma mirabilis, cum illas celeris volucrisque

[1] tamen tanta *Voss.*: tanta tamen *BNL*.
[2] quod velocitas navium mari iuvaretur *post* amplectitur *add.* *BI*.
[3] Duillio: ad uilio *B*: diullio *L*: duellio *I*.

---

[1] 264 B.C. [2] 260 B.C.

themselves opened a way and an opportunity was offered by the complaints which Messana, a Sicilian State allied by treaty to Rome, made about the tyrannical behaviour of the Carthaginians. This people, like the Romans, coveted Sicily, and both nations at the same time with equally strong desires and equal forces were aiming at the empire of the world. On the pretext, therefore, of aiding their allies, but really stimulated by the desire for spoil, this rude, pastoral people, whose proper element was the land, although the strangeness of the undertaking alarmed them, yet (so great is the confidence inspired by courage) showed that for the brave it is a matter of indifference whether the fight is waged on horseback or on shipboard, on land or on sea.

In the consulship of Appius Claudius[1] they first launched the ships across that strait, so ill-famed for fabulous monsters and swept by so violent a current. Yet so little were they alarmed that they welcomed the violence of the rushing tide as a godsend, and immediately without delay defeated Hiero of Syracuse with a suddenness that made him confess that he was defeated before he set eyes upon the enemy.

In the consulship of Duillius and Cornelius[2] they ventured to meet the enemy at sea also. On this occasion the very speed with which they had constructed their fleet was an omen of victory; for within sixty days of the felling of the timber, a fleet of a hundred and sixty vessels rode at anchor, so that it seemed as if the trees had not been made into ships by the art of man, but changed and altered thereto by a dispensation of heaven. The ordering of the battle too was wonderful, since

hostium navis hae graves tardaeque conprehenderent. Longe illis nauticae artes, detorquere remos
9 et ludificari fuga rostra. Iniectae enim ferreae manus machinaeque validae, ante certamen multum ab hoste derisae, coactique hostes quasi in solido decernere. Victor ergo apud Liparas mersa aut fugata hostium classe primum illum maritimum egit
10 triumphum. Cuius quod gaudium fuit, cum Duillius imperator, non contentus unius diei triumpho, per vitam omnem, ubi a cena rediret, praelucere funalia et praecinere sibi tibias iussit, quasi cotidie
11 triumpharet. Prae tanta huius victoria leve damnum [1] fuit alter consulum interceptus Asina Cornelius, qui simulato colloquio evocatus atque ita oppressus, fuit perfidiae Punicae documentum.

12 Calatino dictatore fere omnia praesidia Poenorum Agrigento, Drepanis, Panhormo, Eryce Lilybaeoque
13 detraxit. Trepidatum est semel circa Camerinensium saltum, sed eximia virtute Calpurni Flammae tribuni militum evasimus. Qui lecta trecentorum manu insessum ab hostibus tumulum occupavit atque moratus hostes est,[2] dum exercitus omnis evaderet.
14 Ac sic pulcherrimo exitu Thermopylarum et Leonidae famam adaequavit, hoc inlustrior noster, quod

[1] leve damnum : leve huius proelii damnum *codd.*
[2] est *add. Iahnius.*

---

[1] *remos retorquere* is the manœuvre of sweeping away the oars by brushing against the enemy's ship; cp. Polyb. xvi. 4, 14, ταρσοὺς παρασύρειν.

the heavy, slow Roman vessels came to grips with the swift and active craft of the enemy. Nought availed their usual manœuvres of sweeping away the enemy's oars[1] or frustrating their charge by flight; for grappling-irons and strong appliances, which before the battle had caused much derision on the part of the enemy, fastened upon their ships and obliged them to fight as it were upon dry land. Thus victorious off the Liparae Islands, after sinking or routing the enemy's fleet, they celebrated their first naval triumph. And how great was their joy! Duillius, who had been in command, not content with a single day's triumph, throughout his life, when he returned from supper, ordered torches to be lighted and pipes to play before him by way of celebrating a daily triumph. In comparison with Duillius' great victory, the death of the other consul, Cornelius Asina, in an ambush was a trifling loss; but his invitation to a pretended conference and consequent seizure was a good example of Carthaginian treachery.

In the dictatorship of Calatinus the Romans expelled almost all the Carthaginian garrisons—from Agrigentum, Drepanum, Panormus, Eryx and Lilybaeum. On one occasion there was a panic in the forest of Camerina, but by the extraordinary bravery of Calpurnius Flamma, a military tribune, we extricated ourselves. He, with a chosen band of three hundred men, seized a knoll, which was beset by the enemy, and so delayed them long enough to give the whole army time to escape. By the glorious result of his action he equalled the fame of Leonidas at Thermopylae, the Roman hero being more illustrious in that he survived his great

expeditioni tantae superfuit,[1] licet nihil inscripserit
sanguine.
15 Lucio Cornelio Scipione consule,[2] cum iam Sicilia
suburbana esset populi Romani provincia, serpente
latius bello Sardiniam adnexamque Corsicam transiit.
16 Olbiae hic, ibi Aleriae[3] urbis excidio incolas terruit,
adeoque omni terra et mari Poenos purgavit, ut iam
victoriae nihil nisi Africa ipsa restaret.
17 Marco Atilio Regulo duce iam in Africam navi-
gabat bellum. Nec defuerant qui ipso Punici maris
nomine ac terrore deficerent, insuper augente
Nautio tribuno metum, in quem, nisi paruisset,
securi destricta imperator metu mortis navigandi
18 fecit audaciam. Mox deinde ventis remisque pro-
peratum est, tantusque terror hostici adventus
Poenis fuit, ut apertis paene portis Carthago
19 caperetur. Prooemium[4] belli fuit civitas Clipea;
prima enim a Punico litore quasi arx et specula
procurrit. Et haec et trecenta amplius castella
20 vastata sunt. Nec cum hominibus, sed cum monstris
quoque dimicatum est, cum quasi in vindictam
Africae nata mirae magnitudinis serpens posita apud
21 Bagradam castra vexaverit. Sed omnium victor

[1] ut supervixit *add. B*, et supervixit *add. NL post* superfuit.

[2] consule *add. Iahnius.*

[3] ibi Aleriae *Salmasius*: ibi alte *B*: baleriae *NL*: ibi ateriae *I.*

[4] prooemium belli *Iahnius*: prima premium (proemium *I*) belli *B*: prima belli praemium *NL.*

---

[1] Florus here confuses Leonidas with another Spartan hero, Othryades, who, being the sole survivor of the three hundred Spartans who fought against the Argives for the possession of Thyrea, slew himself on the battle-field after

exploit, though he did not write anything in his own blood.[1]

In the consulship of Lucius Cornelius Scipio,[2] when Sicily was already a suburban province of the Roman people, the war spread further, and they crossed over to Sardinia and the adjoining island of Corsica. They terrified the inhabitants by the destruction of Olbia in the former island and Aleria in the latter, and so completely cleared land and sea of the Carthaginians that only Africa itself still remained to be conquered.

Under the leadership of Marcus Atilius Regulus the war was now transferred to Africa. There had been some, however, who quailed at the very mention of the Punic sea and the terror which it inspired, their alarm being further increased by the tribune Nautius; but the general, by threatening him with the axe if he refused to obey, inspired them with courage for the journey through the fear of death. All haste was then made with sails and oars, and the approach of the enemy so alarmed the Carthaginians that the gates of Carthage were almost opened and the city captured. The war began with the taking of Clipea, which projects as a citadel or watch-tower from the Carthaginian coast. This and three hundred other fortresses were destroyed. But the Romans had to contend not only with human beings, but also with monsters; for a serpent of wondrous size, which seemed to have been created for the defence of Africa, harassed their camp on the Bagradas. But Regulus, everywhere

writing in blood on his shield that Thyrea belonged to the Spartans (Herod. I. 82. 7).

[2] 259 B.C.

Regulus cum terrorem nominis sui late circumtulisset
cumque magnam vim iuventutis ducesque ipsos aut
cecidisset[1] aut haberet in vinculis, classemque
ingenti praeda onustam et triumpho gravem in
urbem praemisisset, iam ipsam, caput belli, Cartha-
ginem urguebat obsidio ipsisque portis inhaerebat.
22 Hic paululum circumacta fortuna est, tantum ut
plura essent Romanae virtutis insignia, cuius fere
23 magnitudo calamitatibus adprobatur. Nam con-
versis ad externa auxilia hostibus, cum Xanthippum
illis ducem Lacedaemon misisset, a viro militiae
peritissimo vincimur—foeda clades Romanisque usu
incognita—vivus in manus hostium venit fortissimus
imperator. Sed ille quidem par tantae calamitati
fuit; nam nec Punico carcere infractus est nec
24 legatione suscepta. Quippe diversa quam hostis
mandaverat censuit, ne pax fieret, ne commutatio
25 captivorum reciperetur. Sed nec illo voluntario ad
hostis suos reditu nec ultimo sive carceris seu crucis
supplicio deformata maiestas; immo his omnibus
admirabilior quid aliud quam victor de victoribus
atque etiam, quia Carthago non cesserat, de fortuna
26 triumphavit? Populus autem Romanus multo
acrior intentiorque pro ultione Reguli quam pro
victoria fuit.

27 Metello igitur consule spirantibus altius Poenis et

[1] cecidisset *Iordanis cod. Polling.*: coepisset *B*: cepisset *NI*.

---

[1] 250 B.C.

victorious, having spread far and wide the terror of his name and having slain or holding as prisoners a large number of the enemy's troops and even of their generals, and having sent in advance to Rome a fleet laden with immense spoils and full of material for a triumph, was already threatening Carthage itself, the author of the war, with blockade and pressing hard upon its very gates. At this point the breeze of fortune veered somewhat, but only in order to provide more evidence of the Roman valour, the greatness of which is more often put to the proof by misfortunes. For when the enemy had resorted to foreign aid and Lacedaemon had sent Xanthippus to be their general, we were defeated by a very skilful leader—a disgraceful disaster such as the Romans had never before experienced—and the brave commander-in-chief fell alive into the enemies' hands. But he proved himself able to face such a calamity; his spirit was not broken either by a Carthaginian prison or by the mission to Rome which he undertook. For, contrary to the instructions of the enemy, he expressed an opinion against making peace or consenting to an exchange of prisoners. His voluntary return to his enemies and his final sufferings, whether in prison or on the cross, in no way sullied his dignity; nay, rendered by all this only the more worthy of admiration, what did he do but triumph victorious over his victors and, since Carthage had not yielded, over Fortune herself? The Roman people, on their part, were even more eager and intent on avenging Regulus than on obtaining a victory.

In the consulship, therefore, of Metellus,[1] when

reverso in Siciliam bello, apud Panhormum sic hostes
cecidit, ut nec[1] amplius eam insulam adgredi
28 cogitarent. Argumentum ingentis victoriae centum
circiter elephantorum captivitas, sic quoque magna
praeda, si gregem illum non bello, sed venatione
cepisset.
29 Appio Claudio consule non ab hostibus, sed a dis
ipsis superatus est, quorum auspicia contempserat,
ibi[2] statim classe demersa, ubi ille praecipitari
pullos iusserat, quod pugnare ab iis vetaretur.
30 Marco Fabio Buteone consule hostium[3] classem
iam in Africo mari apud Aegimurum in Italiam ultro
31 navigantem cecidit. Quantus, o, tum triumphus
tempestate intercidit, cum opulenta praeda classis
adversis acta ventis naufragio suo Africam et Syrtis
32 et[4] omnium interiacentium[5] insularum litora im-
plevit! Magna clades, sed non sine aliqua principis
populi dignitate, interceptam tempestate victoriam
et triumphum perisse[6] naufragio. Et tamen cum
Punicae praedae omnibus promontoriis insulisque
fluitarent, populus Romanus et sic triumphavit.
33 Lutatio Catulo consulé tandem bello finis inpo-
situs apud insulas, quibus nomen Aegatae, nec maior
34 alias in mari pugna. Aderat quippe commeatibus,
exercitu, propugnaculis, armis gravis classis et in

[1] ut nec *L*: ut ne *N*: ne *BI*.
[2] ibi *IN*: ab his *B*.
[3] hostium *post* Aegimurum *ponit BI*.
[4] et *add. Bentleius*.
[5] interiacentium *Bentleius*: imperiagentium *codd.*
[6] perisse *om. B*.

---

[1] 249 B.C. His name was Publius, not Appius, Claudius.
[2] 245 B.C. [3] And not the enemy. [4] 242 B.C.

the Carthaginians became bolder and the war had been transferred back to Sicily, the Romans inflicted such a defeat upon their foes at Panormus that they gave up all thought of further attacks upon the island. The extent of their victory is proved by the capture of about a hundred elephants —a vast prey even if they had captured them not in war but in the chase.

In the consulship of Appius[1] Claudius the Romans were defeated not by the enemy but by the gods, whose auspices he had despised, their fleet being immediately sunk on the spot where Appius Claudius had ordered the sacred chickens to be thrown overboard, because he was warned by them not to fight.

In the consulship of Marcus Fabius Buteo[2] they defeated the enemy's fleet near Aegimurus in the African sea, while it was actually sailing against Italy. But what a triumph was ruined by the storm which then occurred, when the fleet, loaded with rich booty, driven by contrary winds, covered Africa, the Syrtes and the shores of all the interjacent islands with its wreckage! A great calamity indeed! but it did not fail to redound to the honour of an imperial people that it was a storm[3] which had intercepted their victory, and a shipwreck which had destroyed their triumph. And, seeing that the Carthaginian spoil floated off every promontory and island, even so the Roman people triumphed.

In the consulship of Lutatius Catuius[4] the war was at last brought to a close near the islands called the Aegatae. No greater fight was ever fought at sea. For the enemy's fleet came up loaded with supplies, troops, towers and arms; indeed you might

ea quasi tota Carthago; quod ipsum exitio fuit.
35 Romana classis prompta, levis, expedita et quodam
genere castrensis ad similitudinem pugnae equestris
sic remis quasi habenis agebatur, et in hos vel illos
ictus mobilia rostra speciem viventium praeferebant.
36 Itaque momento temporis laceratae hostium rates
totum inter Siciliam Sardiniamque pelagus naufragio
37 suo operuerunt. Tanta denique fuit illa victoria, ut
de excindendis [1] hostium moenibus non quaereretur.
Supervacuum visum est in arcem murosque saevire,
cum iam in mari esset deleta Carthago.

XVIIII. Bellvm Ligvricvm

II, 3 Peracto Punico bello secuta est brevis sane quasi
ad recuperandum spiritum requies, argumentumque
pacis et bona fide cessantium armorum tum primum
post Numam clausa porta Iani fuit; deinceps statim
2 ac sine mora patuit. Quippe iam Ligures, iam
Insubres Galli, nec non et Illyrici lacessebant,
sitae sub Alpibus, id est sub ipsis Italiae faucibus
gentes, deo quodam incitante adsidue, ne rubiginem
3 ac situm scilicet arma sentirent. Denique utrique
cotidiani et quasi domestici hostes tirocinia militum
inbuebant, nec aliter utraque gente quam quasi
cote quadam populus Romanus ferrum suae virtutis
acuebat.

[1] excindendis *Halmius*; excidendis *codd.*

say that all Carthage was on board it. And it was this that caused its ruin; for the Roman fleet, easily handled, light and unencumbered and in a way resembling a land army, was guided by its oars just as horses are guided by their reins in a cavalry engagement, and the beaks of the ships, moving rapidly to ram now this foe and now that, presented the appearance of living creatures. And so in a moment of time the enemy's vessels were cut to pieces and covered the whole sea between Sicily and Sardinia with their wreckage. In a word, so great was the victory that no question was raised of demolishing the enemy's walls; it seemed superfluous to vent their fury on a citadel and walls when Carthage had already been destroyed upon the sea.

XVIIII. The Ligurian War

3. The Carthaginian war being ended, a period of rest ensued, brief, indeed, for the Roman people to recover their breath. As a proof of peace and a genuine cessation of hostilities, the door of the Temple of Janus was closed for the first time since the reign of Numa; but immediately afterwards it was quickly opened again. For first the Ligurians and then the Insubrian Gauls, and also the Illyrians, races living at the foot of the Alps, that is, at the very entrance of Italy, began to give trouble at the continual instigation of some god, who feared that Rome's arms should suffer from rust and decay. In a word, both these races, continually active and, as it were, at our very doors, provided our recruits with practice in warfare, and the Roman people sharpened the edge of their valour on these two people as on the whetstone.

4 Liguras, imis Alpium iugis adhaerentis inter Varum et Magram flumen inplicitosque dumis silvestribus, maior aliquanto labor erat invenire quam vincere. Tuti locis et fuga, durum atque velox genus, ex occasione latrocinia magis quam bella
5 faciebant. Itaque cum diu multumque eluderent[1] Saluvii,[2] Deciates,[3] Oxubii,[4] Euburiates,[5] Ingauni, tandem Fulvius latebras eorum igni saepsit, Baebius in plana deduxit, Postumius ita exarmavit, ut vix reliquerit ferrum quo terra coleretur.

XX. Bellvm Gallicvm

II, 4 Gallis Insubribus, et his accolis Alpium, animi ferarum, corpora plus quam humana erant, sed—experimento deprehensum est, quippe sicut primus impetus eis maior quam virorum est, ita sequens
2 minor quam feminarum—Alpina corpora umente caelo educata habent quiddam simile nivibus suis: quum mox[6] caluere pugna, statim in sudorem eunt
3 et levi motu quasi sole laxantur. Hi saepe et alias et Brittomaro duce non prius posituros se baltea quam Capitolium ascendissent iuraverant. Factum est; victos enim Aemilius in Capitolio discinxit.
4 Mox Ariovisto duce vovere de nostrorum militum praeda Marti suo torquem. Intercepit Iuppiter

[1] eluderent: ludere *B*: eluderet *NL*.
[2] Saluvii: salui *B*: saltus *NL*: saltu viis *I*.
[3] Deciates: decilates *BI*: deciate *L*.
[4] Oxubii: exuuii *B*.
[5] Euburiates: et buriates *B*.
[6] quum mox *scripsi*: quam mox *B*: cum mox *I*: quae mox ut *NL*: cum vix *Bezzenbergerus*.

The Ligurians, who dwelt close to the foot of the Alps between the rivers Varus and Magra, encircled by thickly-wooded undergrowth, were rather more difficult to find than to conquer. Protected by their position and their facilities for escape, this hardy and active race carried on depredations rather than war, as occasion allowed. And so after their tribes, the Saluvii, the Deciates, the Oxubii, the Euburiates, and the Ingauni had long successfully eluded defeat, Fulvius at last surrounded their lairs with a ring of fire, Baebius brought them down into the plains, and Postumius so thoroughly disarmed them as scarcely to leave them any iron to till the soil.

XX. The Gallic War

4. The Insubrian Gauls, who also dwelt near the Alps, possessed the spirit of wild beasts and stature greater than human, but, as experience proved—for just as their first onslaught was mightier than that of men, so their subsequent attack was feebler than that of women—the bodies of the Alpine races, reared in a moist climate, have a certain similarity to their own snows, for as soon as they become heated in the fray, they immediately break into sweat and are dissolved by slight exertion, as snow is melted by the sun. As often on previous occasions, so when Brittomarus was their leader, they swore that they would not doff their belts until they had scaled the Capitol. And so it came to pass; for Aemilius defeated them and ungirt them on the Capitol. Soon afterwards, when Ariovistus was their leader, they vowed to dedicate to their War-god a necklet made from the spoils of our soldiers. Jupiter intercepted their dedication; for

votum; nam de torquibus eorum aureum tropaeum
5 Iovi Flaminius erexit. Viridomaro rege Romana arma Volcano promiserant. Aliorsum vota ceciderunt; occiso enim rege Marcellus tertia post Romulum patrem Feretrio Iovi opima suspendit.

XXI. Bellvm Illyricvm

II, 5 Illyrii seu Liburni sub extremis Alpium radicibus agunt inter Arsiam Titiumque[1] flumen, longissime
2 per totum Hadriani maris litus effusi. Hi regnante Teutana muliere populationibus non contenti licentiae
3 scelus addiderunt. Legatos quippe nostros, ob ea quae deliquerant iure agentes, ne gladio quidem, sed ut victimas securi percutiunt, praefectos navium igne comburunt; idque, quo indignius foret, mulier
4 imperavit. Itaque Gnaeo Fulvio Centimalo[2] duce late domantur. Strictae secures in principum colla legatorum manibus litavere.

XXII. Bellvm Pvnicvm Secvndvm.

II, 6 Post primum Punicum bellum vix quadriennii requies: ecce alterum bellum, minus quidem spatio —nec enim amplius decem et octo annos habet—, sed adeo cladium atrocitate terribilius, ut si quis conferat damna utriusque populi, similior victo sit

[1] Titiumque: titullumque *B*: titulumque *I*.

[2] Centimalo: gentimalo *BI*; Centumalum *appellant fast. Capit. CIL I*[1], *p.* 456.

Flaminius set up in honour of Jupiter a golden trophy made from their necklets. During the reign of Viridomarus they had promised to offer up Roman armour to Vulcan; but their vows turned out otherwise, for their king was slain and Marcellus hung up in the temple of Jupiter Feretrius the *spolia opima* for the second time since father Romulus had done so.

XXI. The Illyrian War

5. The Illyrians, or Liburnians, dwelt at the very roots of the Alps between the rivers Arsia and Titius and spread widely along the coast of the Adriatic Sea. Under the rule of their queen Teutana, not content with depredations, they added crime to lawlessness. When our ambassadors came to protest against their delinquencies, they slew them, not with the sword, but like sacrificial victims, with the axe, and burnt to death the commanders of our ships. To make their action still more insulting, it was a woman that gave the order. They were, therefore, thoroughly subdued by an army under Gnaeus Fulvius Centimalus; and the axe wielded against the necks of the chiefs made atonement to the shades of our ambassadors.

XXII. The Second Punic War

6. After the First Punic War there was peace for barely four years, and then, lo, a second war broke out, less indeed in duration—for it lasted not more than eighteen years—but so much more terrible in the awfulness of the calamities which it involved, that, if one were to compare the losses on both sides, the people which conquered was more like

2 populus ille qui vicit. Urebat nobilem populum mare ablatum, raptae insulae, dare tributa, quae iubere consueverat. Hinc ultionem puer Annibal
3 ad aram patri iuraverat, nec morabatur. Igitur in causam belli Saguntos electa est, vetus Hispaniae civitas et opulenta fideique erga Romanos magnum
4 quidem sed triste monimentum, quam in libertatem communi foedere exceptam Annibal, causas novorum motuum quaerens, et suis et ipsorum manibus evertit, ut Italiam sibi rupto foedere aperiret.
5 Summa foederum Romanis religio est; itaque ad auditum sociae civitatis obsidium, memores icti cum Poenis quoque foederis, non statim ad arma procurrunt, dum prius more legitimo queri malunt.
6 Saguntini interim iam novem mensibus fessi fame machinis ferro, versa denique in rabiem fide inmanem in foro excitant rogum, tum desuper se suosque cum omnibus opibus suis ferro et igne
7 corrumpunt. Huius tantae cladis auctor Annibal poscitur. Tergiversantibus Poenis dux legationis "quae" inquit "mora est?" [Fabius][1] "in hoc ego sinu bellum pacemque porto; utrum eligitis?" Succlamantibus bellum, "bellum igitur" inquit

[1] Fabius *del. Graevius.*

one that had been defeated. A high-spirited people chafed at its exclusion from the sea, the seizure of its islands and the payment of tribute which it had been accustomed to demand from others. Hence Hannibal, while still a boy, had sworn to his father at the altar that he would exact vengeance; and he was not slow to do so. Saguntum, therefore, was chosen as a pretext for war, an ancient and wealthy Spanish city, a notable but sad example of loyalty towards the Roman people. This city, although it had been granted special immunity under a common treaty, Hannibal, seeking pretexts for fresh disturbances, destroyed, partly by his own hands and partly by those of the citizens themselves, in order that, by the violation of the treaty, he might open to himself the path to Italy. The Romans are most scrupulous in their observation of treaties; and so, on hearing of the siege of an allied city, mindful of the treaty which had also been signed by the Carthaginians, they did not immediately rush to arms, but preferred first to lodge a complaint in a legal form. Meanwhile the Saguntines, worn out by nine months of famine, the assaults of machines and the sword, their loyalty at last turning to rage, piled up a huge pyre in the middle of the market-place and, on the top of it, destroyed with fire and the sword themselves and their families together with all their possessions. The surrender of Hannibal was demanded as the author of this great calamity. When the Carthaginians prevaricated, the chief of the embassy exclaimed, "Why this delay? In the folds of this robe I bear war and peace; which do you choose?" And when they cried out "War," he answered, "Take war then," and shaking out the front of his

"accipite." Et excusso in media curia togae gremio non sine horrore, quasi plane sinu bellum ferret, effudit.

8 Similis exitus belli initiis fuit. Nam quasi has inferias sibi Saguntinorum ultimae dirae in illo publico parricidio incendioque mandassent, ita manibus eorum vastatione Italiae, captivitate Africae, ducum et regum qui id gessere bellum exitio
9 parentatum est. Igitur ubi semel se in Hispania movit illa gravis et luctuosa Punici belli vis atque tempestas destinatumque Romanis iam diu fulmen Saguntino igne conflavit, statim quodam impetu rapta medias perfregit Alpes et in Italiam ab illis fabulosae altitudinis nivibus velut caelo missa descendit.

10 Ac primi quidem impetus turbo inter Padum atque Ticinum valido statim fragore detonuit. Tum Scipione duce fusus exercitus; saucius etiam ipse venisset in hostium manus imperator, nisi protectum patrem praetextatus admodum filius ab ipsa morte
11 rapuisset. Hic erit Scipio, qui in exitium Africae crescit, nomen ex malis eius habiturus.

12 Ticino Trebia succedit. Hic secunda Punici belli procella desaevit Sempronio consule. Tum callidissimi hostes, frigidum et nivalem nancti diem, cum

---

[1] 218 B.C.

toga in the midst of the senate-house, he spread it out with a gesture which did not fail to produce the alarm which might have been expected had he really carried war in its folds.

The course of the war resembled its beginning; for, as though the last curses of the Saguntines at their public self-immolation and burning had demanded such funeral rites, atonement was made to their shades by the devastation of Italy, the subjugation of Africa and the destruction of the leaders and kings who waged the war. As soon, therefore, as the dire and dismal stress and storm of the Punic War had arisen in Spain and had forged in the flames of Saguntum the thunderbolt which had long been destined to fall upon the Romans, immediately, hurried along by some compelling force, it burst its way through the midst of the Alps and swooped down upon Italy from those snows of fabulous heights like a missile hurled from the skies.

The tempest of the first assault crashed with a mighty roar between the Padus and the Ticinus. The Roman army under Scipio was scattered, and the general himself would have fallen wounded into the enemy's hands had not his son, still a mere youth, protected his father and rescued him from the very jaws of death. This youth was destined to be that Scipio who grew up to be the conqueror of Africa and was to win a title of honour from its misfortunes.

After the battle of Ticinus came that of Trebia. It was here that in the consulship of Sempronius,[1] the second storm of the Punic War wreaked its fury. On this occasion the crafty enemy, finding the day cold and snowy, after warming themselves

se ignibus prius oleoque fovissent—horribile dictu—
homines a meridie et sole venientes, nostra nos hieme
vicerunt.

13 Thrasymennus lacus, tertium fulmen Annibalis,
imperatore Flaminio.[1] Ars nova Punicae fraudis;
quippe nebula lacus palustribusque virgultis tectus
14 equitatus terga subito pugnantium invasit. Nec de
dis possumus queri. Inminentem temerario duci
cladem praedixerant insidentia signis examina et
aquilae prodire nolentes et commissam aciem
secutus ingens terrae tremor; nisi illum horrorem
soli equitum virorumque discursus et mota vehe-
mentius arma fecerunt.

15 Quartum id et[2] paene ultimum volnus imperii
Cannae, ignobilis Apuliae vicus; sed magnitudine
cladis emersit et sexaginta milium caede parta
nobilitas. Ibi in excidium infelicis exercitus dux,
terra, caelum, dies, tota rerum natura consensit.
16 Si quidem non contentus simulatis transfugis
Annibal, qui mox terga pugnantium ceciderunt,[3]
insuper callidus imperator in patentibus campis
observato loci ingenio, quod et sol ibi acerrimus
et plurimus pulvis et eurus ab oriente semper quasi
ex constituto, ita instruxit aciem, ut, Romanis

[1] Flaminio *N*: flamminino *BL*: flamminio *I*.
[2] et *scripsi*: est *codd.*
[3] ceciderunt *Aldus*: ceciderant *BIL*.

---

[1] The standards were only with difficulty pulled out of the ground in which they were fixed (Liv. XXII, 3, 12).

at their fires and oiling themselves, defeated us (horrible to relate) though they came from the warmth of the southern sunshine, by the aid of our own winter.

Hannibal's third thunderbolt was launched at Lake Trasimene, where Flaminius commanded the Romans. Here Carthaginian craft devised a new stratagem; for their cavalry, under the cover of a mist from the lake and the undergrowth of the marshes, suddenly attacked the rear of our fighters. Nor can we blame the gods; for swarms of bees settling on our standards and the reluctance of the eagles to advance,[1] and a violent earthquake which ensued upon the beginning of the engagement—unless, indeed, it was the rush of horses and men and the unusually violent clash of arms which caused this trembling of the earth—had warned its rash commander of the impending disaster.

The fourth and almost mortal wound received by the Roman Empire was dealt at Cannae, an insignificant Apulian village, which emerged from its obscurity as the scene of a great disaster and gained fame from the slaughter of 60,000 men. There the general, the battle-field, the atmosphere and the weather—in fact, all nature—conspired to bring about the destruction of the unhappy army. For the wily Hannibal, not content with sending pretended deserters who presently fell upon the rear of the fighters, having, moreover, noticed the character of the ground in the open plains (where the sun is very hot and the dust abundant and the wind blows constantly, as though on a fixed principle, from the east) drew up his army in such a way that, while the Romans had all these factors

adversus haec omnia obversis, secundum caelum
17 tenens vento pulvere et sole pugnaret. Itaque duo maximi exercitus caesi ad hostium satietatem, donec Annibal diceret militi suo "parce ferro." Ducum fugit alter, alter occisus est; dubium, uter maiore animo: Paulum puduit, Varro non desperavit.
18 Documenta cladis cruentus aliquandiu Aufidus, pons de cadaveribus iussu ducis factus in torrente Vergello, modii duo anulorum Carthaginem missi
19 dignitasque equestris taxata mensura. Dubium deinde non erit quin ultimum illum diem habitura fuerit Roma quintumque intra diem epulari Annibal in Capitolio potuerit, si, quod Poenum illum dixisse Maharbalem Bomilcaris ferunt, Annibal quem ad
20 modum sciret vincere, sic uti victoria scisset. Sed tum quidem illum, ut dici volgo solet, aut fatum urbis imperaturae aut ipsius mens mala et aversi
21 a Carthagine di in diversum abstulerunt. Cum victoria posset uti, frui maluit, relictaque Roma Campaniam Tarentumque perrexit; ubi mox et ipsius et exercitus[1] ardor elanguit, adeo ut vere
22 dictum sit Capuam Annibali Cannas fuisse. Si quidem invictum Alpibus indomitumque armis Campani—quis crederet?—soles et tepentes fontibus Baiae subegerunt.

[1] et ipsius et exercitus *Dukerus*: et ipse et ipsius exercitus *B*.

against them, he himself fought with the elements on his side, aided by the wind, the dust and the sun. Thus two great Roman armies were slaughtered till the enemy were satiated and Hannibal bade his soldiers stay their swords. One of our generals fled, the other was captured. It is difficult to decide which showed the greater courage: Paulus, who was ashamed to survive, or Varro, who refused to despair. As proofs of the vastness of the slaughter the Aufidus for a long time ran with blood; a bridge of corpses was constructed by order of the general over the torrent of Vergellus; two pecks of rings were sent to Carthage and the services of the equestrian order thus estimated by measure. After this no doubt will be entertained that Rome would have seen its last day and Hannibal might within five days have feasted on the Capitol, if (as they say Maharbal, the Carthaginian, the son of Bomilcar, observed) he had known how to use his victory as well as he knew how to obtain it. However, at the time, as is generally said, either the destiny of Rome as the future ruler of the world, or Hannibal's mistaken judgment, and the hostility of the gods to Carthage, diverted him elsewhere. When he might have exploited his victory, he preferred the enjoyments which it offered and, neglecting Rome, marched to Campania and Tarentum, where the vigour both of himself and of his army soon languished to such an extent that it has been remarked with truth that "Capua was Hannibal's Cannae." For, though it is scarcely credible, the sunshine of Campania and the hot springs of Baiae overcame him who had been undefeated by the Alps and unconquered on the battle-field.

23 Permissum est interim respirare Romanis et quasi
ab inferis emergere. Arma non erant: detracta
sunt templis. Deerat iuventus: in sacramentum
24 liberata servitia. Egebat aerarium: opes suas sena-
tus in medium libens protulit, nec praeter quod in
bullis singulisque anulis erat quicquam sibi auri
reliquerunt. Eques secutus exemplum imitataeque
25 equitem tribus. Denique vix suffecere tabulae, vix
scribarum manus Laevino Marcelloque consulibus,
26 cum privatorum opes in publicum referrentur. Quid
autem? In eligendis magistratibus quae centu-
riarum sapientia, cum iuniores a senioribus consilium
de creandis consulibus petiverunt. Quippe adver-
sus hostem totiens victorem, tam callidum, non
virtute tantum, sed suis etiam pugnare consiliis
oportebat.

27 Prima redeuntis et, ut ita dixerim, revivescentis
imperii spes Fabius fuit, qui novam de Annibale
victoriam commentus est, non pugnare. Hinc illi
cognomen novum et rei publicae salutare Cunctator;
hinc illud ex populo, ut imperii scutum vocaretur.
28 Itaque per Samnium totum, per Falernos Gaura-
nosque saltus sic maceravit Annibalem, ut, quia
frangi virtute non poterat, mora comminueretur.
29 Inde Claudio Marcello duce etiam congredi ausus

---

[1] Golden ornaments which free-born Roman children wore suspended round their necks.

[2] 210 B.C.

Meanwhile the Romans had the opportunity to recover their breath and rise, as it were, from the dead. They had no arms; they took down the arms fixed up in the temples. They had no men; slaves were set free and took the oath of service. The treasury was empty; the senators voluntarily offered their wealth to the State, retaining not a particle of gold except in the *bullae*[1] and in the single ring which each of them wore. The example of the senate was followed by the knights, who, in their turn, were imitated by the tribes, with the result that when, in the consulship of Laevinus and Marcellus,[2] the resources of private individuals were poured into the public treasury, the registers and the hands of the clerks scarcely sufficed to record them. Furthermore, what wisdom the centuries showed in the choice of magistrates, when the younger men sought from their seniors advice about the election of the consuls! For against a foe so often victorious and so crafty it behoved them to fight not only with courage but with stratagem also on their side.

The first hope of the Empire, as it began to recover and, so to speak, return to life, was Fabius, who devised a new method of defeating Hannibal—by not fighting him. Hence he received a new title, significant of the way in which he saved the State, namely, Cunctator ("the Delayer"); hence too the people paid him the tribute of calling him "the Shield of the Empire." And so through the whole of Samnium and the Falernian and Gauran forests he so wore Hannibal down that, since he could not be broken by valour, he was reduced by delay. Then, under the leadership of Claudius Marcellus, they at last ventured to meet

est: comminus venit et perculit[1] in Campania sua
30 et ab obsidione Nolae urbis exclusit. Ausus et
Sempronio Graccho duce per Lucaniam sequi
et premere terga cedentis, quamvis tum—o
pudor![2]—servili pugnaret exercitu;[3] nam huc-
usque tot mala conpulerant. Sed libertate donati
31 fecerunt de servis se virtute[4] Romanos. O horri-
bilem in tot adversis fiduciam! O singularem
animum ac spiritum populi Romani! Tam artis
adflictisque rebus, ut de Italia sua dubitare[5] de-
buisset, ausus tamen est in diversa respicere,
32 cumque hostis in iugulo[6] per Campaniam Apuliam-
que volitaret mediaque[7] de Italia Africam faceret,
eodem tempore et hunc sustinebat et in Siciliam,
Sardiniam, Hispaniam divisa per terrarum orbem
arma mittebat.

33 Sicilia mandata Marcello. Nec diu restitit; tota
enim insula in una urbe superata est. Grande illud
et ante id tempus invictum caput, Syracusae,
quamvis Archimedis ingenio defenderentur, ali-
34 quando cesserunt. Longe illi triplex murus toti-
demque arces, portus ille marmoreus et fons cele-
bratus Arethusae; nisi quod hactenus profuere, ut
pulchritudini victae urbis parceretur.

[1] perculit *Salmasius*: perpulit *BI*: pepulit *N*.
[2] o pudor *I*: pudor *B*: o pudor manu *NL*.
[3] exercitu *I*: exercitum *B*.
[4] de servis se virtute *Salmasius*: de servitute *codd.*
[5] dubitare *I*: decedere *B*.
[6] hostis in iugulo *I*: hosti singulo *B*.
[7] mediaque *Heinsius*: mediamque *codd.*

him in battle; they came to close quarters with him, smote him in his beloved Campania, and forced him to abandon the siege of Nola. They also ventured, under the leadership of Sempronius Gracchus, to pursue him through Lucania, and to press hard upon his rearguard as he retired, though on this occasion they fought him with an army of slaves—a sad disgrace; for their many misfortunes had reduced them to this expedient. But these men, presented with their liberty, made themselves, by their valour, Romans instead of slaves. How amazing was the confidence of the Roman people amid so many adversities! How extraordinary their courage and spirit! Though their fortunes were so reduced and brought low that they might well have had misgivings about their own land of Italy, they yet ventured to turn their eyes in various other directions; and while the enemy, clinging to their very throat, were rushing hither and thither through Campania and Apulia and creating another Africa in the very heart of Italy, they not only withstood them but at the same time spread their troops over the face of the earth, sending them to Sicily, Sardinia and Spain.

Sicily was the area assigned to Marcellus; and it did not long resist him; for the whole island was subjugated by the defeat of a single city. Syracuse, the mighty and hitherto unconquered capital, though it was defended by the genius of Archimedes, at length yielded. Of no avail were its triple walls, its three citadels, its harbour of marble and the celebrated Fountain of Arethusa; the only advantage which they conferred was that the beauties of the conquered city were spared.

35 Sardiniam Gracchus arripuit. Sed nihil illi gentium feritas Insanorumque—nam sic vocantur—inmanitas montium profuere. Saevitum in urbes urbemque urbium Caralim, ut gens contumax vilisque mortis saltem desiderio patrii soli domaretur.

36 In Hispaniam missi Gnaeus et Publius Scipiones
paene totam Poenis eripuerant, sed insidiis Punicae
fraudis oppressi rursum amiserant, magnis quidem
illi proeliis cum Punicas opes cecidissent. Sed
Punicae insidiae alterum ferro castra metantem,
alterum, cum vix[1] evasisset in turrem, cinctum
37 facibus oppresserant. Igitur in ultionem patris ac
patrui missus cum exercitu Scipio, cui iam grande
38 de Africa nomen fata decreverant, bellatricem illam,
viris armisque nobilem Hispaniam, illam seminarium
hostilis exercitus, pusilli illam iam[2] Annibalis eruditricem—incredibile dictu—totam a Pyrenaeis montibus in Herculis columnas et Oceanum recuperavit,
39 nescias citius an felicius. Quam velociter, quattuor
anni fatentur; quam facile, vel una civitas probat.
Eodem quippe quo obsessa est die capta est,
omenque[3] Africanae victoriae fuit, quod tam facile
40 victa est Hispaniae Carthago. Certum est tamen
ad profligandam provinciam maxime profecisse

[1] vix *Rossbachius*: vim *B*.

[2] pusilli illam iam: pusilli iam *B*: illam *NL*: illam iam *I*.

[3] omenque: nomenque *B*: omnemque *LI*.

Gracchus secured Sardinia; the savagery of the inhabitants and the vastness of the Mad Mountains —for such is their name—availed it nothing. Its cities, including Caralis, the capital, were treated with severity, that a race which was obstinate and contemptuous of life might at any rate be tamed by the loss of the soil which it cultivated.

The two Scipios, Gnaeus and Publius, were sent into Spain and had wrested practically the whole of the country from the Carthaginians; but, surprised by the wiles of Carthaginian craft, they had lost it again, although they had defeated their forces in important battles. But the stratagems of the Carthaginians had overwhelmed one of them by attacking him as he was measuring out a camp, and the other by surrounding him with flames in a tower to which he had with difficulty escaped. And so a third Scipio, for whom the fate had already destined a great name to be won in Africa, was sent with an army to avenge his father and uncle, and recovered the whole of Spain (an almost incredible feat) from the Pyrenees to the Pillars of Hercules, that land of warriors, so famous for its heroes and its warlike exploits, that nursery of the enemy's forces which had taught the youthful Hannibal the art of war. It is difficult to say which was greater, his speed or his good fortune. To his speed, the four years of his operations bear witness; the ease of his conquest is proved by the example of a single city, which was captured on the very day on which the siege began, while it was an omen of future victory in Africa that the Spanish Carthage was so easily subdued. It is certain, however, that the remarkable austerity of the general contributed greatly to the subjugation

singularem ducis sanctitatem, quippe qui captivos pueros puellasque praecipuae pulchritudinis barbaris restitueret, ne in conspectum suum quidem passus adduci, ne quid de virginitatis integritate delibasse saltem oculis videretur.

41 Haec in diversa terrarum populus Romanus, nec ideo tamen visceribus Italiae inhaerentem summovere poterat Annibalem. Pleraque ad hostem defecerant, et dux acerrimus contra Romanos Italicis
42 quoque viribus utebatur. Iam tamen eum plerisque oppidis et regionibus excusseramus, iam Tarentum ad nos redierat, iam et Capua, sedes domus et patria altera Annibalis, tenebatur, cuius amissio tantum Poeno duci dolorem dedit, ut inde totis
43 viribus Romam converteretur. O populum dignum orbis imperio dignumque omnium favore et admiratione hominum ac deorum! Conpulsus ad ultimos metus ab incepto non destitit, et de sua urbe sollicitus Capuam tamen non omisit; sed parte exercitus sub Appio consule relicta, parte Flaccum in urbem secuta, absens simul praesensque pugnabat.
44 Quid ergo miramur moventi castra a tertio lapide Annibali iterum ipsos deos—deos inquam, nec fateri
45 pudebit—restitisse?[1] Tanta enim ad singulos illius motus vis imbrium effusa est, tanta ventorum violentia coorta est, ut divinitus hostem summoveri non a caelo, sed ab urbis ipsius moenibus et Capi-

[1] restitisse *post* deos *inser*. *B*.

---

[1] *i.e.* as after Cannae.
[2] As were the Giants in the legend.

of the province; for he restored to the barbarians some captive boys and girls of extraordinary beauty without having allowed them to be brought into his presence, lest even by a glance he should seem to have sullied their virgin purity.

Though such were their achievements in various other parts of the world, the Romans were yet unable to dislodge Hannibal, who still held his grip upon the very vitals of Italy. Many places had deserted to the enemy, whose indefatigable leader was employing Italian aid also against the Romans. We had, however, by this time driven Hannibal out of many towns and districts; Tarentum had already returned to our side, and Capua, his headquarters, his home and his second fatherland (the loss of which caused the Carthaginian leader such grief that he promptly directed his whole forces against Rome) was in our hands. How well did the Roman people deserve the empire of the world and the favour and admiration of all, both gods and men! Compelled to fear the worst, they did not abandon their purpose, and, though alarmed for their own city, did not lose their hold upon Capua; but, part of their army having been left there under the Consul Appius and the rest having followed Flaccus to the capital, they fought at home and away from home at the same time. Why then are we surprised that, when Hannibal was moving his camp forward from the third milestone, the gods, the gods, I say (and we shall feel no shame in admitting their aid), again [1] resisted his progress? For, at each advance of his, such a flood of rain fell and such violent gales arose that he seemed to be repelled by the gods not from heaven,[2] but from the walls of the city

46 tolio videretur. Fugit et cessit et in ultimum se
Italiae recepit sinum, cum urbem tantum non
47 adoratam reliquisset. Parva res dictu sed ad
magnanimitatem populi Romani probandam satis
efficax, quod illis ipsis quibus obsidebatur diebus
ager, quem Annibal castris insederat, venalis Romae
48 fuit hastaeque subiectus invenit emptorem. Voluit
Annibal contra imitari fiduciam subiecitque argenta-
rias urbis tabernas; nec sector inventus est, ut scias
etiam praesagia fatis adfuisse.

49 Nihil actum erat tanta virtute, tanto favore etiam
deorum, si quidem ab Hispania Hasdrubal frater
Annibalis cum exercitu novo, novis viribus, nova
50 belli mole veniebat. Actum erat procul dubio, si
vir ille se cum fratre iunxisset. Sed hunc quoque
iam tum quom[1] ab Alpe descenderat, apud Me-
taurum castra metantem Claudius Nero cum Livio
51 Salinatore debellat. Nero in ultimum Italiae angu-
lum[2] summoverat Annibalem, Livius in diversissi-
mam partem, id est in ipsas nascentis Italiae fauces
52 signa converterat. Tanto, id est omni, qua longissi-
ma est[3] Italia, solo interiacente, quo consilio, qua
celeritate consules castra coniunxerint, inopina-
tumque hostem conlatis signis oppresserint, neque
53 id fieri Annibal senserit, difficile dictu est. Certe
Annibal re cognita cum proiectum fratris caput ad
sua castra vidisset, "agnosco" inquit "infelicita-

[1] iam tum quom *Rossbachius*: tantum quod *codd.*
[2] in ultimum Italiae angulum *Halmius*: in ultimo Italiae angulo *codd.*
[3] est *I*: fuit *B*.

itself and the Capitol. Hannibal fled and departed, withdrawing to the furthermost corner of Italy, abandoning the city, the object almost of his worship. It is a small detail but rather a striking proof of the stout-heartedness of the Romans that, during the very days when the city was being besieged, the land upon which Hannibal had set up his camp came up for sale at Rome, and, on being put up for auction, found a purchaser. Hannibal on his part, wishing to imitate this confidence, put up for sale the banking establishments in the city; but no bidder could be found, a fact which shows that future events cast their shadow before them.

All this valour and even the powerful support of the gods had produced no result, since Hasdrubal, Hannibal's brother, was coming from Spain with a new army, new strength and new resources for war; the fate of Rome had certainly been sealed if he had effected a junction with his brother. However, when Hasdrubal had just descended from the Alps, as he was planning out a camp near the Metaurus, Claudius Nero, together with Livius Salinator, defeated him also. Nero had driven Hannibal into the uttermost corner of Italy, while Livius had advanced to the very opposite end of the country, the very entrance of the Italian frontier. Since so vast a space, the utmost length of Italy, lay between them, it is difficult to do justice to the skill and speed with which the consuls joined their forces and, with their combined armies, surprised their unsuspecting foe without Hannibal's knowing that they were doing so. Hannibal, at any rate, on learning what had happened by seeing his brother's head thrown into his camp, exclaimed, "I recognize the ill-luck of

tem Carthaginis." Haec fuit illius viri non sine
praesagio quodam fati inminentis prima confessio.
54 Iam certum erat Annibalem etiam ipsius con-
fessione posse vinci; sed tot rerum prosperarum
fiducia plenus populus Romanus magni aestimabat
55 asperrimum hostem in sua Africa debellare. Duce
igitur Scipione in ipsam Africam tota mole con-
versus imitari coepit Annibalem et Italiae suae
56 clades in Africa vindicare. Quas ille, dii boni,
Hasdrubalis copias fudit, quos Syphacis Numidici
regis equitatus! Quae quantaque utriusque[1] castra
facibus inlatis una nocte delevit! Denique iam non
a tertio lapide, sed ipsas Carthaginis portas obsi-
57 dione quatiebat. Sic factum ut inhaerentem atque
58 incubantem Italiae extorqueret Annibalem. Non
fuit maior sub imperio Romano dies quam ille, cum
duo omnium et antea et postea ducum maximi[2]
duces, ille Italiae, hic Hispaniae victor, conlatis
comminus signis direxere aciem. Sed et conlo-
quium fuit inter ipsos de legibus pacis, et steterunt
59 diu mutua admiratione defixi. Ubi de pace non
60 convenit, signa cecinere. Constat utriusque con-
fessione nec melius instrui aciem nec acrius potuisse
pugnari; hoc Scipio de Annibalis, Annibal de
61 Scipionis exercitu praedicaverunt. Sed tamen Anni-

[1] *post* utriusque *add.* clasis *B*, classis *I*.
[2] maximi *I*: maxime *BN*.

Carthage." This was his first confession, fraught with foreknowledge of approaching failure.

It was now certain that Hannibal, even by his own confession, could be defeated; but the Roman people, full of the confidence inspired by so much success, set great store upon defeating their bitterest enemy on his own soil of Africa. Under the leadership, therefore, of Scipio, they directed the whole mass of their forces upon Africa itself and began to imitate the example of Hannibal and avenge upon Africa the disasters which had befallen their own land of Italy. Ye gods, what forces of Hasdrubal, what cavalry of Syphax, king of Numidia, did Scipio put to flight! What mighty camps of both these leaders did he destroy in a single night by bringing firebrands against them! At last, not at three miles distance but by a close siege, he shook the very gates of Carthage. He thus succeeded in making Hannibal release his grip upon Italy, to which he was still clinging and over which he still brooded. In the whole history of the Roman Empire there was no more notable occasion than when the two generals, greater than any before or since, the one the conqueror of Italy, the other of Spain, drew up their armies for a pitched battle. But first a conference was held between them about terms of peace, and they stood for a while motionless in mutual admiration. When, however, no agreement was reached about peace, the signal was given for battle. It is agreed from the admission of both sides that no armies could have been better arrayed and no battle more obstinately contested; Scipio acknowedged this about Hannibal's army and Hannibal about that of Scipio. But Hannibal had

bal cessit, praemiumque victoriae Africa fuit et secutus Africam statim terrarum orbis.

XXIII. Bellvm Macedonicvm Primvm

II, 7 Post Carthaginem vinci neminem puduit. Statim
Africam secutae sunt gentes, Macedonia, Graecia,
Syria ceteraque omnia quodam quasi aestu et
2 torrente fortunae, sed primi omnium Macedones,
adfectator quondam imperii populus. Itaque
quamvis tum Philippus regno praesideret, Romani
tamen dimicare sibi cum rege Alexandro videbantur.
3 Macedonicum bellum nomine amplius quam specta-
4 tione gentis fuit. Causa coepit a foedere Philippi,
quo rex iam pridem dominantem in Italia Annibalem
sibi socium iunxerat; postea crevit inplorantibus
Athenis auxilium contra regis iniurias, cum ille
ultra ius victoriae in templa et aras et sepulcra
5 ipsa saeviret. Placuit senatui opem tantis ferre
supplicibus. Quippe iam gentium reges, duces,
populi, nationes, praesidia sibi ab hac urbe repe-
6 tebant. Primum igitur Laevino consule populus
Romanus Ionium mare ingressus, tota Graeciae
7 litora velut triumphanti classe peragravit. Spolia
quippe Siciliae, Sardiniae, Hispaniae, Africae prae-

[1] 210 B.C.

to yield, and Africa became the prize of victory; and the whole world soon followed the fate of Africa.

XXIII. The First Macedonian War

7. After the conquest of Carthage, no nation felt ashamed of being conquered. The peoples of Macedonia, Greece, Syria and all the other countries immediately followed in the wake of Africa, as if borne along by the flood and torrent of fortune. Of all these the first were the Macedonians, a people who had once aimed at imperial power; and so, though at the time King Philip occupied the throne, the Romans nevertheless felt as if they were fighting against King Alexander. The Macedonian War gained importance rather from its name than from any consideration of the nation with whom it was waged. The original cause of the war was a treaty by which Philip had joined himself in alliance with Hannibal at a time when he had long been dominating Italy. Subsequently an additional pretext was afforded when the Athenians implored help against the injuries of the king, who was venting his fury, beyond any rights which victory conferred, on their temples, altars and even sepulchres. The senate resolved to grant help to such important suppliants; for by this time kings and leaders, peoples and nations of the world were beginning to seek protection from this city. In the consulship of Laevinus,[1] therefore, the Roman people first entered the Ionian Sea and coasted along all the shores of Greece with their fleet in a kind of triumphal procession; for they bore in the front of their vessels the trophies of Sicily, Sardinia, Spain and Africa, and the bay tree

ferebat, et manifestam victoriam nata in praetoria
8 puppi laurus pollicebatur. Aderat sponte in
auxilium Attalus rex Pergamenorum, aderant Rho-
dii, nauticus populus, qui navibus a mari,[1] consul
9 a terris omnia equis virisque quatiebat. Bis victus,
bis fugatus rex, bis exutus castris, cum tamen
nihil terribilius Macedonibus fuit ipso volnerum
aspectu, quae non spiculis nec sagittis nec ullo
Graeculo ferro, sed ingentibus pilis nec minoribus
10 adacta gladiis ultra mortem patebant. Enimvero
Flaminino[2] duce invios antea Chaonum montes
Aoumque[3] amnem per abrupta[4] vadentem et ipsa[5]
11 Macedoniae claustra penetravimus. Introisse victo-
ria fuit. Nam postea numquam ausus congredi rex
ad tumulos, quos Cynocephalas vocant, uno ac ne
12 hoc quidem iusto proelio opprimitur. Et illi quidem
consul pacem dedit regnumque concessit, mox, ne
quid esset hostile, Thebas et Euboeam et grassantem
sub Nabide[6] tyranno suo Lacedaemona conpescuit.
13 Graeciae vero veterem statum reddidit, ut legibus
14 viveret suis et avita libertate frueretur. Quae
gaudia, quae vociferationes fuerunt, cum hoc forte
Nemeae in theatro quinquennalibus ludis a prae-
cone caneretur! Quo certavere plausu! Quid
15 florum in consulem profuderunt! Et iterum ite-

[1] qui navibus a mari *Freinshemius* : quibus a mari *codd.*

[2] Flaminino: flamminio *BI*: flaminio *NL*.

[3] Aoumque *Vinetus*: savum que *B*: dumque *NL*: saumque *I*.

[4] abrupta *L*: abruta *B*.

[5] et ipsa *NL*: ad ipsa *B*: et ad ipsa *I*.

[6] sub Nabide: sub nam | bide *B*: sum mauide *N*: summa uide *L*.

which sprouted on the prow of the flagship promised certain victory. Attalus, king of Pergamon, was there of his own accord to help us; the Rhodians were there, a naval people who spread consternation everywhere at sea with their ships, as did the consul on land with his horsemen and foot-soldiers. King Philip was twice defeated, twice driven into flight, twice despoiled of his camp; but nothing caused the Macedonians greater fear than the sight of their wounds, which, having been dealt not with darts or arrows or any Greek weapon but by huge javelins and no less huge swords, gaped wider than was necessary to cause death. Indeed under the leadership of Flamininus we penetrated into the mountains of the Chaonians, hitherto impassable, and the river Aous which flows through deep gorges, the very gates of Macedonia. To have effected an entrance into this country meant victory; for afterwards the king, who had never ventured to meet us in the field, was overwhelmed, near the hills which they call Cynoscephalae, in a single engagement which could hardly be called a regular battle. To Philip, then, the consul granted peace and restored to him his kingdom, and afterwards, that no foe might remain, subdued Thebes and Euboea and Lacedaemon, which attempted resistance under its tyrant Nabis. To Greece Flamininus restored its ancient constitution, that it might live under its old laws and enjoy its ancestral liberty. What joy there was, what cries of delight there were, when this proclamation was made, as it happened, at the quinquennial games in the theatre at Nemea! How they vied with one another in their applause! What flowers they showered upon the consul! Again and again

rumque praeconem repetere vocem illam iubebant, qua libertas Achaiae pronuntiabatur, nec aliter illa consulari sententia quam modulatissimo aliquo tibiarum aut fidium cantu fruebantur.

XXIIII. Bellvm Syriacvm Regis Antiochi

II, 8 Macedoniam Asia[1] statim et regem Philippum Antiochus excepit quodam casu, quasi de industria sic adgubernante fortuna, ut quem ad modum ab Africa in Europam,[2] sic ab Europa[3] in Asiam ultro se suggerentibus causis imperium procederet, et cum terrarum orbis situ ipse ordo victoriarum
2 navigaret. Non aliud formidolosius fama bellum fuit; quippe cum Persas et orientem, Xerxen atque Darium cogitarent, quando perfossi invii montes,
3 quando velis opertum mare nuntiaretur. Ad hoc caelestes minae territabant, cum umore continuo Cumanus Apollo sudaret; sed hic faventis Asiae
4 suae numinis timor erat. Nec sane viris opibus armisque quicquam copiosius Syria; sed in manus tam ignavi regis inciderat, ut nihil fuerit in Antiocho speciosius quam quod a Romanis victus
5 est. Inpulere regem in id bellum illinc Thoas, Aetoliae princeps, inhonoratam apud Romanos querens adversus Macedonas militiae suae societa-

[1] Asia *add. Halmius.* [2] Europam *L* : Achaiam *B.*
[3] Europa : Achaia *B.*

they bade the herald repeat the declaration by which the liberty of Achaea was proclaimed; and they took as much delight in the consul's decision as in the most harmonious concert of pipes and strings.

XXIIII. The Syrian War against King Antiochus

8. Asia then immediately took the place of Macedonia, and Antiochus that of King Philip, a mere coincidence making it seem as if fortune designedly so arranged matters that, just as the empire had advanced from Africa into Europe, so now, owing to causes which spontaneously presented themselves, it should spread from Europe into Asia, and that the series of victories might follow a geographical sequence. Report never represented any war as more formidable than this, as the Romans bethought them of the Persians and the East, of Xerxes and Darius, of the days when impassable mountains were said to have been cut through and the sea hidden with sails. Moreover, threats from heaven alarmed them; for the statue of Apollo at Cumae was in a constant sweat, though it was really due to the fear of the god in his affection for his beloved Asia. No land indeed is richer than Syria in men, resources and arms, but it had fallen into the hands of so poor-spirited a king that the most notable fact about Antiochus was his conquest by the Romans. The two persons who instigated the king to undertake this war were, on the one hand, Thoas, prince of Aetolia, who complained that he had not received due credit from the Romans for the support given by his army against the Macedonians, and, on the other

tem, hinc Annibal, qui in Africa victus, profugus
et pacis inpatiens hostem populo Romano toto orbe
6 quaerebat. Et quod illud fuisset periculum, si se
consiliis eius rex tradidisset, id est si Asiae viribus
usus fuisset miser Annibal? Sed rex suis opibus
et nomine regio fretus satis habuit bellum movere.
7 Europa iam dubio procul iure belli ad Romanos
pertinebat. Hic Lysimachiam, urbem in litore
Thracio positam a maioribus suis, Antiochus ut
8 hereditario iure repetebat. Hoc velut sidere
Asiatici belli mota tempestas. Sed maximus regum,
contentus fortiter indixisse bellum, cum ingenti
strepitu ac tumultu movisset ex Asia, occupatis
statim insulis Graeciaeque litoribus otia et luxus
9 quasi victor agitabat. Euboan insulam continenti
adhaerentem tenui freto reciprocantibus aquis
Euripus abscindit. Hic ille positis aureis sericisque
tentoriis sub ipso freti murmure, cum praefluentes
aquae tibiis fidibusque concinerent, conlatis undique
quamvis per hiemem rosis, ne non aliquo genere
ducem agere videretur,[1] virginum puerorumque
10 dilectus habebat. Talem ergo regem iam luxuria
sua debellatum Acilio Glabrione consule populus
Romanus in insula adgressus ipso statim adventus

[1] agere videretur *om. B.*

---

[1] Cicero uses a similar figure (*pro Murena*, 17).
[2] 191 B.C.

hand, Hannibal, who, defeated in Africa, now a fugitive and unable to rest in peace, was scouring the whole world to find an enemy to fight against the Roman people. And, indeed, how great would have been the peril if King Antiochus had entrusted himself to his guidance and the unhappy Hannibal had had all the resources of Asia at his command! The king, however, confident in his own powers and royal title, thought it enough merely to set war in motion. Europe without doubt belonged to the Romans by right of conquest; yet Antiochus demanded back, as of hereditary right, a European city, Lysimachia, which had been founded by his ancestors on the coast of Thrace. This action, like the rising of some star,[1] stirred up the storm of war in Asia. This mightiest of kings, however, content with his bold declaration of war, marched out of Asia with loud noise and tumult, and immediately seizing the islands and coasts of Greece, spent his time in ease and luxury as though he had already won the day. The island of Euboea, lying close to the mainland, is separated therefrom by the narrow straits of the Euripus, whose waters continually ebb and flow. Here he set up his tents of cloth of gold and silk within the very sound of the straits, whose waters as they flowed past murmured in harmony with the music of pipes and strings, and having collected roses, although it was winter, from every quarter, that he might seem in some way at any rate to act the general, held his levies of maidens and boys. Against this king then, already defeated by his own luxury, the Roman people, in the consulship of Acilius Glabrio,[2] advanced while he was in the island, and immediately drove him into flight by the mere

11 sui nuntio coëgit ab insula fugere. Tum praeci-
pitem apud Thermopylas adsecutus, locum tre-
centorum Laconum speciosa clade memorandum, ne
ibi quidem fiducia loci resistentem, mari ac terra
12 cedere coëgit. Statim et e vestigio itur in Syriam.
Classis regia Polyxenidae Annibalique commissa—
nam rex proelium nec spectare poterat,—duce
Aemilio Regillo, adremigantibus Rhodiis tota lace-
13 ratur. Ne sibi placeant Athenae; in Antiocho
vicimus Xerxen, in Aemilio Alcibiaden aequavimus,
14 Epheso Salamina pensavimus. Tum consule Sci-
pione, cui frater, ille modo victor Carthaginis
Africanus, aderat voluntaria legatione, debellari
regem placet. Et iam toto cesserat mari, sed nos
15 imus ulterius. Maeandrum ad amnem montemque
Sipylum castra ponuntur. Hic rex, incredibile dictu
16 quibus auxiliis, quibus copiis consederat. Trecenta
milia peditum, equitum falcatorumque curruum non
minor numerus. Elephantis ad hoc inmensae
magnitudinis, auro purpura argento et suo ebore
17 fulgentibus, aciem utrimque vallaverat.[1] Sed haec
omnia praepedita magnitudine sua, ad hoc imbre,
qui subito superfusus mira felicitate Persicos arcus
corruperat.[2] Primum trepidatio, mox fuga, deinde
18 triumphus fuerunt. Victo et supplici pacem par-

[1] vallaverat: vallaverant *NL*: variaverat *B*.
[2] corruperat: perruperat *B*.

announcement of their approach. They pursued him in his headlong flight, and at Thermopylae, a spot memorable for the glorious defeat of the three hundred Spartans (even this scene did not inspire him with confidence enough to make a stand), forced him to own them victors by land and sea. Then instantly, without delay, they set out for Syria. The royal fleet entrusted to the charge of Polyxenidas and Hannibal—for the king could not even bear to look upon a battle—was completely destroyed by the Romans under Aemilius Regillus, with the aid of the Rhodian fleet. Let not Athens be over-proud : in Antiochus we defeated a Xerxes ; in Aemilius we had the equal of an Alcibiades ; at Ephesus we rivalled Salamis. Then, under the consul Scipio, whose brother, the great Africanus, the recent conqueror of Carthage, was serving voluntarily under him as second-in-command, it was decided utterly to defeat King Antiochus. He had entirely abandoned the sea, but we carried the war beyond it, and our camp was pitched near the river Maeander and Mount Sipylus. Here the king had taken up a position with an incredible number of auxiliaries and other troops. He had 300,000 foot-soldiers and an equal number of cavalry and chariots armed with scythes. He had also protected both his flanks with elephants of huge size, brilliant with gold, purple and silver and the sheen of their own ivory. But all this great force was embarrassed by its very size, as well as by a shower of rain, which, suddenly descending, had, by a piece of wonderful good luck, destroyed the efficiency of the Persian bows. First there was panic, then flight, and finally complete triumph. To the conquered and suppliant Antiochus

temque regni dari placuit eo libentius, quod tam facile cessisset.

XXV. Bellvm Aetolvm

II, 9 Syriaco bello successit, et debebat, Aetolum. Victo quippe Romanus Antiocho faces Asiatici belli persequebatur. Ergo Fulvio Nobiliori mandata
2 ultio est. Hic protinus caput gentis Ambraciam, regiam Pyrrhi, machinis quatit. Secuta deditio est.
3 Aderant Aetolorum precibus Attici, Rhodii, et
4 memineramus auxilii: sic placuit ignoscere. Serpsit tamen latius in proximos bellum, omnisque late Cephallenia, Zacynthos[1] et quidquid insularum in eo mari inter Ceraunios montes iugumque Maleum Aetoli belli accessio fuerunt.

XXVI. Bellvm Histricvm

II, 10 Histri secuntur Aetolos; quippe bellantes eos
2 nuper adiuverant. Et initia pugnae hosti prospera fuerunt,[2] eademque exitii causa. Nam cum Gnaei Manlii[3] castra cepissent opimaeque praedae incubarent, epulantes ac ludibundos plerosque, qui aut ubi essent prae poculis nescientes, Appius Pulcher

[1] omnisque late Cephallenia, Zacynthos *Freinshemius*: omnemque late Cephalleniam, Zacynthon *codd.*
[2] fuerunt: fuerant *B.*
[3] Manlii: manilii *B*: mali *NL.*

it was decided to grant peace and a portion of his kingdom, and this all the more willingly because he had yielded so easily.

XXV. The Aetolian War

9. The Syrian war was followed, as it was bound to happen, by an Aetolian war; for after the conquest of Antiochus, the Romans pursued those who had kindled the war in Asia. And so the task of vengeance was committed to Fulvius Nobilior. He immediately attacked Ambracia, the capital of the nation and the royal abode of Pyrrhus, with his engines of war. Its surrender quickly followed. The Athenians and Rhodians supported the supplications of the Aetolians, and we remembered their former services and decided to pardon them. Hostilities, however, spread more widely among the neighbouring peoples; and all Cephallenia and Zacynthus and all the islands in that sea between the Ceraunian mountains and Cape Malea were involved in the Aetolian war.

XXVI. The Istrian War

10. The Istrians were dealt with after the Aetolians, for they had recently assisted them in war. The beginnings of the struggle were favourable to the enemy, and this very success was the cause of their ruin. For when they had captured the camp of Gnaeus Manlius and were gloating over their rich spoil, Appius Pulcher fell upon most of them feasting and enjoying themselves and so deep in their cups that they were unconscious and did not know

3 invadit. Sic cum sanguine et spiritu male partam
revomuere victoriam. Ipse rex Aepulo[1] equo inpositus, cum subinde crapula et capitis errore lapsaret,
captum sese vix et aegre, postquam expergefactus
est, didicit.

XXVII. Bellvm Gallograecvm

II, 11 Gallograeciam quoque Syriaci belli ruina con-
2 volvit. Fuerint inter auxilia regis Antiochi, an fuisse
cupidus triumphi Manlius Vulso[2] simulaverit, du-
3 bium; at certe[3] negatus est victori triumphus, quia
causam belli non adprobavit. Ceterum gens Gallograecorum, sicut ipsum nomen indicio est, mixta
et adulterata est: reliquiae Gallorum, qui Brenno
duce vastaverant Graeciam, orientem secuti, in
4 media Asiae parte sederunt; itaque, uti frugum
semina[4] mutato solo degenerant, sic illa genuina
feritas eorum Asiatica amoenitate mollita est.
5 Duobus itaque proeliis fusi fugatique sunt, quamvis
sub adventu hostis relictis sedibus in altissimos se
montes recepissent. Tolostobogi[5] Olympum, Tectosagi Magabam[6] insederant. Utrimque fundis sagittisque detracti in perpetuam se pacem dediderunt.
6 Sed alligati miraculo quidam[7] fuere, cum catenas

[1] Aepulo *Livius*, XLI. 11: apulo *BNL*.

[2] Manlius Vulso *Mommsenus*: visos *B*: aneos visos *NL*: visus *I*.

[3] at certe *Iahnius*: hac | perte *B*: certe *NL*.

[4] semina: seminam *B*.

[5] Tolostobogi: colos cobegi *B*: colosobegit *I*.

[6] Magabam *H. Muellerus*: magabant *B*: magaba *I*.

[7] quidam: quodam *codd.*

where they were. Thus, as they yielded up their blood and breath, they disgorged the ill-gotten spoils of victory. Their king Aepulo himself, who had been placed upon a horse, from which he frequently fell in his intoxicated and dizzy condition, was with difficulty at last made to understand, when he woke up, that he was a prisoner.

XXVII. The Gallo-Greek War

11. The disastrous termination of the Syrian war involved Gallo-Graecia also. Whether its inhabitants had really been among the auxiliaries of King Antiochus, or whether Manlius Vulso, in his eagerness for a triumph, had pretended that they were so, is uncertain. In any case, though he was victorious, he was refused a triumph, because the Romans did not approve of the pretext under which he had gone to war. The race of the Gallo-Greeks, as their very name implies, was of mixed and confused origin; they were the remnants of those Gauls who had laid Greece waste under the leadership of Brennus, and then, taking an easterly direction, settled in the middle of Asia. And so, just as seeds of cereals degenerate in a different soil, so their natural ferocity was softened by the mild climate of Asia. They were, therefore, routed and put to flight in two engagements, although, at the approach of the enemy, they had left their homes and retired to the highest mountains. The Tolostobogi had occupied Olympus, the Tectosagi Magaba. Dislodged from both these places by slings and arrows, they surrendered under a promise of perpetual peace. Some of them, however, after they had been bound, caused astonishment by trying to sever their bonds by

morsibus et ore temptassent, cum offocandas invicem fauces praebuissent. Nam Orgiacontis regis[1] uxor a centurione stuprum passa[2] memorabili exemplo custodiam evasit, revolsumque adulteri hostis caput ad maritum reportavit.

XXVIII. Bellvm Macedonicvm Secvndvm

II, 12 Dum aliae aliaeque gentes Syriaci belli secuntur
2 ruinam, Macedonia rursus se erexit. Fortissimum populum memoria et recordatio suae nobilitatis agitabat, et successerat Philippo filius Perses, qui semel in perpetuum victam esse Macedoniam non
3 putabat ex gentis dignitate. Multo vehementius sub hoc Macedones quam sub patre exurgunt. Quippe Thracas in res[3] suas traxerant, atque ita industriam Macedonum viribus Thracum, ferociam
4 Thracum disciplina Macedonica temperavere. Accessit his consilium ducis, qui situm regionum suarum a summo speculatus Haemo, positis per abrupta[4] castris, ita Macedoniam suam armis ferroque vallaverat, ut non reliquisse aditum nisi a
5 caelo venturis hostibus videretur. Tamen Marcio Philippo consule eam[5] provinciam ingressus populus Romanus, exploratis diligenter accessibus per Ascurida[6] paludem Perrhaebosque tumulos illa volucribus

[1] regis *om. B.*
[2] passa *om. BI.*
[3] res *Iahnius*: vires *codd.*
[4] abrupta : abruta *codd.*
[5] eam *Heinsius* : nam *codd.*
[6] Ascurida *Heinsius; cf. Livius* XLIV. 2, 3: astudam *B*: astundam *NL*.

[1] 186 B.C.

biting them with their teeth and offering their throats to one another to be strangled. The wife of their king Orgiacon, who had suffered violation at the hands of a centurion, achieved the remarkable exploit of escaping from custody and carrying to her husband the head of her licentious foe which she had cut off.

XXVIII. The Second Macedonian War

12. While nation after nation was involved in the disaster of the Syrian war, Macedonia again raised her head. The memory and recollection of its former greatness spurred that valiant people to action. Also Philip had been succeeded by his son Perses, who thought that it ill accorded with the high repute of the nation that Macedonia, once conquered, should remain for ever conquered. Under his leadership, therefore, the Macedonians rose with much more vigour than under his father. They had induced the Thracians to support their efforts and had thus tempered the Macedonian persistence with Thracian energy, and Thracian savagery with Macedonian discipline. A further advantage was the skill of their leader, who, having surveyed the topography of his territory from the summit of Mount Haemus, pitched his camp in an inaccessible spot, and so fortified his realm with arms and the sword that he seemed to have left no means of access except to an enemy who should descend from the sky. But the Roman people, under the consul Marcius Philippus,[1] having entered the province and having carefully explored the approaches by the Lake of Ascuris and the Perrhaebian Mountains,

quoque, ut videbantur, invia accessit, regemque
securum et nihil tale metuentem subita belli in-
6 ruptione deprehendit. Cuius tanta trepidatio fuit,
ut pecuniam omnem in mare iusserit mergi ne
7 periret, et classem cremari ne incenderetur. Paulo
consule, cum maiora et crebriora essent inposita
praesidia, per alias vias Macedonia deprensa est,
summa quidem arte et industria ducis, cum alia
8 minatus alia inrupisset. Cuius adventus ipse adeo
terribilis regi fuit, ut interesse non auderet, sed
9 gerenda ducibus bella mandaverit. Absens ergo
victus fugit in maria insulamque Samothracen, fretus
celebri religione, quasi templa et arae possent
defendere, quem nec montes sui nec arma potuissent.
10 Nemo regum diutius amissae fortunae conscientiam
retinuit. Supplex cum scriberet ad imperatorem
ab illo quo confugerat templo nomenque epistolae
notaret suum, regem addidit. Sed nec reverentior
11 captae maiestatis alius Paulo fuit. Cum in con-
spectum venisset hostis, in tribunali recepit et
conviviis adhibuit liberosque admonuit suos ut
12 fortunam, cui tantum liceret, revererentur. Inter
pulcherrimos hunc quoque populus Romanus de
Macedonia duxit ac vidit triumphum, quippe cuius
13 spectaculo triduum impleverit. Primus dies signa

---

[1] For the paradox cp. Martial, II. 80:

Hostem cum fugeret, se Fannius ipse peremit.
Hic, rogo, non furor est, ne moriare, mori?

[2] 182 B.C.

effected an entrance over heights which seemed inaccessible even to birds, and by a sudden inroad surprised the king, who thought himself safe and feared no such attack. Such was his alarm that he ordered all his money to be thrown into the sea, lest it should be lost,[1] and his fleet to be burned, lest it should be set on fire. Under the consul Paulus,[2] after larger and more frequent garrisons had been established, other methods were used to take Macedonia by surprise through the remarkable skill and perseverance of the general, who threatened an attack at one point and broke through at another. His mere approach so alarmed the king that he did not dare to take an active part in the war, but committed the management of it to his generals. Being defeated, therefore, in his absence he fled to the sea, and to the island of Samothrace, relying on the well-known sanctity of the place, as though temples and altars could protect one whom his own mountains and arms had been unable to save. No king ever clung more tenaciously to the memory of the great position which he had lost. When he wrote to the Roman general as a suppliant from the temple in which he had taken refuge and signed the letter with his name, he added the title of king. On the other hand, no one ever showed more respect than Paulus for captured majesty. When his enemy came into his presence, he received him upon his tribunal, invited him to his own table, and warned his own children to respect Fortune whose power was so great. The triumph in honour of the conquest of Macedonia was among the most splendid which the Roman people ever held and witnessed. The spectacle occupied three days; on

tabulasque, sequens arma pecuniam transvexit,
tertius captivos ipsumque regem adtonitum adhuc
14 tamquam subito malo et stupentem. Sed multo
prius gaudium victoriae populus Romanus quam
epistulis victoris praeceperat. Quippe eodem die,
quo victus est Perses in Macedonia, Romae cogni-
15 tum est, cum duo iuvenes candidis equis apud
Iuturnae lacum pulverem et cruorem abluebant.
Hi nuntiavere. Castorem et Pollucem fuisse credi-
tum volgo, quod gemini fuissent; interfuisse bello,
quod sanguine maderent; a Macedonia venire, quod
adhuc anhelarent.

XXVIIII. Bellvm Illyricvm Secvndvm

II, 13 Macedonici belli contagio traxit Illyrios; si qui-
dem,[1] ut Romanum a tergo distringerent, a Perse
2 rege conducti pecunia militaverunt. Sine mora ab
Anicio praetore subiguntur. Scodram,[2] caput gentis,
delesse suffecit; statim secuta deditio est. Denique
hoc bellum ante finitum est quam geri Romae
nuntiaretur.

XXX. Bellvm Macedonicvm Tertivm

II, 14 Quodam fato, quasi ita convenisset inter Poenos
et Macedonas ut tertio quoque vincerentur, eodem

[1] si quidem *Iahnius*: ipsi quidem *BN*: sed ipsi quidem *L*.
[2] Scodram: scoriadam *B*: scordam *NL*.

the first day the statues and pictures were displayed in procession, on the next day the arms and treasure, on the third day the captives, including the king himself, who seemed still to be dazed and stupefied by the suddenness of the disaster. But the Roman people had already received the glad news of the victory long before it was announced by the victorious general's despatches. For it was known in Rome on the very day on which Perses was defeated through the presence of two young men with white horses washing off dust and gore at the pool of Juturna. These brought the news, and were popularly believed to have been Castor and Pollux because they were twins, and to have taken part in battle because they were dripping with blood, and to come from Macedonia because they were still out of breath.

XXVIIII. The Second Illyrian War

13. The contagion of the Macedonian war involved the Illyrians, since they served as mercenaries in the pay of King Perses in order to cause a diversion in the rear of the Romans. They were subjugated without delay by the praetor Anicius. It sufficed to destroy Scodra, their capital, and their submission immediately followed. Indeed, the end of the war occurred before the news that it had begun could reach Rome.

XXX. The Third Macedonian War

14. By a dispensation of fate which made it seem as if the Carthaginians and Macedonians had made compact together that they should both be con-

2 tempore utrique arma moverunt. Sed prior iugum
excutit Macedo, aliquanto quam ante gravior, dum
3 contemnitur. Causa belli prope erubescenda.
Quippe regnum pariter et bellum vir ultimae sortis
Andriscus invaserat, dubium liber an servus, mer-
cennarius certe; sed quia vulgo Philippus ex
similitudine Philippi Persae filii vocabatur,[1] regiam
formam, regium nomen, animum quoque regis
4 implevit. Igitur dum haec ipsa contemnit populus
Romanus, Iuventio praetore contentus, virum non
Macedonicis modo sed Thraciae quoque auxiliis
ingentibus validum temere temptavit, invictusque[2] a
veris regibus, ab illo imaginario et scaenico rege
5 superatus est. Sed consul Metellus amissum cum
legione praetorem plenissime ultus est. Nam et
Macedoniam servitute multavit et ducem belli,
deditum ab eo ad quem confugerat Thraciae regulo,
in urbem in catenis reduxit, hoc quoque illi in malis
suis indulgente fortuna, ut de eo populus Romanus
quasi de rege vero triumpharet.

[1] Philippus ex similitudine Philippi Persae filii vocabatur *Sauppius*: philippus persae filius vocabatur *B*: philippus ex similitudine philippi pseudo filippus (philippus *L*) vocabatur *NL*.

quered for a third time, both nations began hostilities at the same time. The Macedonians were the first to throw off the yoke, having grown far more formidable than before, because they were treated with contempt. The cause of the war almost makes one blush for shame. Andriscus, a man of the lowest origin, had seized the throne and begun war at the same moment. It is uncertain whether he was a freeman or a slave, but he had certainly served as a hired labourer; however, being popularly called Philip from his resemblance to Philip, son of Perses, he supplied a royal presence, a royal name and a royal spirit as well. The Roman people then, despising all these pretensions and considering the praeter Juventius as a match for him, rashly engaged him when he was strongly supported not only by the Macedonians but by vast numbers of Thracian auxiliaries, and though they had never been beaten by real kings, were defeated by this pretended and stage-play monarch. However, ample vengeance was taken by the consul Metellus[1] for the loss of the praetor and his legion. For he not only punished the Macedonians by enslaving them, but also brought back in chains to the city the instigator of the war, who was surrendered to them by a Thracian prince with whom he had taken refuge. Fortune, however, thus far smiled upon him in his misfortune that the Roman people triumphed over him as though he had been a real king.

[1] 168 B.C.

---

[2] invictusque a veris regibus *Freinshemius*: invictusque non a veris regibus sed *NL*: invalidus que non veris regibus sed *B*.

XXXI. Bellvm Pvnicvm Tertivm

II, 15 Tertium Punicum bellum et tempore exiguum
(nam quadriennio patratum[1] est) et in comparatio-
nem priorum minimum labore (non enim tam cum
viris quam cum ipsa urbe pugnatum est) sed[2] plane
maximum eventu: quippe tandem Carthago finita
2 est. Atquin si quis trium temporum momenta
consideret, primo commissum est Punicum bellum,
3 profligatum secundo, tertio vero confectum est. Sed
huius causa belli, quod contra foederis legem ad-
versus Numidas quidem, sed parassent classem et
4 exercitum. Frequens autem Massinissa[3] finis terri-
tabat; sed huic ut bono socioque regi favebatur.
Cum de bello sederet, de belli fine tractatum est.
Cato inexpiabili odio delendam esse Carthaginem,
5 et cum de alio consuleretur, pronuntiabat, Scipio
Nasica servandam, ne metu ablato aemulae urbis
luxuriari felicitas[4] inciperet; medium senatus
6 elegit, ut urbs tantum loco moveretur. Nihil enim
speciosius videbatur quam esse Carthaginem, quae
7 non timeretur. Igitur Manilio Censorinoque con-
sulibus populus Romanus adgressus Carthaginem
spe pacis iniecta traditam a volentibus classem sub
8 ipso ore urbis incendit. Tum evocatis principibus,

[1] patratum: raptum *B.* [2] sed: et *B.*
[3] Massinissa *Iahnius*: massinissae *BNL.*
[4] urbis *post* felicitas *BNL.*

---

[1] 149 B.C.

XXXI. The Third Punic War

15. The Third Punic War was brief in its duration (for it was brought to an end within four years), and much less difficult in comparison with the earlier wars (for it was fought not so much against an army in the field as against the city itself). In its results, however, it was by far the most important, for at last an end was made of Carthage. If one considers the significance of the three periods, the first saw the beginning of the war, the second saw it given a decisive turn, the third saw its final end. The pretext of the war was that, contrary to an article in the treaty, the Carthaginians had equipped a fleet and army—though it was only against the Numidians. Massinissa, it is true, caused frequent alarms on their frontier; but the Romans supported this monarch as a good friend and ally. Deciding upon war, they discussed what was to happen when it was concluded. Cato, with implacable hatred, kept declaring, even when he was consulted on other subjects, that Carthage must be destroyed. Scipio Nasica thought that it ought to be preserved, lest, if the fear of the rival city were removed, prosperity should begin to have a demoralizing effect. The senate decided upon the middle course, namely, that the city should merely be removed to another site; for they could imagine nothing which redounded more to their credit than that Carthage should still exist, but a Carthage which they need not fear. And so, in the consulship of Manilius and Censorinus,[1] the Roman people attacked Carthage and burnt within the very sight of the city the fleet which had been voluntarily surrendered because hopes of peace had been raised. They then summoned the chief citizens and ordered

si salvi esse vellent, ut migrarent finibus imperavit.
Quod pro rei atrocitate adeo movit iras, ut extrema
mallent. Comploratum igitur publice statim et pari
9 voce clamatum est "ad arma," seditque sententia
quoquo modo rebellandum; non quia iam spes ulla
superesset, sed quia patriam suam mallent hostium
10 quam suis manibus everti. Qui rebellantium fuerit
furor, vel hinc intellegi potest, quod in usum novae
classis tecta domuum resciderunt; in armorum
officinis aurum et argentum pro aere ferroque
conflatum est, in tormentorum vincula crinis suos
matronae contulerunt. Mancino deinde consule
11 terra marique fervebat obsidio. Operti portus,
nudatus est primus et sequens, iam et tertius murus,
cum tamen Byrsa, quod nomen arci fuit, quasi
12 altera civitas resistebat. Quamvis profligato urbis
excidio tamen fatale Africae nomen Scipionum
videbatur. Igitur in alium Scipionem conversa res
publica finem belli reposcebat. Hunc Paulo Mace-
donico procreatum Africani illius magni filius in [1]
decus gentis adsumpserat, hoc scilicet fato, ut, quam
13 urbem concusserat avus, nepos eius everteret. Sed
quem ad modum maxime mortiferi morsus solent
esse morientium bestiarum, sic plus negotii fuit cum
semiruta Carthagine quam cum integra. Con-
14 pulsis in unam arcem hostibus portum quoque mari

[1] in *om. B.*

---

[1] Cf. Liv. XXII. 53, 4, *desperata et complorata republica.*

them to leave Carthaginian territory, if they wished to save their lives. This demand, by its severity, so kindled their wrath that they preferred to suffer any extremity. And so they immediately gave up all hope of the national cause,[1] and with one voice the cry was raised, "To arms!" and it was resolved to resist by every means in their power—not that any hope remained, but because they preferred that their country should be ruined by the hands of the enemy rather than by their own. Their spirit of furious resistance may be understood from the facts that they tore off the roofs of their houses for material to construct a new fleet, and that, in the munition factories, gold and silver were melted down instead of bronze and iron, while the women contributed their hair to form cords for the engines of war. Under the consul Mancinus a hot siege was kept up by land and sea. The harbours were blocked up; the first, then the second, and finally the third wall was dismantled; but the Byrsa, as they called their citadel, held out like a second city. Though the destruction of the city was thus as good as certain, yet it seemed as if fate required a Scipio to make an end of Africa. The State, therefore, turned to another Scipio and demanded that he should complete the war. This man, the offspring of Paulus Macedonicus, had been adopted by the son of the great Africanus for the glory of the family, for the grandson was destined by fate to overthrow the city which his grandfather had shattered. But, just as the bite of a dying animal is always most deadly, even so Carthage, half destroyed, caused more trouble than when it was whole. While the enemy had been driven into the sole remaining

Romanus obstruxerat. Illi alterum[1] sibi portum ab
alia urbis parte foderunt, nec ut fugerent; sed qua
nemo illos nec evadere posse credebat, inde quasi nata[2]
15 subito classis erupit, cum interim iam diebus, iam nocti-
bus nova aliqua moles, nova machina, nova perditorum
hominum manus quasi ex obruto incendio subita de
16 cineribus flamma prodibat. Deploratis novissime
rebus triginta sex milia virorum se dediderunt, quo
17 minus credas, duce Hasdrubale. Quanto fortius
femina et uxor ducis! Quae conprehensis duobus
liberis a culmine se domus in medium misit in-
cendium, imitata reginam quae Carthaginem con-
18 didit. Quanta urbs deleta sit, ut de ceteris taceam,
de ignis mora probari potest. Quippe per continuos
decem et septem dies vix potuit incendium extingui
quod domibus ac templis suis sponte hostes inmise-
rant; ut, quatenus urbs eripi Romanis non poterat,
triumphus arderet.

XXXII. Bellvm Achaicvm

II, 16 Quasi saeculum illud eversionibus urbium curreret, Carthaginis ruinam statim Corinthus excepit, Achaiae caput, Graeciae decus, inter duo maria, Ionium et Aegaeum, quasi spectaculo exposita. Haec—facinus

[1] alterum *NL*: autem *B*. [2] nata: nota *B*.

stronghold, the Romans had also blocked up the harbour from the sea. The Carthaginians thereupon excavated another harbour on another side of the city, though not with the object of escaping; but at a point where no one imagined that they could break out, a fleet, as it were, sprang suddenly into birth and sallied forth, while at the same time, now by day and now by night, some new structure or engine of war or some fresh band of desperate men started forth like a sudden flame from the ashes of a buried fire. When the position finally became hopeless, 36,000 men led—though it is scarcely credible—by Hasdrubal surrendered themselves. How much braver was the conduct of a woman, the wife of the commander, who, with her two children in her arms, hurled herself from the roof of her house into the midst of the flames, following the example of the queen who founded Carthage![1] How mighty was the city which was destroyed is shown, to mention only a single fact, by the long duration of the fire; for it was only after seventeen days of continual effort that the flames were with difficulty put out which the enemy had themselves kindled in their houses and temples, in order that, since the city could not be saved from the Romans, the material for a triumph might be burnt.

XXXII. The Achaean War

16. As though that age could only run its course by the destruction of cities, the ruin of Carthage was immediately followed by that of Corinth, the capital of Achaea, the glory of Greece, set for all men to behold between the Ionian and Aegean seas.

[1] *i.e.* Dido.

indignum—ante oppressa est quam in numero certo-
2 rum hostium referretur. Critolaus causa belli, qui
libertate a Romanis data adversus ipsos usus est
3 legatosque Romanos, dubium an et manu, certe
oratione violavit. Igitur Metello ordinanti tum[1]
maxime Macedoniam[2] mandata est ultio; et hinc
Achaicum bellum. Ac primum Critolai manum
Metellus consul per patentis Elidos campos toto
4 cecidit Alphio. Et uno proelio peractum erat
bellum; iam enim urbem ipsam terrebat obsidio;
sed—fata rerum—cum Metellus dimicasset, ad
5 victoriam Mummius intervenit.[3] Hic alterius ducis
Diaei[4] late exercitum sub ipsis Isthmi faucibus fudit
geminosque portus sanguine infecit. Tum ab incolis
deserta civitas direpta primum, deinde tuba[5]
6 praecinente deleta est. Quid signorum, quid ve-
stium quidve tabularum raptum incensumque atque
proiectum est! Quantas opes et abstulerit et cre-
maverit, hinc scias, quod quidquid Corinthii aeris
toto orbe laudatur incendio superfuisse comperimus.
7 Nam et aeris notam pretiosiorem ipsa opulentissimae
urbis fecit iniuria,[6] quia incendio permixtis plurimis
statuis atque simulacris aeris auri argentique venae
in commune fluxerunt.

[1] tum: cum *codd.*
[2] Macedoniam: Macedoniae *codd.*
[3] intervenit *Woelfflinus*: inuenit *B.*
[4] Diaei *Pighius*: dinei *B*: dignitate *NL.*
[5] tuba *L. Voss. Palat.*: turba *BN.*
[6] iniuria: syniuria *B*: ruina *Hauptius.*

---

[1] Head of the Achaean League.

This city, by an act unworthy of the Romans, was overwhelmed before it could be accounted in the number of their declared enemies. The cause of the war was the action of Critolaus,[1] who used against the Romans the liberty which they themselves had granted, and insulted the Roman ambassadors, certainly by his words and perhaps also by personal violence. The task of vengeance was therefore entrusted to Metellus, who just at the time was settling matters in Macedonia. Thus the Achaean war began. First of all the consul Metellus[2] defeated the forces of Critolaus all along the Alpheus in the wide plains of Elis. The war was thus finished by a single battle, and a siege already threatened the city itself; but—so fate decreed—though Metellus had fought the battle, Mummius interposed to reap the fruits of the victory. He completely routed the army of the other general, Diaeus, in the very neck of the Isthmus and dyed the twin harbours with blood. The city, deserted by its inhabitants, was first plundered and then destroyed at a signal given by trumpets. What a vast quantity of statues, garments and pictures was carried off, burnt, and thrown away! How great was the wealth which was plundered or burnt may be judged from the fact that we are told that all the Corinthian bronze-work, which enjoys so high a repute throughout the world, was a survival from the conflagration. For the damage inflicted on this rich city in itself caused a higher value to be placed upon Corinthian bronze, because, by the melting together of countless statues and images by the flames, brass, gold and silver ore were fused into one common mass.

[2] Consul in 146 B.C.

XXXIII. Res in Hispania Gestae

II, 17 Vt Carthaginem Corinthus, ita Corinthum Nu-
mantia secuta est; nec deinde orbe toto quicquam
2 intactum armis fuit. Post illa duo clarissimarum[1]
urbium incendia late atque passim, nec per vices,
sed simul pariter quasi unum undique bellum fuit;
prorsus ut illae[2] quasi agitantibus ventis diffudisse
quaedam belli incendia orbe toto viderentur.

3 Hispaniae numquam animus fuit adversum nos
universae consurgere, numquam conferre vires suas
libuit, neque aut imperium experiri aut libertatem
tueri suam publice. Alioquin ita undique mari
Pyrenaeoque vallata est, ut ingenio situs ne adiri
4 quidem potuerit. Sed ante a Romanis obsessa est
quam se ipsa cognosceret, et sola omnium provincia-
5 rum vires suas postquam victa est intellexit. In
hac prope ducentos per annos dimicatum est a
primis Scipionibus in primum Caesarem Augustum,
non continuo nec cohaerenter, sed prout causae
lacessierant, nec cum Hispanis initio, sed cum
Poenis in Hispania; inde contagium serpens[3]
causaeque bellorum.

6 Prima per Pyrenaeum iugum signa Romana
Publius et Gnaeus Scipiones intulerunt proeliisque
ingentibus Annonem et Hasdrubalem fratres Anni-
balis ceciderunt; raptaque erat impetu Hispania,

[1] clarissimarum *Freinshemius*: clarissima *codd.*
[2] illae: ille *BN*: favillae *Iahnius*: scintillae *Woelfflinus.*
[3] serpens *Mommsenus*: ad series *B*: et series *NL.*

XXXIII. Operations in Spain

17. As the fate of Corinth followed upon that of Carthage, so the fate of Numantia followed upon that of Corinth; and thereafter not a single place in the whole world was left unassailed by the arms of Rome. After the burning of these two famous cities, a single war was waged far and wide everywhere at once, and not merely against one nation after another; so that it seemed as if these two cities, as by the action of winds, had scattered the flames of war over the whole world.

Spain as a whole never had any desire to rise against us; it never thought of pitting its strength against us, and either making a bid for empire or a united defence of its liberty. Otherwise it is so well protected on all sides by the sea and the Pyrenees that, owing to its geographical conformation, it would be unassailable. But it was beset by the Romans before it recognized its own possibilities, and was the only one of the provinces that discovered its strength only after it had been defeated. Fighting continued in Spain over a period of nearly two hundred years, from the earliest of the Scipios down to the first Caesar Augustus, yet not continuously and without intermission, but at the call of circumstances; and the first hostilities were directed not against the Spanish but against the Carthaginians in Spain, from whom the contagion spread and who were the cause of all the wars.

The two Scipios, Publius and Gnaeus, bore the first Roman standards over the Pyrenees, and defeated Hanno and Hasdrubal, the brothers of Hannibal, in important encounters. Spain would

nisi fortissimi viri in ipsa victoria sua oppressi
Punica fraude cecidissent, terra marique victores.
7 Igitur quasi novam integramque provinciam ultor
patris et patrui Scipio ille mox Africanus invasit,
isque statim capta Carthagine et aliis urbibus, non
contentus Poenos expulisse, stipendiariam nobis
provinciam fecit, omnes citra ultraque Hiberum
subiecit imperio, primusque Romanorum ducum
victor ad Gades et Oceani ora pervenit. Plus est
8 provinciam retinere quam facere. Itaque per partes
iam huc, iam illuc missi duces, qui ferocissimas et in
id tempus liberas gentes ideoque inpatientes iugi
multo labore nec incruentis certaminibus servire
9 docuerunt. Cato ille censorius Celtiberos, id est
robur Hispaniae, aliquot proeliis fregit. Gracchus,
pater ille Gracchorum, eosdem centum et quinqua-
10 ginta urbium eversione multavit. Metellus ille, qui
ex Macedonia cognomen meruerat, et Celtibericus
fieri meruit, cum et Contrebiam [1] memorabili ce-
pisset exemplo et Nertobrigae [2] maiore gloria
11 pepercisset. Lucullus Turdulos atque Vaccaeos,
de quibus ille Scipio posterior singulari certamine,
12 cum rex fuisset provocator, opima rettulerat. Deci-
mus Brutus aliquanto latius Celticos Lusitanosque et

[1] Contrebiam : cantabriam *B* : cum | trebiam *L*.
[2] Nertobrigae : nectobricae *B* : nersobrigis *L*.

---

[1] New Carthage, the modern Cartagena.

have been carried by assault had not the gallant Roman leaders, in the hour of victory, been surprised and killed by Carthaginian craft, when they had been successful by land and sea. And so, that other Scipio, afterwards to be known as Africanus, coming to avenge his father and uncle, entered as it were a new and unimpaired province. After immediately capturing Carthage[1] and other cities, not content with having expelled the Carthaginians, he made Spain into a province paying tribute to Rome, and subdued all the inhabitants on both sides of the Iberus, and was the first Roman general to reach Gades and the shores of the Ocean as a conqueror. It is easier to create than to retain a province. Generals were, therefore, sent to deal with the inhabitants in detail, now to this region and now to that, who, with much toil and after sanguinary encounters, taught submission to savage races who had hitherto been free and were, therefore, impatient of the yoke. Cato, the well-known censor, broke the resistance of the Celtiberians, the flower of Spanish manhood, in several battles. Gracchus, the famous father of the Gracchi, punished the same race by the destruction of a hundred and fifty cities. Metellus, who had won in Macedonia the title of Macedonicus, deserved also that of Celtibericus, after he had achieved a notable exploit in the capture of Contrebia and had gained still greater glory by sparing Nertobriga. Lucullus conquered the Turduli and Vaccaei, from whom the younger Scipio had won the *spolia opima* in a single combat to which their king had challenged him. Decimus Brutus conquered a much wider district, which included the Celts and Lusitanians

omnis Callaeciae populos formidatumque militibus
flumen Oblivionis, peragratoque victor Oceani litore
non prius signa convertit quam cadentem in maria
solem obrutumque aquis ignem non sine quodam
sacrilegii metu et horrore deprendit.
13 Sed tota certaminum moles cum Lusitanis fuit et
Numantinis. Nec inmerito. Quippe solis gentium
Hispaniae duces contigerunt. Fuisset et cum
omnibus Celtiberis, nisi dux illius motus initio belli
vi[1] oppressus esset, summi vir[2] astus et audaciae, si
14 processisset, Olyndicus, qui hastam argenteam qua-
tiens quasi caelo missam vaticinanti similis omnium
in se mentes converterat. Sed cum pari temeritate
sub nocte castra consulis adisset, iuxta tentorium
15 ipsum pilo vigilis exceptus est. Ceterum Lusitanos
Viriatus erexit, vir calliditatis acerrimae. Qui ex
venatore latro, ex latrone subito dux atque imperator
et, si fortuna cessisset, Hispaniae Romulus, non
contentus libertatem suorum defendere, per quat-
tuordecim[3] annos omnia citra ultraque Hiberum et
16 Tagum igni ferroque populatus, castra etiam prae-
torum et praesidia[4] adgressus, Claudium Vnimanum
paene ad internicionem exercitus cecidit[5] et insignia
trabeis et fascibus nostris quae ceperat in montibus

[1] vi *Iahnius*: ut *B*.

[2] summi vir astus et audaciae *scripsi*: summae uir audaciae *B*: summus uir astutus et audaciae *NL*.

[3] quattuordecim: quattuor *B*: XIIII *NL*.

[4] praesidia *Halmius*: praesidium *codd.*

[5] cecidit et *Freinshemius*: cecidisset *codd.*

---

[1] Also called the Limaea (Strabo, III, p. 153).

and all the peoples of Callaecia and the River of Oblivion,[1] much dreaded by the soldiers, and, after marching victorious along the shores of the Ocean, did not turn back until, not without a certain dread of impiety and a feeling of awe, he beheld the sun sinking into the sea and its fires quenched in the waters.

But the chief trouble in the contest lay with the Lusitanians and the Numantines, and not without reason; for they were the only Spanish tribes that possessed leaders. There would have been trouble also with all the Celtiberians had not the leader of their rising, Olyndicus—a man of great craft and daring, if only fortune had favoured him—been put out of the way early in the war. This man, brandishing a silver spear which he claimed had been sent from heaven, and behaving like a prophet, had attracted general attention; but having, with corresponding temerity, approached the consul's camp under the cover of night, he ended his career by the javelin of a sentry close to the very tent of the consul. The Lusitanians were stirred to revolt by Viriatus, a man of extreme cunning, who from being a hunter became a brigand, and from a brigand suddenly became a leader and general, and, if fortune had favoured him, would have become the Romulus of Spain. Not content with defending the liberty of his countrymen, for fourteen years he laid waste with fire and sword all the land on both sides of the Iberus and Tagus; attacked the camps of the praetors and the Roman garrisons; defeated Claudius Unimanus, almost completely exterminating his army; and fixed up in his native mountains trophies adorned with the official robes and fasces which he had

17 suis tropaea fixit.[1] Tandem et eum [2] Fabius Maximus consul oppresserat; sed a successore Popilio violata victoria est. Quippe qui conficiendae rei cupidus, fractum ducem et extrema deditionis agitantem per fraudem et insidias et domesticos percussores adgressus, hanc hosti gloriam dedit, ut videretur aliter vinci non posse.

XXXIIII. Bellvm Nvmantinvm

II, 18 Numantia quantum Carthaginis, Capuae, Corinthi opibus inferior, ita virtutis nomine et honore par omnibus, summumque, si vero aestimes, Hispaniae
2 decus. Quippe quae sine muro, sine turribus, modice edito in tumulo apud flumen sita, quattuor milibus Celtiberorum quadraginta exercitum per annos undecim sola sustinuit, nec sustinuit modo, sed saevius aliquando [3] perculit pudendisque foederibus adfecit. Novissime, cum invictam esse constaret, opus fuit eo qui Carthaginem everterat.

3 Non temere, si fateri licet, ullius causa belli iniustior. Segidenses, socios et consanguineos suos,
4 Romanorum manibus elapsos, exceperant.[4] Habita pro his deprecatio nihil valuit. Cum se ab omni bellorum contagione removerent, in legitimi foederis pretium iussi arma deponere. Hoc sic a barbaris

[1] fixit *Freinshemius*: fixisset *codd.*
[2] et eum *scripsi*: etiam *codd.*
[3] aliquando *Lipsius*: aliquanto *codd.*
[4] exceperant: susceperant *B.*

captured from us. At last Fabius Maximus had overcome him also; but his victory was spoilt by the conduct of his successor Popilius, who, in his eagerness to finish the campaign, assailed the enemy leader, when he was already defeated and was contemplating the final step of surrender, by craft and stratagem and private assassins, and so gave him the credit of seeming to have been invincible by any other method.

XXXIIII. The Numantine War

18. Numantia, however inferior in wealth to Carthage, Capua and Corinth, in respect of valour and distinction was the equal of any of them, and, if one judges it aright, was the greatest glory of Spain. This city, without any walls or fortifications and situated on only a slight eminence on the banks of a stream, with a garrison of 4,000 Celtiberians, held out alone against an army of 40,000 men for eleven years, and not only held out but repulsed its foes with considerable vigour on several occasions and drove them to make discreditable terms. Finally, when they found that the city was undefeated, they were forced to call in the general who had overthrown Carthage.

Scarcely ever, if the truth may be confessed, was the pretext for any war more unjust. The Numantines had harboured their allies and kinsmen the Segidians who had escaped from the hands of the Romans. The intercession which they made on their behalf produced no result. When they offered to withdraw from all participation in the war, they were ordered to lay down their arms as the price of a regular treaty. This demand was interpreted

acceptum, quasi manus absciderentur. Itaque
statim Megaravico fortissimo duce ad arma conversi.
Pompeium proelio adgressi, foedus tamen maluerunt,
cum debellare potuissent; Hostilium deinde Manci-
5 num: hunc quoque adsiduis caedibus ita subegerunt,
ut ne oculos quidem aut vocem Numantini viri
6 quisquam sustineret. Tamen cum hoc quoque
foedus maluere, contenti armorum manubiis, cum
7 ad internicionem saevire potuissent. Sed non minus
Numantini quam Caudini illius foederis flagrans
ignominia aut pudore populus Romanus dedecus
quidem praesentis flagitii deditione Mancini expiavit,
8 ceterum duce Scipione, Carthaginis incendiis ad
excidium urbium inbuto, tandem etiam in ultionem
excanduit. Sed tum acrius in castris quam in
9 campo, nostro cum milite quam cum Numantino
10 proeliandum fuit. Quippe adsiduis et iniustis et
servilibus maxime operibus adtriti ferre plenius
vallum, qui arma nescirent, luto inquinari, quia
sanguine nollent, iubebantur. Ad hoc scorta,
calones, sarcinae nisi ad usum necessariae ampu-
11 tantur. Tanti esse exercitum quanti imperatorem
vere proditum est. Sic redacto in disciplinam

---

1 Mancinus was placed unarmed and bound before the gates of Numantia, but the Numantines refused to take him prisoner (Vell. Pater. II, 1, 5).

2 Cp. Liv. *Epit.* 57 (where the incident is referred to): *militem triginta dierum frumenta ac septenos vallos ferre coegit.*

by the barbarians as equivalent to the cutting off of their hands; and so they immediately had recourse to arms under the leadership of the brave Megaravicus. They attacked Pompeius, but, when they might have utterly defeated him, they preferred to conclude a treaty. They next attacked Hostilius Mancinus; him too they reduced by inflicting continual losses upon him, so that no one could endure even to look in the eyes or hear the voice of a Numantine. Nevertheless, when they might have wreaked their fury in wholesale destruction, they preferred to make a treaty with him, being content to despoil his men of their arms. But the Roman people, as much incensed at the dishonour and shame of this Numantine treaty as they had been at that of the Caudine Forks, wiped out the disgrace of the disaster of the moment by surrendering Mancinus to the enemy,[1] and then, under the leadership of Scipio, who had been trained for the destruction of cities by the burning of Carthage, at last their desire for vengeance burst into flames. At first he had a harder struggle in the camp than in the field, and more with our own soldiers than with the Numantines; for, worn out with continual, excessive and, for the most part, servile tasks, on the ground that they did not know how to fight they were ordered to carry more than the usual number of stakes,[2] and because they refused to stain themselves with blood, they were bidden to befoul themselves with mud. In addition to this, the women and camp-followers and all the baggage except what was absolutely necessary were dispensed with. It is a true proverb which says that a general has the army which he deserves. The troops having been thus reduced to

milite commissa acies, quodque nemo visurum se
umquam speraverat factum, ut fugientes Numantinos
12 quisquam videret. Dedere etiam se volebant, si
toleranda viris imperarentur. Sed cum Scipio veram
vellet et sine exceptione victoriam, eo necessitatum
conpulsi primum ut destinata morte in proelium
ruerent, cum se prius epulis quasi inferiis implevis-
sent carnis semicrudae et caeliae;[1] sic vocant in-
13 digenam ex frumento potionem. Intellectum ab
imperatore consilium, itaque non est permissa pugna
morituris. Cum fossa atque lorica quattuorque
castris circumdatos fames premeret, a duce orantes
proelium, ut tamquam viros occideret, ubi non
14 impetrabant, placuit eruptio. Sic conserta manu
plurimi occisi, et cum urgueret fames, aliquantisper
inde vixerunt.[2] Novissime consilium fugae sedit;
sed hoc quoque ruptis equorum cingulis[3] uxores
15 ademere, summo scelere per amorem. Itaque
deplorato exitu in ultimam rabiem furoremque
conversi, postremo Rhoecogene duce se, suos,
patriam ferro veneno, subiecto igne undique pere-
16 gerunt. Macte[4] fortissimam et meo iudicio beatissi-
mam in ipsis malis civitatem. Adseruit cum fide
socios, populum orbis terrarum viribus fultum tam
parva manu aetate tam longa sustinuit. Novissime

[1] caeliae *NL* : praellae *B*. [2] vixerunt: vicerunt *B*.
[3] cingulis: singuli *B*.
[4] esse *post* macte *add. codd. del. Aldus*.

---

[1] A kind of beer; cf. Pliny *N.H.* XXII. 25. 82.
[2] This interpretation of *inde* is confirmed by the account given by Val. Max. VII. 6, 2.

discipline, a battle was fought, and the sight of the Numantines in flight, which no one had even expected to see, was actually realized. They were willing to surrender if conditions were imposed to which men of spirit could submit. But since Scipio desired a complete and unqualified victory, they were first reduced to the necessity of rushing into the fray resolved to die, after they had first gorged themselves with, as it were, a funeral banquet of half-raw flesh and *caelia*,[1] a name which they give to a local drink made from corn. Their intention was perceived by the general, and so, ready though they were to die, no opportunity was given them of fighting. When famine pressed hard upon them—for they were surrounded by a trench and breastwork and four camps—they begged the general to allow them to engage him, so that he might slay them like men, and, when their request was refused, they determined to make a sortie. This resulted in a battle in which very many of them were slain and, as hunger pressed them hard, they lived for a while on the dead bodies.[2] Finally, they made up their minds to flee, but this was prevented by their wives, who cut the girths of their horses—a grievous wrong, but due to their affection. Despairing, therefore, of escape and in a revulsion of rage and fury, they, at last, under the leadership of Rhoecogenes, made an end of themselves, their families and their native city with the sword, with poison and with a general conflagration. All glory to a brave city, a city blessed, so it seems to me, even in its misfortunes; for it loyally helped its allies and with so small a force withstood for so long a period a people which was supported by the resources of the whole world.

maximo duce oppressa civitas nullum de se gaudium
17 hosti reliquit. Unus enim vir Numantinus non
fuit qui in catenis duceretur; praeda, ut de pauper-
rimis, nulla: arma ipsi cremaverunt. Triumphus
fuit tantum [1] de nomine.

II, 19 Hactenus populus Romanus pulcher, egregius,
pius, sanctus atque magnificus; reliqua saeculi, ut
grandia aeque, ita vel magis turbida et foeda,
crescentibus cum ipsa magnitudine imperii vitiis;
2 adeo ut, si quis hanc tertiam eius aetatem trans-
marinam, quam ducentorum annorum fecimus,
dividat, centum hos priores, quibus Africam,
Macedoniam, Siciliam,[2] Hispaniam domuit, aureos,
3 sicut poëtae canunt, iure meritoque fateatur, centum
sequentes ferreos plane et cruentos et si quid
immanius; quippe qui Iugurthinis, Cimbricis, Mith-
ridaticis, Parthicis, piraticis bellis, Gallicis atque
Germanicis, quibus caelum ipsum gloria ascendit,
Gracchanas Drusianasque caedes, ad hoc servilia
bella miscuerint et, ne quid turpitudini desit,
4 gladiatoria. Denique in se ipse conversus Marianis
atque Sullanis,[3] novissime Pompei et Caesaris mani-
bus, quasi per rabiem et furorem—nefas!—semet
5 ipse laceravit. Quae etsi [4] iuncta inter se sunt
omnia atque confusa, tamen quo melius appareant,

[1] tantum: tantus *B*.
[2] Siciliam *om. B*: Syriam *Iahnius*.
[3] Sullanis: Sillanis *B*.
[4] quae etsi *L. Voss*: quasi *B*: quaesi *N*.

Having been finally overcome by the greatest of generals, it left the enemy no cause for exultation; for not a single Numantine was left to be led in triumph as a prisoner; the city, being poor, provided no spoil; their arms they themselves burned. Only the name of the city remained over which they could triumph.

19. Hitherto the Roman people had been glorious, illustrious, humane, upright and high-minded; the rest of their history during this period, though equally grand, was more disturbed and disgraced by the vices which increased with the very greatness of their empire; so much so that, if one were to subdivide this third age, which saw conquests beyond the seas and to which we have allotted two hundred years, he would reasonably and justly admit that the first hundred years, during which they subdued Africa, Macedonia, Sicily and Spain, might be named, in the language of the poets, golden, and the following hundred years an age of iron and bloodshed or whatever is still more terrible. For these years included not only the Jugurthine, Cimbrian, Mithridatic, Parthian and piratical wars, and the wars in Gaul and Germany (when the glory of Rome rose to the very heavens), but the murders of the Gracchi and Drusus, and also the wars against the slaves, and also (that nothing might be wanting to their infamy) those against the gladiators. Lastly, the Romans, turning upon themselves, as though in madness and fury, rent themselves to pieces—a crime indeed—by the hands of the Marian and Sullan parties, and finally by those of Pompeius and Caesar. These events, though they are closely connected and involved with one another, nevertheless, in order that they may be set forth more clearly, and

simul et ne scelera virtutibus obstrepant, separatim referentur,[1] priusque, ut coepimus, iusta illa et pia cum exteris gentibus bella memorabimus, ut magnitudo crescentis in dies imperii appareat; tum ad illa civium scelera turpesque et inpias pugnas revertemur.

XXXV. Bellvm Asiaticvm

II, 20 Victa ad occasum Hispania populus Romanus ad orientem pacem agebat, nec pacem modo, sed inusitata et incognita quadam felicitate relictae regiis hereditatibus opes et tota insemel regna
2 veniebant. Attalus rex Pergamenorum, regis Eumenis filius, socii quondam commilitonisque nostri, testamentum reliquit: "Populus Romanus bonorum meorum heres esto. In bonis regiis haec
3 fuerunt." Adita igitur hereditate provinciam populus Romanus non quidem bello nec armis, sed,
4 quod aequius, testamenti iure retinebat. Sed hanc difficile dictu est utrum facilius amiserit populus Romanus an recuperaverit. Aristonicus, regii sanguinis ferox iuvenis, urbis regibus parere consuetas partim facile sollicitat, paucas resistentis, Myndon,[2] Samon, Colophona vi recepit; Crassi quoque praetoris cecidit[3] exercitum ipsumque cepit.

[1] referentur *Halmius*: perferentur *codd.*
[2] Myndon: myndam *B.* [3] cecidit *Rehd.*: caede *codd.*

---

[1] *fuerunt* appears to be a sort of epistolary perfect: "were, when I made my will."

also that the crimes may not obscure the virtues, shall be related separately. And so, in the first place, in accordance with our original plan, we will describe the just and honourable wars waged against foreign nations, in order that the greatness of the daily increasing empire may be made manifest; and afterwards we will turn to the crimes and to the disgraceful and impious struggles of the citizens amongst themselves.

XXXV. The Asiatic War

20. When Spain had been conquered in the West, the Roman people had peace in the East; and they not only had peace, but, by an unparalleled and unheard-of dispensation of fortune, wealth was left to them by royal bequests and whole kingdoms at a time passed into their hands. Attalus, king of Pergamon, son of King Eumenes, who had been our former ally and supporter in war, left a will which said, "Let the Roman people be heir to my estate: the following possessions now constitute the royal property."[1] Entering, therefore, into this inheritance, the Roman people took possession of a province not by war or force of arms but, what is more equitable, by the right conferred by a will. It is difficult to say whether the Roman people lost or recovered this province with greater ease. Aristonicus, a high-spirited young man of the royal blood, easily won over some of the cities which had been accustomed to obey the kings, and compelled a few others—Myndos, Samos and Colophon—which refused to join him. He also defeated the army of the praetor Crassus and captured its commander.

5 Sed ille memor et familiae et Romani nominis
custodem[1] barbarum virgula excaecat et in exitium
6 sui, quod volebat, ita concitat. Mox a Perperna
domitus et captus et per deditionem in vinculis
7 habitus. Aquilius Asiatici belli reliquias confecit,
mixtis—nefas—veneno fontibus ad deditionem qua-
rundam urbium. Quae res ut maturam, ita infamem
fecit victoriam, quippe cum contra fas deum mores-
que maiorum medicaminibus inpuris in id tempus
sacrosancta Romana arma violasset.

XXXVI. Bellvm Ivgvrthinvm

III, 1 Haec ad orientem; sed non ad meridianam
plagam eadem quies. Quis speraret post Cartha-
2 ginem aliquod in Africa bellum? Atquin non
leviter se Numidia concussit, et fuit in Iugurtha
quod post Annibalem timeretur. Quippe rex calli-
dissimus populum Romanum armis invictum opibus
adgressus est; citra spem omnium fortuna cessit,
3 ut rex fraude praecipuus fraude caperetur. Hic,
Massinissa avo, Micipsa patre per adoptionem, cum
interficere fratres statuisset agitatus regni cupidi-
tate, nec illos magis quam senatum populumque
Romanum, quorum in fide et in clientela regnum

[1] sui *post* custodem *delevi.*

The latter, however, not forgetful of the traditions of his family and of the Roman name, blinded with a stick the barbarian who was guarding him and thus provoked him, as was his purpose, to put him to death. Aristonicus was soon afterwards overcome by Perperna and taken prisoner, and was kept in chains after resigning his claims. Aquilius finally brought the Asiatic war to a close by the wicked expedient of poisoning the springs in order to procure the surrender of certain cities. This, though it hastened his victory, brought shame upon it, for he had disgraced the Roman arms, which had hitherto been unsullied, by the use of foul drugs in violation of the laws of heaven and the practice of our forefathers.

XXXVI. The Jugurthine War

1. So much for events in the East; in the South there was not the same tranquillity. Who, after the fate of Carthage, could expect another war to arise in Africa? Yet Numidia bestirred herself in a serious effort, and there was something in Jugurtha to make him an object of dread as the successor of Hannibal. This crafty king used his wealth to attack the Roman people when they were invincible with arms. Contrary to general expectation, fate decreed that a king pre-eminent in stratagem should himself be ensnared by a stratagem. Jugurtha, the grandson of Massinissa and the adopted son of Micipsa, having, in his hurry to possess kingly power, determined to put his brothers to death, was less afraid of them than of the Roman senate and people, in whose allegiance and under whose protection the kingdom then was; he, therefore, relied

erat, metueret, primum scelus mandat insidiis.
4 Potitus Hiempsalis capite cum se in Adherbalem convertisset isque Romam profugisset, missa per legatos pecunia traxit in sententiam suam senatum.
5 Et haec eius fuit de nobis prima victoria. Missos deinde, qui regnum inter illum Adherbalemque dividerent, similiter adgressus, cum in Scauro ipsos Romani imperii mores expugnasset, inchoatum nefas
6 perfecit audacia. Sed non diu latent scelera. Corruptae nefas legationis erupit, placuitque persequi
7 bello parricidam. Primus in Numidiam Calpurnius Bestia consul inmittitur; sed rex, peritus fortius adversus Romanos aurum esse quam ferrum, pacem
8 emit. Cuius flagitii reus cum interveniente publica fide a senatu arcesseretur, pari audacia et venit et conpetitorem imperii Massivam inmisso percussore
9 confecit. Haec altera contra regem causa belli fuit. Igitur sequens ultio mandatur Albino. Sed huius quoque—pro dedecus—frater ita corrupit exercitum, ut voluntaria nostrorum fuga vinceret Numida castrisque poteretur, addito etiam turpi foedere in pretium salutis, quo[1] quos emerat dimisit exercitus.
10 Tandem in ultionem non tam imperii Romani

[1] quo *Perizonius*: quod *codd.*

---

[1] Consul in 111 B.C.

[2] Aulus Albinus, who was left in Africa, as pro-praetor (Sall., *Jug.* 38).

on treachery in the commission of his first crime. Having possessed himself of the head of Hiempsal, he had turned his attention to Adherbal, who had fled to Rome, and sending ambassadors with money he won over the senate to his side. This was his first victory over us. Adopting similar methods with the commissioners who had been sent to partition the kingdom between him and Adherbal, and having carried by assault the very embodiment of the character of the Roman Empire by bribing Scaurus, he trusted to audacity to complete the evil with which he had begun. But crimes do not long remain undetected. The scandal of the bribed commission came to light, and it was resolved to begin hostilities against the murderer of his own kinsman. The consul Calpurnius Bestia [1] was the first general to be sent against Numidia; but the king, who knew by experience that gold was more efficacious against the Romans than steel, purchased peace from him. Jugurtha, being accused of this criminal action and having been summoned to appear before the senate under promise of safe-conduct, showed equal effrontery in coming to Rome and sending an assassin and murdering Massiva, his rival for the throne. This act was an additional pretext for war against the king. The vengeance that was to follow was entrusted to Albinus. But his brother [2] too (shameful to relate) so corrupted the army that, through the spontaneous flight of our troops, the Numidian was victorious and gained possession of our camp. This was followed by a disgraceful treaty fixing the terms of their safety, under which he allowed the armies which he had brought to depart. At last Metellus arose

quam pudoris Metellus adsurgit, qui callidissime
hostem nunc precibus nunc minis, iam simulata
iam vera fuga eludentem artibus suis adgressus est.
11 Agrorum atque vicorum populatione non[1] contentus[2]
in ipsa Numidiae capita impetum fecit; et Zamam
quidem frustra adsiluit,[3] ceterum Thalam, gravem
12 armis thensaurisque regiis,[4] diripuit. Tunc urbibus
exutum regem et iam finium suorum regnique
fugitivum per Mauros atque Gaetuliam sequebatur.
13 Postremo Marius auctis admodum copiis, cum pro
obscuritate generis sui capite censos sacramento
adegisset, iam fusum et saucium regem adortus, non
facilius tamen vicit quam si integrum ac recentem.
14 Hic et urbem ab Hercule conditam Capsam, in
media Africa siti anguibus harenisque vallatam,
mira quadam felicitate superavit, et saxeo inditam
monti Molucham[5] urbem per Ligurem aditu arduo
15 inaccessoque penetravit. Mox non ipsum modo,
sed Bocchum quoque Mauretaniae regem, iure
sanguinis Numidas vindicantem, apud oppidum
16 Cirtam graviter cecidit. Qui ubi diffisus rebus suis
alienae cladis accessio fieri timet, pretium foederis
17 atque amicitiae regem facit. Sic fraudulentissimus
regum fraude gener soceri sui in insidias deductus

[1] non *add. Aldus.* [2] contentus: contemptus *codd.*
[3] adsiluit *Freudenbergius*: diuoluit *B*: diu uoluit *NL.*
[4] regiis *Halmius*: regii *B*: regis *NL.*
[5] Molucham *Aldus*: molucam *B.*

---

[1] The incident is described by Sallust (*Jug.* 93, 2).

to defend not so much the might as the honour of the Roman Empire. With great skill he used their own wiles against the enemy, who sought to delude him now with entreaties and now with threats, at one moment by pretended and at another by actual flight. Not content with laying waste the fields and villages, he attacked the principal cities of Numidia. He was unsuccessful indeed in his assault upon Zama, but plundered Thala, a storehouse of arms and royal treasures. He then pursued the king, stripped of his cities and now a fugitive from his country and kingdom, through Mauretania and Gaetulia. Finally, Marius with considerably increased forces (for, acting as one would expect a low-born man to act, he had forced the lowest class of citizens to enlist), though he attacked the king when he was already routed and wounded, did not, however, defeat him any more easily than if his strength had been fresh and unimpaired. Marius not only captured, by a wonderful stroke of good fortune, the city of Capsa founded by Hercules in the middle of Africa, defended by waterless tracts, snakes and sand, but he also penetrated, thanks to a Ligurian soldier,[1] to Molucha, a city built on a rocky height, the approach to which was steep and inaccessible. Presently he defeated not only Jugurtha himself but also Bocchus, king of Mauretania, who from ties of kinship was supporting the Numidians, near the city of Cirta. Bocchus, apprehensive about his own interests and afraid of being involved in another's ruin, offered the person of Jugurtha as the price of a treaty and friendship. Thus the most treacherous of kings was entrapped by the treachery of his own father-in-law

Sullae[1] in manum traditur, tandemque opertum catenis Iugurtham in triumpho populus Romanus
18 aspexit. Sed ille quoque, quamvis victus ac vinctus, vidit urbem, quam venalem et quandoque perituram, si habuisset emptorem, frustra cecinerat. Iam, ut venalis fuisset, habuit emptorem; cum illum evaserat, certum erat non esse perituram.

XXXVII. Bellvm Allobrogvm

III, 2 Sic ad meridiem populus Romanus. Multo atrocius et multipliciter magis a septentrione venientem * * *.[2]
2 Nihil hac plaga infestius. Atrox caelum, perinde ingenia. Omni igitur tractu violentus hostis, a dextris atque laevis et a medio septentrionis erupit.
3 Prima trans Alpes arma nostra sensere Saluvii, cum de eis fidissima atque amicissima civitas Mas-
4 silia quereretur; Allobroges deinde et Arveni, cum adversus eos[3] similes Haeduorum querellae opem et auxilium nostrum flagitarent: utriusque[4] victoriae testes[5] Isara et Vindelicus amnes et inpiger flumi-
5 num Rhodanus. Maximus barbaris terror elephanti[6] fuere, inmanitati gentium pares. Nihil tam conspicuum in triumpho quam rex ipse Bituitus[7] dis-

[1] sullae *N*: sillae *B*.
[2] *lacunam post* venientem *indicavit Mommsenus*: saevitum *vel* saeviente *Aldus*: venit malum *vel* exitium *Rossbachius*.
[3] eos *add. Voss. Rehd. Monac. Palat.*
[4] utriusque *Iahnius*: variusque *codd.*
[5] testes *Dukerus*: testis *codd.*
[6] elephanti *N L*: elephantis *B*.
[7] Bituitus: vituitus *B*: bis visus *N L*.

and handed over to Sulla, and at last the Roman people saw Jugurtha led in triumph loaded with chains; and he himself, too, conquered and in chains, saw the city of which he had vainly prophesied that it could be bought and would one day perish if it could find a purchaser. In Jugurtha it had a purchaser—if it had been for sale; but once it had escaped his hands, it was certain that it was not doomed to perish.

XXXVII. The War with the Allobroges

2. So much for the activities of the Roman people in the South. A much more formidable and widespread danger threatened them from the North.[1] Nothing is more inclement than this region. The climate is harsh, and the disposition of the inhabitants resembles it. Along the whole extent, on the right and left and in the centre of the country to the north, violent foes broke forth.

The Saluvii felt the first shock of our arms on the other side of the Alps, when the loyal and friendly city of Marseilles complained of their behaviour. The Allobroges and Arveni were next attacked, when similar complaints against them on the part of the Aedui demanded our help and assistance. The rivers Isara and Vindelicus and the Rhone, swiftest of streams, can bear witness to the victories which we won over each of them. Our elephants, whose ferocity matched that of the barbarians, caused great alarm amongst them. The most conspicuous figure in the triumph was King Bituitus

[1] The reading here is uncertain (see critical note), but the general sense is clear.

coloribus in armis argenteoque carpento, qualis
6 pugnaverat. Utriusque victoriae quod quantumque gaudium fuerit, vel hinc aestimari potest, quod et Domitius Ahenobarbus et Fabius Maximus ipsis quibus dimicaverant locis saxeas erexere turres, et desuper exornata armis hostilibus tropaea fixerunt, cum hic mos inusitatus fuerit nostris. Numquam enim populus Romanus hostibus domitis victoriam exprobravit.

XXXVIII. Bellvm Cimbricvm Tevtonicvm Tigvrinvm

III, 3 Cimbri, Teutoni atque Tigurini ab extremis Galliae profugi, cum terras eorum inundasset Oceanus,
2 novas sedes toto orbe quaerebant, exclusique et Gallia et Hispania cum in Italiam demigrarent, misere legatos in castra Silani, inde ad senatum, petentes ut Martius populus aliquid sibi terrae daret quasi stipendium, ceterum ut vellet manibus
3 atque armis suis uteretur. Sed quas daret terras populus Romanus agrariis legibus inter se dimicaturus? Repulsi igitur, quod nequiverant precibus,
4 armis petere coeperunt.[1] Sed nec primum impetum barbarorum Silanus, nec secundum Manilius, nec tertium Caepio sustinere potuerunt; omnes fugati,
5 exuti castris. Actum erat, nisi Marius illi saeculo contigisset. Ille quoque non ausus congredi statim militem tenuit in castris, donec invicta illa rabies

[1] coeperunt: ceperunt *B*: constituunt *N L*.

himself, in his vari-coloured arms and silver chariot, just as he had appeared in battle. The great joy caused by both these victories may be judged from the fact that both Domitius Ahenobarbus and Fabius Maximus set up towers of stone on the actual sites of the battles which they had fought, and fixed on the top of them trophies adorned with the enemy's arms. This practice was unusual with our generals; for the Roman people never cast their defeats in the teeth of their conquered enemies.

XXXVIII. The War with the Cimbri, Teutones and Tigurini

3. The Cimbri, Teutones and Tigurini, fugitives from the extreme parts of Gaul, since the Ocean had inundated their territories, began to seek new settlements throughout the world, and excluded from Gaul and Spain, descended into Italy and sent representatives to the camp of Silanus and thence to the senate asking that "the people of Mars should give them some land by way of pay and use their hands and weapons for any purpose it wished." But what land could the Roman people give them when they were on the eve of a struggle amongst themselves about agrarian legislation? Thus repulsed they began to seek by force of arms what they had failed to obtain by entreaties. Silanus could not withstand the first attack of the barbarians, nor Manilius the second, nor Caepio the third; they were all routed and their camps captured. There would have been an end of Rome if that age had not had the good fortune to possess Marius. Even he did not dare to meet the enemy immediately, but kept his soldiers in camp until the irresistible

et impetus, quem pro virtute barbari habent, con-
6 senesceret. Recessere igitur increpantes et—tanta
erat capiendae urbis fiducia—consulentes, si quid ad
uxores suas mandarent. Nec segnius quam minati
fuerant tripertito agmine in Alpes, id est claustra
7 Italiae, ferebantur. Marius mira statim velocitate
occupatis compendiis praevenit hostem, prioresque
Teutonas sub ipsis Alpium radicibus adsecutus in
loco quem Aquas Sextias vocant quo—fidem[1] nu-
8 minum—proelio oppressit! Vallem fluviumque
medium hostes tenebant, nostris aquarum nulla
copia. Consultone id egerit imperator, an errorem
in consilium verterit, dubium; certe necessitate
9 acta virtus victoriae causa fuit. Nam flagitante
aquam exercitu,[2] "Si viri estis," inquit "en, illic
habetis." Itaque tanto ardore pugnatum est, ea
caedes hostium fuit, ut victor Romanus cruento
flumine non plus aquae biberit quam sanguinis
10 barbarorum. Certe rex ipse Teutobodus,[3] quaternos
senosque equos transilire solitus, vix unum, cum
fugeret, ascendit, proximoque in saltu conprehensus
insigne spectaculum triumphi fuit Quippe vir pro-
ceritatis eximiae super tropaea sua eminebat.

11 Sublatis funditus Teutonis in Cimbros convertitur.

[1] quo fidem *Salmasius*: pro fide *B*: qua fide *L*.
[2] flagitante aquam exercitu: flagitantem aquam exercitum *B*.
[3] Teutobodus: teuto vocatus *B*: teutobocus *NL*.

fury and rage, which in barbarians takes the place of courage, spent itself. The barbarians, therefore, made off, jeering at our men and—such was their confidence that they would capture Rome—advising them to give them any messages which they had for their wives. With a speed which amply fulfilled their threats, they bore down towards the Alps, which form the barriers of Italy, in three detachments. Marius with wonderful celerity immediately, by taking shorter routes, outstripped the enemy, and coming upon the Teutones first at the very foot of the Alps, what a defeat he inflicted upon them, ye heavenly powers, at the place called Aquae Sextiae! The enemy held the valley and the river flowing through it, while our men had no water-supply. It is uncertain whether the general acted designedly or whether he converted a mistake into a stratagem; at any rate the valour of the Romans under the constraint of necessity gave them victory. For when the men demanded water, Marius replied, "If you are men, there it is yonder for you." With such ardour, then, did they fight and such was the slaughter of the enemy that the victorious Romans drank quite as much barbarian gore as water from the blood-stained stream. Their king, Teutobodus himself, who had been accustomed to vault over four or even six horses, could scarcely find one to mount when he fled, and having been captured in a neighbouring forest was a striking figure in the triumphal procession; for, being a man of extraordinary stature, he towered above the trophies of his defeat.

The Teutones having been thus absolutely destroyed, attention was next directed to the Cimbri.

Hi iam—quis crederet?—per hiemem, quae altius
Alpes levat, Tridentinis iugis in Italiam provoluti
12 veluti[1] ruina descenderant. Atesim[2] flumen non
ponte nec navibus, sed quadam stoliditate barbarica
primum corporibus adgressi, postquam retinere
amnem manibus et clipeis frustra temptaverant,
13 ingesta silva obrutum transiluere. Si statim infesto
agmine urbem petissent, grande discrimen; sed in
Venetia, quo fere tractu Italia mollissima est, ipsa
soli caelique clementia robur elanguit. Ad hoc
panis usu carnisque coctae et dulcedine vini miti-
14 gatos Marius in tempore adgressus est. Venere
ipsi—nam metus in barbaris nulla vestigia—et[3]
diem pugnae a nostro imperatore petierunt; et
sic proximum dedit. In patentissimo, quem Raudium
vocant, campo concurrere. Inde milia sexaginta
quinque cecidere, hinc trecentis minus; per omnem
15 diem conciditur barbarus. Istic quoque imperator
addiderat virtuti dolum, secutus Annibalem artem-
que Cannarum; primum nebulosum nanctus diem,
ut hosti inopinatus occurreret, tum ventosum quo-
que, ut pulvis in oculos et ora ferretur, tum acie
conversa in orientem, ut, quod ex captivis mox
cognitum est, ex splendore galearum aere reper-
16 cusso[4] quasi ardere caelum videretur. Nec minor

[1] veluti *add. N. Heinsius.*

[2] Atesim *Salmasius*: adęsim *B*: ad hostes in *NL.*

[3] *locus valde corruptus*: est—vestigia *om. B*: venere—vestigia *om. L*: venere illi quam et in barbaris multa vestigia *ceteri*: venere ipsi—nam metus in barbaris nulla vestigia—et *etc. Halmius.*

[4] aere repercusso *Iahnius*: aere percusso *B.*

This people, though it is scarcely credible, had already descended during the winter (which increases the height of the Alps) from the Tridentine ranges like an avalanche into Italy. Attempting at first to cross the river Atesis, not by a bridge or in boats, but, with the stupidity of barbarians, by swimming, when they had vainly tried to stem the current with their hands and shields, they blocked it by hurling trees into it, and so crossed. If they had immediately marched upon Rome with hostile intent, the danger would have been great; but in Venetia, a district in which the Italian climate is almost at its softest, the very mildness of the country and of the air sapped their vigour. When they had been further demoralized by the use of bread and cooked meat and the delights of wine, Marius opportunely approached them. They came of their own accord—for the barbarians have no trace of fear[1]—and asked our general to name a day for the battle; and so he appointed the morrow. The armies met in a very wide plain which they call the Raudian Plain. On the side of the enemy 65,000 men fell, on our side less than 300; the slaughter of the barbarians continued all day. On this occasion too our general had added craft to courage, imitating Hannibal and his stratagem at Cannae. For, in the first place, the day he had chosen was misty, so that he could charge the enemy unawares, and it was also windy, so that the dust was driven into the eyes and faces of the enemy; finally, he had drawn up his line facing the west, so that, as was afterwards learned from the prisoners, the sky seemed to be on fire with the glint reflected from the bronze of the Roman helmets. There

[1] The text here is very uncertain; see critical note.

cum uxoribus eorum pugna quam cum ipsis fuit;
cum obiectis undique plaustris atque carpentis altae
17 desuper securibus contisque pugnarent. Perinde
speciosa mors earum fuit quam pugna. Nam cum
missa ad Marium legatione libertatem ac sacerdotium
non inpetrassent (nec fas erat), suffocatis elisisque
passim infantibus suis aut mutuis concidere vul-
neribus aut vinculo e crinibus suis facto ab arboribus
18 iugisque plaustrorum pependerunt. Boiorix[1] rex
in prima acie dimicans inpigre nec inultus occiditur.

Tertia Tigurinorum manus, quae quasi in sub-
sidio Noricos insederat Alpium tumulos, in diversa
19 elapsa fuga ignobili et[2] latrociniis evanuit. Hunc
tam laetum tamque felicem liberatae Italiae adserti-
que imperii nuntium non per homines, ut solebat,
populus Romanus accepit, sed per ipsos, si credere
20 fas est,[3] deos. Quippe eodem die quo gesta res
est visi pro aede Pollucis et Castoris iuvenes
laureatas praetori litteras dare, frequensque in
spectaculo rumor victoriae Cimbricae.[4] * * *
21 "feliciter!" dixit. Quo quid admirabilius, quid
insignius fieri potest? Quippe velut elata montibus
suis Roma spectaculo belli interesset, quod in

[1] Boiorix: Boleris *BL*: bo eloris *N*.
[2] et *NL*: e *B*.
[3] si credere fas est: fas est si credere *B*.
[4] *post* Cimbricae *lacunam statuit Iahnius*.

---

[1] They had asked to be sent as a gift to the Vestal Virgins and promised to take vows of chastity (Val. Max. VI, 1).
[2] There is a lacuna in the text at this point.

was quite as severe a struggle with the women-folk of the barbarians as with the men; for they had formed a barricade of their waggons and carts and, mounting on the top of it, fought with axes and pikes. Their death was as honourable as their resistance; for when, after sending a delegation to Marius, they had failed to secure their liberty and to be made priestesses [1]—a request which could not lawfully be granted—they strangled all their infants or dashed them to pieces, and themselves either fell by wounds inflicted by one another, or else, making ropes of their own hair, hanged themselves on trees or the yokes of their waggons. Their king Boiorix fell fighting energetically in the forefront of the battle, and not without having inflicted vengeance on his foes.

The third body, consisting of the Tigurini, who had taken up their position as a reserve force among the Norican ranges of the Alps, dispersing in different directions, resorted to ignoble flight and depredations and finally vanished away. The joyful and happy news of the deliverance of Italy and the salvation of the empire was received by the Roman people not, as usual, through human agency but from the lips of the gods themselves, if we may believe the tale. For on the same day as that on which the battle was fought, young men were seen to present to the praetor a despatch decked with laurels in front of the temple of Pollux and Castor, and the rumour of a victory over the Cimbri spread far and wide through the theatre. . . . [2] exclaimed, "May it be a good omen." What could be more wonderful or remarkable than this? For just as though Rome, raised aloft on her hills, was present watching the battle, the people in the

gladiatorio munere fieri solet, uno eodemque momento, cum in acie Cimbri succumberent, populus in urbe plaudebat.

XXXVIIII. Bellvm Thracicvm

III, 4 Post Macedonas, si dis placet, Thraces rebellant, illi quondam tributarii Macedonum; nec in proximas modo provincias contenti incurrere, Thessaliam atque Dalmatiam, in Adriaticum mare usque venerunt; eoque fine retenti,[1] quasi interveniente natura,
2 contorta in ipsas aquas tela miserunt. Nihil interim per id omne[2] tempus residuum crudelitatis fuit in captivos saevientibus: litare dis sanguine humano, bibere in ossibus capitum, cuiusque modi ludibriis foedare mortem tam igni quam fumo, partus quoque
3 gravidarum mulierum extorquere tormentis. Saevissimi omnium Thracum Scordisci fuere, sed calli-
4 ditas quoque ad robur accesserat: silvarum et montium situs cum ingenio consentiebant. Itaque non fusus modo ab his aut fugatus, sed—simile[3] prodigio—omnino totus interceptus exercitus quem
5 duxerat Cato. Didius vagos et libera populatione diffusos intra suam reppulit Thraciam. Drusus ulterius egit et vetuit transire Danuvium. Minucius toto vastavit Hebro, multis quidem amissis, dum per[4]

[1] retenti *Graevius*: contenti *codd.*
[2] per id omne: peridomne *L*: perdi omne *N*: per imperium donec *B*.
[3] simile *Aldus*: simili *BL*.
[4] per *om. B*.

[1] Cp. Cicero, *in Verr.* II, i, 17 (45), where torture by fumigation is described.

city were raising the usual applause which is given at a gladiatorial show at the very moment when the Cimbri were falling on the field of battle.

XXXVIIII. The Thracian War

4. After the Macedonians (heaven save the mark), the Thracians, former tributaries of the Macedonians, rebelled and, not content with making incursions merely into the neighbouring provinces of Thessaly and Dalmatia, penetrated as far as the Adriatic; checked by the boundary which it formed, since nature apparently stayed their advance, they hurled their weapons against the very waters. Throughout the period of their advance they left no cruelty untried, as they vented their fury on their prisoners; they sacrificed to the gods with human blood; they drank out of human skulls; by every kind of insult inflicted by burning and fumigation[1] they made death more foul; they even forced infants from their mothers' wombs by torture. The cruellest of all the Thracians were the Scordisci, and to their strength was added cunning as well; their haunts among the woods and mountains harmonized well with their fierce temper. An army, therefore, was not only routed and put to flight by them, but—what almost seemed like a miracle—entirely cut up under the command of a Cato. Didius, finding them wandering about and dispersed in undisciplined plundering, drove them back into their own land of Thrace. Drusus forced them still further and prevented them from recrossing the Danube. Minucius laid waste all the country along the Hebrus, losing, however, many of his men as they rode across a river covered

6 perfidum glacie flumen equitatur. Volso Rhodopen Caucasumque[1] penetravit. Curio Dacia tenus venit, sed tenebras saltuum expavit. Appius in Sarmatas usque pervenit, Lucullus ad terminum gentium
7 Tanain lacumque Maeotim. Nec aliter cruentissimi hostium quam suis moribus domiti. Quippe in captivos igni ferroque saevitum est; sed nihil barbaris atrocius visum est quam quod abscisis manibus relicti vivere superstites poenae suae iubebantur.

XL. Bellvm Mithridaticvm

III, 5 Ponticae gentes a septentrione in sinistrum iacent, a Pontico cognominatae mari. Harum gentium atque regionum rex antiquissimus Aeetas,[2] post Artabazes, a septem Persis oriundus, inde Mithri-
2 dates, omnium longe maximus. Quippe cum quattuor Pyrrho, tredecim[3] anni Annibali suffecerint, ille per quadraginta annos restitit, donec tribus ingentibus bellis subactus felicitate Sullae,[4] virtute
3 Luculli, magnitudine Pompei consumeretur. Causam quidem illius belli praetenderat apud Cassium legatum, adtrectari terminos suos a Nicomede Bithyno; ceterum elatus animis ingentibus Asiae totius et,

[1] Caucasumque: cauca umque *B*: Haemumque *Iahnius.*
[2] Aeetas: œtas *N*: aetas *B*: etas *L.*
[3] tredecim *B*: quattuordecim *NL.*
[4] Sullae: syllae *NL*: sillae *B.*

---

[1] The mention here of the Caucasus is a good example of the gross exaggeration in which Florus sometimes indulges.
[2] The meaning apparently is that the Pontus (Black Sea) was regarded as lying to the left of ships sailing to Asia.

with treacherous ice. Volso penetrated to Rhodope and the Caucasus.[1] Curio reached Dacia, but shrank from its gloomy forests. Appius advanced as far as the Sarmatians, while Lucullus reached the Tanais, the boundary of those tribes, and Lake Maeotis. These savage enemies could only be reduced by the employment of their own methods against them; severe cruelties were inflicted upon the captives by fire and the sword, but nothing was regarded by the barbarians as more horrible than that they should be left with their hands cut off and be forced to survive their punishment.

XL. The Mithridatic War

5. The Pontic races lie to the North on the left[2] and derive their name from the sea of Pontus. The earliest king of these regions and races was Aeetas, after him came Artabazes, who was sprung from one of the seven Persians,[3] and then came Mithridates, by far the greatest of their rulers; for, while four years sufficed to defeat Pyrrhus and thirteen to defeat Hannibal, Mithridates resisted for forty years, until, defeated in three great wars, he was brought to nought by the good fortune of Sulla, the valour of Lucullus and the might of Pompeius. He had alleged to our ambassador Cassius as the cause of the war that his frontiers were being violated by Nicomedes, king of Bithynia; but, in fact, carried away by boundless ambition, he was consumed by a

[3] Polyb. v. 43, 2 says "Mithridates boasted that he was a descendant of one of the seven Persians who destroyed the Magus" (see Herod. III, 61), "and that he had received from his forefathers in direct succession the dominion along the Black Sea originally bestowed upon them by Darius."

4 si posset, Europae cupiditate flagrabat. Spem ac
fiduciam dabant nostra vitia. Quippe cum civilibus
bellis distringeremur, invitabat occasio, nudumque
latus imperii ostendebant procul Marius, Sulla,
5 Sertorius. Inter haec rei publicae vulnera et hos
tumultus repente quasi captato tempore in lassos
simul atque districtos subitus turbo Pontici belli ab
ultima veluti specula septentrionis erupit.

6 Primus statim impetus belli Bithyniam rapuit,
Asia inde pari terrore correpta est, nec cunctanter
ad regem ab urbibus nostris populisque descitum
7 est. Aderat, instabat, saevitia quasi virtute ute-
batur. Nam quid atrocius uno eius edicto, cum
omnes qui in Asia forent Romanae civitatis homines
interfici iussit? tum quidem domus, templa et arae,
8 humana omnia atque divina iura violata sunt. Sed
hic terror Asiae Europam quoque regi aperiebat.
Itaque missis Archelao Neoptolemoque praefectis,
excepta Rhodo, quae pro nobis firmius stetit, ceterae
Cyclades, Delos, Euboea et ipsum Graeciae decus
9 Athenae tenebantur. Italiam iam ipsamque urbem
Romam regius terror adflabat. Itaque L. Sulla
festinat, vir armis optimus, parique violentia ruentem
10 ulterius hostem quadam quasi manu reppulit. Pri-
mumque Athenas urbem,—quis crederet?—frugum

burning desire to possess himself of all Asia and, if he could, of Europe also. Our weaknesses gave him hope and confidence; for a tempting opportunity was offered while we were preoccupied by civil wars, and the activities of Marius, Sulla and Sertorius made it known far and wide that the flank of the empire was unprotected. While the State was thus wounded and distracted, suddenly, as though it had chosen the opportune moment, the tempest of the Pontic war broke forth from the furthest outpost of the North against a people who were both weary and preoccupied.

The first assault immediately won Bithynia; whereupon Asia was seized by a general panic, and without delay our cities and peoples revolted to the king. He was on the spot, he was insistent, he practised cruelty as though it were a virtue. For what could be more outrageous than that one decree of his by which he gave orders for the murder of all those in Asia who were of Roman citizenship? At the same time the sanctity of private houses, temples and altars, and all laws, human and divine, were violated. The alarm thus inspired in Asia also opened to the king the gates of Europe. He, therefore, sent his generals, Archelaus and Neoptolemus, and (except Rhodes, which supported us more loyally than ever) all the Cyclades, Delos, Euboea and Athens itself, the glory of Greece, were occupied. The dread of the king now spread to Italy and Rome itself. Our great commander, Sulla, therefore, hastened to oppose him and, as he advanced with violence unabated, stayed his further progress by, as it were, a mere gesture of the hand. First, he compelled Athens, where corn was first discovered, by siege

parentem, obsidione ac fame ad humanos cibos
conpulit; mox subrutus Piraei portus sex aut
amplius muris cinctus. Postquam domuerat ingra-
tissimos hominum, tamen, ut ipse dixit, in honorem
11 mortuorum sacris suis famaeque donavit. Mox cum
Euboea atque Boeotia praesidia regis depulisset,[1]
omnis copias uno apud Chaeroniam, apud Orcho-
menon altero bello dissipavit, statimque in Asiam
transgressus ipsum opprimit. Et debellatum foret,
nisi de Mithridate triumphare cito quam vere
12 maluisset. Ac tum quidem hunc Asiae statum
Sulla dederat. Ictum cum Ponticis foedus, recepit
Bithyniam a[2] rege Nicomedes, Ariobarzanes[3] Cappa-
dociam, Asia rursus nostra, ut coeperat, Mithridates
tantum[4] repulsus. Itaque non fregit ea res Ponticos,
13 sed incendit. Quippe rex Asia et Europa quodam
modo inescatus non iam quasi alienas,[5] sed, quia
14 amiserat, quasi raptas[5] belli iure repetebat. Igitur
ut extincta parum fideliter incendia maiore flamma
revivescunt, ita ille de integro, auctis maiorem in
modum copiis, tota denique regni sui mole in Asiam
rursus mari terra fluminibusque veniebat.

15 Cyzicus,[6] nobilis civitas, arce, moenibus, portu
turribusque marmoreis Asiaticae plagae litora inlus-
trat. Hanc ille quasi alteram Romam toto invaserat

[1] depulisset: dispulisset *BL*. [2] a: et *B*.
[3] Nicomedes, Ariobarzanes: nichomede abariobar zenae *B*.
[4] tantum: tantus *B*.
[5] alienas . . . raptas *scripsi*: alienam . . . raptam *codd.*
[6] Cyzicus: ci zicus *B*: Cyzicum *NL*.

and famine (the story is scarcely credible) to feed on human flesh; then the harbour of Piraeus, surrounded by six or more walls, was destroyed. When he had subdued the most ungrateful of men, he nevertheless (to use his own words) "spared them because of their shrines and past glory, as an act of respect towards their dead forefathers." Then, when he had driven the king's garrisons out of Euboea and Boeotia, he scattered the whole of his forces in one battle at Chaeronea and in another at Orchomenus, and then, immediately crossing over into Asia, overwhelmed the king himself. The war would have been brought to an end if Sulla had not preferred a speedy rather than a thorough triumph over Mithridates. The following was the state of affairs which Sulla had established in Asia: a treaty was made with the people of Pontus; Bithynia was handed over by Mithridates to Nicomedes, Cappadocia to Ariobarzanes, Asia was again ours, as before; but Mithridates had been only repulsed. This condition of affairs, so far from breaking the spirit of the people of Pontus, only inflamed them; for the king, lured on as it were by the bait of Asia and Europe, now sought to recover them by right of arms, as though they did not belong to others but had been snatched from him, because he had failed to retain his conquests. And so, just as fire not wholly extinguished bursts forth again into greater flames, so Mithridates, with greatly increased forces and indeed with the whole weight of his kingdom, overran Asia afresh by land and sea and river.

The noble city of Cyzicus with its citadel, walls, harbour and marble towers is the glory of the coast of Asia. This he had attacked with all his forces,

16 bello. Sed fiduciam oppidanis resistendi nuntius
fecit, docens adventare Lucullum, qui—horribile
dictu—per medias hostium naves utre suspensus et
pedibus iter gubernans, videntibus procul quasi
17 marina pristis evaserat. Mox clade conversa, cum
ex mora obsidii regem fames et ex fame pestilentia
urgueret, recedentem Lucullus adsequitur adeoque
cecidit,[1] ut Granicus et Aesepus[2] amnes cruenti
18 redderentur. Rex callidus Romanaeque avaritiae
peritus spargi aurum a fugientibus et pecuniam
iussit, qua sequentes moraretur. Nec felicior in
mari quam terra fuga. Quippe centum[3] amplius
navium classem apparatu belli gravem Pontico[4]
mari adgressa tempestas tam foeda strage laceravit,
19 ut navalis belli instar efficeret, planeque ut Lucullus
quodam cum fluctibus procellisque commercio de-
20 bellandum tradidisse regem ventis videretur. Ad-
tritae iam omnes validissimi regni vires erant, sed
21 animus malis augebatur. Itaque conversus ad
proximas gentes totum paene orientem ac septen-
trionem ruina sua involvit. Hiberi, Caspii, Albani
et utraeque sollicitantur Armeniae, per quae omnia
decus et nomen et titulos gloriae Pompeio suo
22 Fortuna quaerebat. Qui ubi novis motibus ardere
Asiam videt aliosque ex aliis prodire reges, nihil

[1] cecidit *L* : caedit *B* : caecidit *N*.
[2] Aesepus *Salmasius*: aesopus *codd.*
[3] centum *om. B*.
[4] Pontico: in pontico *NL*: pontu *B*.

---

[1] *i.e.* Greater and Lesser Armenia.

as though it were a second Rome. But a messenger who, by an extraordinary feat, had made his way through the midst of the enemy's fleet buoyed up by an inflated skin, steering with his feet and presenting to distant observers the appearance of some sea-monster, had inspired the townspeople with confidence to resist by the news of Lucullus' approach. Soon afterwards, when ill-fortune went over to the king's side and, owing to the length of the siege, famine afflicted him and pestilence as a result of famine, he retreated. Lucullus followed him and dealt him so heavy a blow that the rivers Granicus and Aesepus ran with blood. The crafty king, who had had experience of Roman avarice, ordered that gold and money should be scattered in their path by his flying troops in order to delay his pursuers. His flight by sea was no more fortunate than by land; for a tempest which arose in the Black Sea attacked his fleet of more than a hundred ships laden with material of war, and shattered them with such terrible loss as to produce the effect of a naval defeat and make it appear as if Lucullus, by some compact with the waves and storms, had handed over the king to the wind to be defeated. All the resources of his powerful kingdom were now exhausted, but his misfortunes only served to raise his spirit. Turning, therefore, to the neighbouring peoples he involved almost the whole of the East and the North in his ruin. The Iberians, the Caspians, the Albanians, and both the Armenian peoples[1] were rallied to his cause, Fortune thus seeking fresh opportunities to win honour, fame and new titles of glory for her favourite Pompeius. He, seeing that fresh flames of rebellion were being kindled in Asia

cunctandum ratus, priusquam inter se gentium
robora coirent, statim ponte navibus facto omnium
ante se primus transiit Euphratem regemque fugi-
entem media nanctus Armenia—quanta felicitas
23 viri—uno proelio confecit. Nocturna ea dimicatio
fuit et Luna in partibus. Quippe quasi commilitans
cum[1] dea a tergo se hostibus, a facie Romanis
praebuisset, Pontici per errorem longius cadentis
24 umbras suas quasi hostium corpora petebant. Et
Mithridates quidem nocte illa debellatus est. Nihil
enim postea valuit,[2] quamquam omnia expertus
more anguium, qui optrito capite postremum cauda
25 minantur. Quippe cum effugisset hostem Colchis
tenus, iungere Bosporon, inde per Thracen Mace-
doniamque et Graeciam transilire, sic Italiam nec
26 opinatus invadere—tantum cogitavit. Sed defectione
civium Pharnacisque filii scelere praeventus male
temptatum veneno spiritum ferro expulit.

27 Gnaeus interim Magnus rebellis Asiae reliquias
sequens per diversa gentium terrarumque volitabat.
Nam sub orientem secutus Armenios, captis, ipso
capite gentis, Artaxatis, supplicem[3] iussit regnare
28 Tigranen. At in septentrione Scythicum iter tam-
quam in mari stellis secutus Colchos cecidit, ignovit
Hiberiae, pepercit Albanis. Regem horum[4] Oroden[5]

[1] quasi *post* cum *add. B.* [2] valuit *om. B.*

[3] captis, ipso capite gentis, Artaxatis *NL* : captae gentis atrapens supplicem *ceteris omissis B.*

[4] horum *Graevius* : colchorum *codd.*

[5] Oroden : orhozen *B.*

and that one king after another was rising, considered that he ought not to delay, and before the nations could consolidate their strength, built a bridge of boats over the Euphrates, and was the first to cross that river by this means, and coming up with the king as he was fleeing through the middle of Armenia, defeated him, with his usual good luck, in a single battle. The engagement took place at night, and the moon took sides in it; for when the goddess, as if fighting on Pompeius' side, had placed herself behind the enemy and facing the Romans, the men of Pontus aimed at their own unusually long shadows, thinking that they were the bodies of their foes. That night saw the final defeat of Mithridates; for he never again effected anything, although, like a snake, which, though its head is crushed, threatens to the last with its tail, he tried every expedient. For, after escaping from the enemy to the Colchians, he formed a plan (though it remained *only* a plan) of bridging the Bosporus and then crossing through Thrace, Macedonia and Greece and making a sudden inroad in Italy; but, baulked by the desertion of his subjects and the treachery of his son Pharnaces, he ended by the sword a life which he had in vain tried to destroy with poison.

Meanwhile Gnaeus Pompeius Magnus, pursuing the remnants of rebellious Asia, was hastening through nations and lands lying far apart. Following the Armenians eastward he captured Artaxata, the very capital of that race, and bade Tigranes, who implored his pardon, retain his kingdom. To the North, following the route to Scythia by the stars, as sailors steer at sea, he defeated the Colchians, pardoned the Iberians, and spared the Albanians.

positis sub ipso Caucaso castris iussit in plana descendere, at Arthocen, qui Hiberis imperabat,[1] obsides liberos dare; Oroden[2] etiam muneravit, ultro ab Albania sua lectum aureum et alia dona mittentem.
29 Nec non in meridiem verso agmine Libanum Syriae Damascumque transgressus per nemora illa odorata, per turis et balsami silvas Romana signa circumtulit.
30 Arabes, si quid imperaret, praesto fuere. Hierosolyma[3] defendere temptavere Iudaei; verum haec quoque et intravit et vidit illud grande inpiae gentis arcanum patens, sub aurea vite caelum.[4] Dissidentibusque de regno fratribus arbiter factus regnare iussit Hyrcanum; Aristobolum, quia renovabat
31 imperium, in catenas dedit. Sic Pompeio duce populus Romanus totam,[5] qua latissima est, Asiam pervagatus, quam extremam imperii habebat provinciam mediam fecit. Exceptis quippe Parthis, qui foedus maluerunt, et Indis, qui adhuc nos nec noverant, omnis Asia inter Rubrum et Caspium et Oceanum Pompeianis domita vel oppressa signis tenebatur.

[1] *post* imperabat *add.* et *codd.*, *del. Iahnius.*
[2] Oroden: horolen *B.*
[3] Hierosolyma: ierosolimam *B*: hierosolymam *N.*
[4] vite: vitae *B.*
[5] totam: tota *B*: totum (-am *man. sec.*) *N.*

Having pitched his camp at the very foot of the Caucasus, he ordered their king, Orodes, to descend into the plain, while he commanded Arthoces, who was ruler of the Iberians, to hand over his children as hostages; he even rewarded Orodes, who actually sent a golden bed and other gifts from his kingdom of Albania. Furthermore, turning his army southwards, he passed through the Lebanon in Syria and through Damascus, and bore the Roman standards through the famous scented groves and woods of frankincense and balm. He found the Arabs ready to carry out any orders which he might give. The Jews attempted to defend Jerusalem; but this also he entered and saw the great secret of that impious nation laid open to view, the heavens beneath a golden vine.[1] Being appointed arbitrator between the two brothers who were disputing the throne, he decided in favour of Hyrcanus and threw Aristobolus into prison, because he was seeking to restore his power. Thus the Roman people, under the leadership of Pompeius, traversed the whole of Asia in its widest extent and made what had been the furthest province into a central province;[2] for with the exception of the Parthians, who preferred to make a treaty, and the Indians, who as yet knew nothing of us, all Asia between the Red and Caspian Seas and the Ocean was in our power, conquered or overawed by the arms of Pompeius.

[1] That is, the image of the God of the Sky (Jehovah); cf. Juvenal, VI, 545: *interpres legum Solymarum et magna sacerdos | arboris ac summi fida internuntia caeli*: see also Perrot and Chipiez, *Hist. de l'art dans l'antiq.*, II, fig. 8, 235.

[2] *i.e.* brought under Roman rule territory beyond the province of Asia.

XLI. Bellvm Piraticvm

III, 6 Interim cum populus Romanus per diversa terra-
rum districtus est, Cilices invaserant maria sublatis-
que commerciis, rupto foedere generis humani, sic
2 maria bello quasi tempestate praecluserant. Auda-
ciam perditis furiosisque latronibus dabat inquieta
Mithridaticis proeliis Asia, dum sub alieni belli
tumultu exterique regis invidia inpune grassantur.
3 Ac primum duce Isidoro contenti proximo mari
Cretam inter atque Cyrenas et Achaiam sinumque
Maleum, quod ab spoliis aureum ipsi vocavere,
4 latrocinabantur. Missusque in eos Publius Servilius,
quamvis leves et fugaces myoparonas gravi et Martia
5 classe turbaret, non incruenta victoria superat. Sed
nec mari summovisse contentus, validissimas urbes
eorum et diutina praeda abundantes, Phaselim et
Olympum evertit Isaurosque ipsam arcem Ciliciae,
unde conscius sibi magni laboris Isaurici cognomen
6 adamavit. Non ideo tamen tot cladibus domiti
terra se continere potuerunt; sed ut quaedam
animalia, quibus aquam terramque incolendi gemina
natura est, sub ipso hostis recessu inpatientes soli

XLI. The War against the Pirates

6. In the meantime, while the Roman people were preoccupied in various parts of the world, the Cilicians had invaded the seas, and, making intercourse impossible and interrupting the peace of the world, had by their warlike operations caused the same result as a tempest in closing the seas to traffic. The disturbed condition brought about in Asia by the Mithridatic wars engendered a spirit of daring in these abandoned and desperate robbers, who, under the cover of the confusion caused by a war in which they took no part and the odium against a foreign prince, ranged over the seas with impunity. At first, under their leader Isodorus, they confined their operations to the neighbouring sea and committed their depredations between Crete and Cyrenae and Achaea and the sea off Cape Malea, which, from the richness of the spoil which it yielded, they themselves named the Golden Sea. Publius Servilius was sent against them, and, although with his heavy and well-equipped ships of war he defeated their light and elusive brigantines, he won a by no means bloodless victory. Not content, however, with having driven them off the seas, he overthrew their strongest cities, full of spoil collected over a long period, Phaselis, Olympus and the city of the Isauri, the very stronghold of Cilicia, from which, conscious of the greatness of his achievement, he assumed the title of Isauricus. But the pirates, though overcome by so many disasters, would not on that account confine themselves to the land, but, like certain animals whose nature fits them equally well for living in the sea and on the earth, as soon as ever the enemy had gone away,

in aquas suas resiluerunt, et aliquanto latius quam prius Siciliae quoque litora et Campaniam nostram
7 subito adventu terrere voluerunt. Sic Cilix dignus victoria Pompei visus est et Mithridaticae provinciae factus accessio. Ille dispersam toto mari pestem semel et in perpetuum volens extinguere divino
8 quodam apparatu adgressus est. Quippe cum classibus et suis et socialibus Rhodiorum abundaret, pluribus legatis atque praefectis utraque Ponti et
9 Oceani ora conplexus est. Gellius Tusco mari inpositus, Plotius Siculo; Atilius[1] Ligusticum sinum, Pomponius[2] Gallicum obsedit, Torquatus Balearicum, Tiberius Nero Gaditanum fretum, qua primum maris nostri limen aperitur; Lentulus Marcellinus Libycum,[3] Aegyptium, Pompei iuvenes
10 Hadriaticum, Varro Terentius Aegaeum et Ionicum,[4] Pamphylium Metellus, Asiaticum Caepio; ipsas Propontidos fauces Porcius Cato sic obditis navibus
11 quasi porta[5] obseravit. Sic per omnis aequoris portus, sinus, latebras, recessus, promontoria, freta, paeninsulas quidquid piratarum fuit quadam indagine
12 inclusum est. Ipse Pompeius in originem fontemque belli Ciliciam; nec hostes detractavere certa-
13 men. Non ex fiducia, sed quia oppressi erant, ausi

[1] Atilius *Gronovius*: gratillus *B*: gratillius *NL*.
[2] Pomponius *Dukerus*: Pompeius *codd.*
[3] Marcellinus Libycum *scripsi*: Libycum Marcellinus *codd.*
[4] Ionicum *Ormerodius*: Ponticum et *codd.*
[5] porta *Lipsius*: portam *codd.*

---

[1] The reading and punctuation adopted in this passage are those of Professor H. A. Ormerod, who in an article published in *Liverpool Annals of Archaeology*, Vol. X, pp. 46 ff., has cleared up the whole question of the distribution of Pompeius' forces in the campaign of 67 B.C.

impatient of remaining ashore they launched forth again upon their natural element, the sea, and, extending their operations over a far wider area than before, were eager to create a panic on the coasts of Sicily and our own Campania by a sudden attack. Cilicia was, therefore, deemed worthy of being conquered by Pompeius and was added to his sphere of operations against Mithridates. Pompeius, determining to make an end once and for all of the pest which had spread over the whole sea, approached his task with almost superhuman measures. Having at his disposal an ample force both of his own ships and of those of our allies the Rhodians, he extended his operations from the mouth of the Black Sea to that of the Ocean with the aid of numerous commanders and captains. Gellius was placed in charge of the Tuscan Sea, Plotius over the Sicilian Sea; Atilius occupied the Ligurian Gulf, Pomponius the Gallic Gulf; Torquatus commanded in the Balearic waters, Tiberius Nero in the Straits of Gades, where the threshold of our sea opens; Lentulus Marcellinus watched over the Libyan and Egyptian Seas, the young sons of Pompeius over the Adriatic, Terentius Varro over the Aegean and Ionian Seas, Metellus over the Pamphylian, and Caepio over the Asiatic Sea, while Porcius Cato sealed the very mouth of the Propontis with ships stationed so close to one another as to form, as it were, a gate.[1] Thus, in every harbour, bay, shelter, creek, promontory, strait and peninsula in the sea, every single pirate was enclosed as it were in a net. Pompeius himself proceeded against Cilicia, the origin and source of the war; nor did the enemy refuse an engagement, though their boldness seemed to be inspired not so

videbantur; sed nihil tamen amplius, quam ut ad primum ictum concurrerent. Mox ubi circumfusa undique rostra viderunt,[1] abiectis statim telis remisque plausu undique pari, quod supplicantium signum
14 fuit, vitam petiverunt. Non alia tam incruenta victoria usi umquam sumus, sed nec fidelior in posterum reperta gens ulla est;[2] idque prospectum singulari consilio ducis, qui maritimum genus a conspectu longe removit maris et mediterraneis agris quasi obligavit, eodemque tempore et usum maris navibus
15 recuperavit et terrae homines suos reddidit. Quid prius in hac mirere victoria? velocitatem? quadragensimo die parta est. An felicitatem? ne una quidem navis amissa est. An vero perpetuitatem? amplius piratae non fuerunt.

XLII. Bellvm Creticvm

III, 7 Creticum bellum, si vera volumus, [nos fecimus][3] sola vincendi nobilem insulam cupiditas fecit. Favisse Mithridati videbatur; hoc placuit armis
2 vindicare. Primus invasit insulam Marcus Antonius cum ingenti quidem victoriae spe atque fiducia, adeo ut pluris catenas in navibus quam arma por-
3 taret. Dedit itaque poenas vaecordiae. Nam plerasque naves intercepit hostis, captivaque corpora religantes velis ac funibus suspendere, ac sic velifi-

[1] viderunt: viderent *B.*
[2] reperta gens ulla est *om. B.*
[3] nos fecimus *secl. Iahnius.*

much by confidence as by the knowledge that they were hard pressed. However, they did no more than meet the first onslaught; for as soon as they saw the beaks of our ships all round them, they immediately threw down their weapons and oars, and with a general clapping of hands, which was their sign of entreaty, begged for quarter. We never gained so bloodless a victory, and no nation was afterwards found more loyal to us. This was secured by the remarkable wisdom of our commander, who removed this maritime people far from the sight of the sea and bound it down to the cultivation of the inland districts, thus at the same time recovering the use of the sea for shipping and restoring to the land its proper cultivators. In this victory what is most worthy of admiration? Its speedy accomplishment—for it was gained in forty days—or the good fortune which attended it—for not a single ship was lost—or its lasting effect—for there never were any pirates again?

XLII. The Cretan War

7. The Cretan war, if the truth is to be told, was due solely to our desire to conquer that famous island. It was thought to have supported Mithridates, an offence which we resolved to punish by force of arms. Marcus Antonius made the first attack upon the island with such expectation of victory and confidence that he carried more fetters than arms on board his ships. And so he paid the penalty of his rashness; for the enemy cut off most of his ships and hung the bodies of their prisoners from the sails and tackle; and then spreading their

cantes triumphantium in modum Cretes portibus
4 suis adremigaverunt. Metellus deinde totam in-
sulam igni ferroque populatus intra castella et urbes
redegit, Cnoson Eleuthernan[1] et, ut Graeci dicere
5 solent, urbium matrem Cydoneam; adeoque saeve
in captivos consulebatur,[2] ut veneno se plerique con-
ficerent, alii deditionem suam ad Pompeium absen-
6 tem mitterent. Et cum ille res in Asia gerens eo
quoque praefectum misisset Antonium in alienam[3]
provinciam, inritus fuit, eoque infestior Metellus in
hostes ius victoris exercuit, victisque Lasthene et
Panare, Cydoneae ducibus, victor rediit. Nec quic-
quam tamen amplius de tam famosa victoria quam
cognomen Creticum reportavit.

XLIII. Bellvm Balearicvm

III, 8 Quatenus Metelli Macedonici domus bellicis agno-
minibus[4] adsueverat, altero ex liberis eius Cretico
facto mora non fuit quin alter quoque Balearicus
2 vocaretur. Baleares per id tempus insulae piratica
rabie maria corruperant. Homines feros atque
silvestres mireris ausos a scopulis suis saltem maria
3 prospicere. Ascendere etiam inconditas rates et
praeternavigantes subinde inopinato impetu terruere.
4 Sed cum venientem ab alto Romanam classem pro-

[1] Eleuthernan: aetery threan *B*: et erythream *N*.
[2] consulebatur: consolebatur *B*: consulabatur *N*.
[3] alienam *Mommsenus*: aliam *B*.
[4] agnominibus: bacnominibus *B*: nominibus *NL*.

sails the Cretans returned in triumph to their harbours. Metellus subsequently laid waste the whole island with fire and sword and drove the inhabitants into their strongholds and cities, Cnossus, Eleutherna and Cydonia, the mother of cities, as the Greeks usually call it. So severe were the measures which he took against the prisoners that most of them put an end to themselves with poison, while others sent an offer of surrender to Pompeius across the sea. Pompeius, although while in command in Asia he had sent his officer Antonius outside his sphere of command to Crete, was powerless to act in the matter, and so Metellus exercised the rights of a conqueror with all the greater severity and, after defeating the Cydonian leaders, Lasthenes and Panares, returned victorious to Rome. However, from his remarkable victory he gained nothing but the title of Creticus.

XLIII. The Balearic War

8. Seeing that the family of Metellus Macedonicus had become accustomed to the assumption of surnames won in war, after one of his sons had become Creticus, it was not long before the other received the name of Balearicus. The Balearic islanders at this period had ravaged the seas with their piratical outrages. You may wonder that savages who dwelt in the woods should venture even to look upon the sea from their native rocks, but they actually went on board roughly constructed ships, and from time to time terrified passing ships by attacking them unexpectedly. When they had espied the Roman fleet approaching from the open sea, thinking it an

spexissent, praedam putantes, ausi etiam occurrere,
et primo impetu ingenti lapidum saxorumque nimbo
5 classem operuerunt. Tribus quisque fundis proe-
liantur. Certos esse quis miretur ictus, cum haec
sola genti arma sint, id unum ab infantia studium?
cibum puer a matre non accipit,[1] nisi quem ipsa
monstrante percusserit. Sed non diu lapidatione
6 Romanos terruere. Nam postquam comminus ven-
tum est expertique rostra et pila venientia, pecudum
in morem clamore sublato petiverunt fuga litora,
dilapsique in proximos tumulos quaerendi fuerunt
ut vincerentur.

XLIIII. Expeditio in Cyprum

III, 9 Aderat fatum insularum. Igitur et Cypros re-
cepta sine bello. Insulam veteribus divitiis abun-
2 dantem et ob hoc Veneri sacram Ptolemaeus regebat.
3 Sed divitiarum tanta erat fama, nec falso, ut victor
gentium populus et donare regna consuetus, P.
Clodio tribuno plebis duce, socii vivique regis con-
4 fiscationem mandaverit. Et ille quidem ad rei
5 famam veneno fata praecepit. Ceterum Porcius
Cato Cyprias opes Liburnis per Tiberinum ostium
invexit. Quae res latius aerarium populi Romani
quam ullus triumphus implevit.

[1] accipit: accepit *B*.

easy prey, they actually dared to assail it, and at the first onslaught covered it with a shower of stones and rocks. They fight with three slings apiece; and who can wonder that their aim is so accurate, seeing that this is their only kind of arm and its employment their sole pursuit from infancy? A boy receives no food from his mother except what he has struck down under her instruction. But the alarm caused among the Romans by their slinging of stones did not last long; when it came to close fighting and they experienced the attack of the beaks of our ships and our javelins, they raised a bellowing like cattle and fled to the shore, and scattering among the neighbouring hills had to be hunted down before they could be conquered.

XLIIII. The Expedition to Cyprus

9. The fate of the islands was sealed; and so Cyprus too was taken over without any fighting. This island, rich in ancient wealth and therefore dedicated to Venus, was under the rule of Ptolemy. But such was the fame of its riches (and not without cause) that a people which had conquered nations and was accustomed to make gifts of kingdoms ordered, on the proposal of Publius Clodius, the tribune of the people, that the property of a king, allied to themselves and still living, should be confiscated. Ptolemy, on hearing the news of this, anticipated fate by taking poison, and Porcius Cato brought the wealth of Cyprus in Liburnian galleys to the mouth of the Tiber. This replenished the treasury of the Roman people more effectively than any triumph.

XLV. Bellvm Gallicvm

III, 10 Asia Pompei manibus subacta reliqua, quae restabant in Europa, Fortuna in Caesarem transtulit.
2 Restabant autem inmanissimi gentium Galli atque Germani et quamvis toto orbe divisi, tamen quia vincere libuit, Britanni.

Primus Galliae motus ab Helvetiis coepit, qui Rhodanum inter et Rhenum siti, non sufficientibus terris venere sedem petitum, incensis moenibus suis;
3 hoc sacramentum fuit, ne redirent. Sed petito tempore ad deliberandum, cum inter moras Caesar Rhodani ponte rescisso fugam abstulisset, statim bellicosissimam gentem sic in sedes suas, quasi
4 greges in stabulum pastor, reduxit. Sequens longe longeque cruentior pugna Belgarum, quippe pro libertate pugnantium. Hic cum multa Romanorum militum insignia, tum illud egregium ipsius ducis, quod, nutante in fugam[1] exercitu, rapto fugientis e manu scuto in primam volitans aciem manu proelium
5 restituit. Inde cum Venetis etiam navale bellum, sed maior cum Oceano quam cum ipsis navibus rixa. Quippe illae rudes et informes et statim naufragae, cum rostra sensissent; sed haerebat in vadis pugna,

[1] fugam *Rhed.* : fuga *cet.*

XLV. The Gallic War

10. Asia having been subdued by the might of Pompeius, fortune handed over to Caesar all that remained to be conquered in Europe. Those who were still left were the most formidable of all races, the Gauls and the Germans, and also the Britons; for we were minded to conquer them, although they are a whole world away.

The first disturbance began with the Helvetii, who, being settled between the Rhone and the Rhine and being possessed of insufficient territory, came to ask us for new lands after burning their cities, an act which stood for an oath that they would not return. But Caesar, after asking for time to consider their request, having during the interval prevented their escape by breaking down the bridge over the Rhone, immediately drove back this warlike nation to its former abode, as a shepherd drives his flocks into the fold. Next followed a far more sanguinary struggle with the Belgae, since they were fighting for their freedom. In this, while there were many notable exploits on the part of Roman soldiers, a remarkable feat was performed by the general himself; for when his troops were wavering and on the point of retiring, snatching a shield out of the hand of a retreating soldier, he rushed to the front line and by his own efforts restored the battle. Next came a naval war with the Veneti; but it was a struggle rather against the ocean than against the enemy's fleet. For their vessels were rude and clumsy and went to pieces as soon as they had felt the beaks of our ships; but the battle was obstructed by the shallow water, since

cum aestibus solitis in ipso certamine subductus
6 Oceanus intercedere bello videretur. Illae quoque
accessere diversitates pro gentium locorumque
natura. Aquitani, callidum genus, in speluncas se
recipiebant: iussit includi; Morini dilabebantur in
silvas:[1] iussit incendi. Nemo tantum feroces
7 dixerit Gallos: fraudibus agunt. Indutiomarus
Treveros, Ambiorix concitavit Eburones. Utrique,
absente Caesare coniuratione facta, invasere legatos.
8 Sed ille fortiter a Dolabella summotus est, relatum-
que regis caput; hic insidiis in valle dispositis dolo
perculit. Itaque et castra direpta sunt et Aurun-
culeium[2] Cottam cum Titurio[3] Sabino legatos
amisimus. Nec ulla de rege mox ultio; quippe
perpetua trans Rhenum fuga latuit.

9 Nec Rhenus ergo inmunis; nec enim fas erat ut
10 liber esset receptator hostium atque defensor. Et
prima contra Germanos illius pugna iustissimis
quidem ex causis. Haedui de incursionibus eorum
11 querebantur. Quae Ariovisti[4] regis superbia! cui
cum legati dicerent "veni ad Caesarem," et "quis
est Caesar?" et "si vult, veniat" inquit, et "quid
12 ad illum, quid agat nostra Germania? num ego me
interpono Romanis?" Itaque tantus gentis novae
terror in castris, ut testamenta passim etiam in

[1] Morini dilabebantur in silvas *Vinetus*: morabantur in silvis *B*: nec mora dilabebantur in silvas *N*.

[2] Aurunculeium *Perizonius*: aurum ablatum *codd.*

[3] Titurio: tirio *B*.

[4] Ariovisti: tario bisti *B*: ario iusti *L*.

the ocean, retiring with usual fall of tide in the very middle of the engagement, seemed to take part in the struggle. The operations of the war varied with the nature of the people and the country. The crafty Aquitani betook themselves to caves; Caesar ordered that they should be blockaded there. The Morini scattered amongst their forests; Caesar ordered that the forests should be burnt. Let no one say that the Gauls are mere savages, for they can act with cunning. Indutiomarus stirred up the Treveri, Ambiorix the Eburones. In Caesar's absence these two tribes banded together and attacked the lieutenant-generals. Indutiomarus was bravely repulsed by Dolabella, and his head was brought back to the camp. Ambiorix, however, defeated us by the stratagem of an ambush set in a valley, with the result that our camp was plundered and we lost the lieutenant-generals Aurunculeius Cotta and Titurius Sabinus. No immediate vengeance was taken upon the king, who eluded our vigilance by perpetual flight across the Rhine.

The Rhine, therefore, was not left unattacked; for indeed it was not right that it should harbour and protect our enemies with impunity. The first battle against the Germans on this river was fought on the most just of pretexts; for the Aedui complained of their incursions. And how great was the insolence of King Ariovistus! When our ambassadors told him to come to Caesar, he replied, "Who is Caesar? Let him come to me if he likes: what does it matter to him what we in Germany do? Do I interfere with the Romans?" So great was the alarm inspired in the camp by this unknown people, that there was a general making of wills even in the

principiis scriberentur. Sed illa inmania corpora
quo maiora erant, eo magis gladiis ferroque patue-
13 runt. Qui calor in proeliando militum fuerit, nullo
magis exprimi potest quam quod, elatis super caput
scutis cum se testudine barbarus tegeret, super ipsa
Romani scuta salierunt, et inde in iugulos gladiis
14 descendebant. Iterum de Germano Tencteri[1]
querebantur. Hic vero iam Caesar ultro Mosellam[2]
navali ponte transgreditur ipsumque Rhenum et
Hercyniis hostem quaerit in silvis; sed in saltus ac
paludes gens omnis diffugerat. Tantum pavoris
15 incussit intra ripam subito Romanus visus.[3] Nec
semel Rhenus, sed iterum quoque, et quidem ponte
facto penetratus est. Maior aliquanto trepidatio.
Quippe cum Rhenum suum sic ponte quasi iugo
captum viderent, fuga rursus in silvas et paludes,
et, quod acerbissimum Caesari fuit, non fuere qui
vincerentur.

16 Omnibus terra marique peragratis respexit Ocea-
num et, quasi hic Romanis orbis non sufficeret, alte-
rum cogitavit. Classe igitur conparata Britanniam
transit mira celeritate; quippe qui tertia vigilia cum
Morinorum solvisset[4] a portu, minus quam medio
17 die insulam ingressus est. Plena erant tumultu
hostico[5] litora, et trepidantia ad conspectum rei

[1] Tencteri: genteri *B*: centeri *NL*: treviri *Aldus*.
[2] Mosellam *Monac.*: musellam *B*: massiliam *NL*.
[3] Romanus visus *Rossbachius*: romana vis *BN*.
[4] cum Morinorum solvisset *Halmius*: com morinos movisset *B*: marino solvisset (*om.* cum) *NL*.
[5] hostico: hostilico (li *in margine additum*) *B*.

camp square. But the vaster the stature of our enemies, the more were they exposed to our swords and other weapons. The ardour of our soldiers in the fray cannot be better illustrated than by the fact that, when the barbarians protected themselves by forming a "tortoise" with their shields raised over their heads, the Romans actually leaped on the top of the shields and from there fell upon their throats with their swords. Further complaints against the Germans were brought by the Tencteri. On this occasion Caesar took the initiative and crossed the Moselle by a bridge of boats and made for the Rhine itself and the enemy in the Hercynian forests; but the whole tribe had fled away to their woods and marshes, so great was the panic caused by the appearance of the Romans on the further bank of the river. Nor was this the only occasion on which the Rhine was crossed, but he penetrated across it a second time by a bridge which he had built. The alarm of the enemy was ever greater this time; for when they saw their Rhine placed as it were a prisoner under the yoke of the bridge, they fled again to their woods and marshes and, to Caesar's bitter disappointment, no enemy remained to be conquered.

Having penetrated everywhere by land and sea, he turned his gaze towards the ocean and, as if this world of ours sufficed not for the Romans, set his thoughts on another. He, therefore, collected a fleet and crossed over to Britain with wonderful speed; for starting from the harbour of the Morini at the third watch he disembarked upon the island before midday. The shores were crowded with a confused throng of the enemy, and their chariots were hurrying to and fro in panic at the strange

novae carpenta volitabant. Itaque trepidatio pro victoria fuit. Arma et obsides accepit a trepidis, et ulterius isset, nisi inprobam classem naufragio
18 castigasset Oceanus. Reversus igitur in Galliam, classe maiore auctisque copiis in eundem rursus Oceanum eosdemque rursus Britannos. Caledonas secutus in silvas unum quoque e[1] regibus Casuella-
19 num[2] in vincla dedit. Contentus his (non enim provinciae, sed nomini studebatur) cum maiore quam prius praeda revectus est, ipso quoque Oceano tranquillo magis et propitio, quasi inparem ei se fateretur.

20 Sed maxima omnium eademque novissima coniuratio fuit Galliarum, cum omnis[3] pariter Arvernos
21 atque Biturigas, Carnuntas simul Sequanosque contraxit[4] corpore armis spirituque terribilis, nomine etiam quasi ad terrorem conposito, Vercingetorix. Ille festis diebus et conciliabulis, cum frequentissimos in lucis haberet, ferocibus dictis ad ius pristi-
22 num libertatis erexit. Aberat tunc Caesar Ravennae dilectum agens, et hieme creverant Alpes: sic interclusum putabant iter. Sed ille qualis erat ad nuntium rei felicissima temeritate[5] per invios ad id tempus montium tumulos, per intactas vias et nives,

[1] e: et *B*.

[2] Casuellanum *Rossbachius* (*cf.* *Dio*, *XL*. 2, 3, *Polyaen.* *VIII*. 23, 5): cas | uella *B*: cavelianis *NL*.

[3] omnis *N*: omnes *L*.

[4] *post* contraxit *add.* hi *B*, ille *NL*.

[5] felicissima temeritate *Salmasius*: felicissimae temeritatis *codd.*

sight before their eyes. This panic was as good as a victory for Caesar, who received arms and hostages from his frightened foes and would have advanced further if the ocean had not taken vengeance on his presumptuous fleet by wrecking it. He, therefore, returned to Gaul and then, with a larger fleet and increased forces, made another attempt against the same ocean and the same Britons. Having pursued them into the Caledonian forests, he made one of their kings, Casuellanus, a prisoner. Content with these achievements (for he sought a reputation rather than a province) he returned with greater spoil than before, the very ocean showing itself more calm and propitious, as though it confessed itself unequal to opposing him.

The greatest, and at the same time the last, of all the risings in Gaul, took place when Vercingetorix, a chief formidable alike for his stature, his skill in arms, and his courage, endowed too with a name which seemed to be intended to inspire terror, formed a league alike of the Arverni and Bituriges, and at the same time of the Carnuntes and Sequani. He at their festivals and councils, when he found them collected in their greatest crowds in their groves, roused them by his ferocious harangues to vindicate their ancient rights of freedom. Caesar was absent at the time holding a levy at Ravenna, and the Alps had been swollen by winter snows; hence they thought that his passage was blocked. But Caesar, starting just as he was on the receipt of the news, by a most successful act of daring made his way across Gaul with a light-armed force through ranges of mountains never before crossed and over ways and snows never trodden

expedita manu emensus Galliam, et ex distantibus hibernis castra contraxit, et ante in media Gallia
23 fuit, quam ab ultima timeretur. Tum ipsa capita belli adgressus urbes, Avaricum[1] quadraginta milium propugnantium [sustulit],[2] Alesiam ducentorum quinquaginta milium iuventute subnixam
24 flammis adaequavit. Circa Gergoviam Avernorum tota belli moles fuit. Quippe cum octoginta milia muro et arce et abruptis ripis defenderent maximam
25 civitatem, vallo sudibus et fossa inductoque fossae flumine, ad hoc decem et octo castellis ingentique lorica circumdatam primum fame domuit, mox audentem eruptiones in vallo sudibusque concidit,
26 novissime in deditionem redegit. Ipse ille rex, maximum victoriae decus, supplex cum in castra venisset, equum et phaleras et sua arma ante Caesaris genua proiecit. "Habe,"[3] inquit, "fortem virum, vir fortissime, vicisti."

XLVI. Bellvm Parthicvm

III, 11 Dum Gallos per Caesarem in septentrione debellat, ipse interim ad orientem grave volnus a Parthis populus Romanus accepit. Nec de fortuna queri
2 possumus; caret solacio clades. Adversis et dis et hominibus cupiditas consulis Crassi, dum Parthico inhiat auro, undecim strage legionum et ipsius

[1] Avaricum: salaricum *B*: alvaricum *N*: aviaricum *in* alvaricum *mut. L.*

[2] sustulit *secl. Iahnius.*

[3] habe *Petrarca* : habes *codd.*

before, and collected his troops from distant winter quarters and was in the middle of Gaul before the terror of his approach had reached its borders. Attacking the cities which were the headquarters of the enemy's forces, he burnt to the ground Avaricum, which was defended by 40,000 men, and Alesia, which had a garrison of 250,000. All the most important operations were concentrated round Gergovia in the territory of the Averni. This mighty city, defended by a wall and citadel and steep river-banks, had a garrison of 80,000 men. Caesar, surrounding it with a rampart, a palisade and a trench, into which he admitted water from the river, and also eighteen towers and a huge breastwork, first reduced it by starvation; and then, when the defenders attempted to make sallies, cut them down at the ramparts and palisades, and finally reduced them to surrender. The king himself, to crown the victory, came as a suppliant to the camp, and placing before Caesar his horse and its trapping and his own arms, exclaimed, "Receive these spoils; thou thyself, bravest of men, hast conquered a brave enemy."

XLVI. The Parthian War

11. While in the north the Roman people by the hand of Caesar were conquering the Gauls, in the east they received a serious blow from the Parthians. Nor can we complain of fortune; for it was a disaster which admitted of no consolation. Both gods and men were defied by the avarice of the consul Crassus, in coveting the gold of Parthia, and its punishment was the slaughter of eleven legions

3 capite multata est. Et tribunus plebi Metellus
exeuntem ducem hostilibus[1] diris devoverat, et cum
Zeugma transisset exercitus, rapta subitis signa
4 turbinibus hausit Euphrates, et cum apud Nice-
phorium castra posuisset, missi ab Orode[2] rege legati
nuntiavere, percussorum cum Pompeio foederum
5 Sullaque meminisset. Regiis inhians ille thensauris,
nihil ne imaginario quidem iure, sed Seleuciae se
6 responsurum esse respondit. Itaque dii foederum
ultores nec insidiis nec virtuti hostium defuerunt.
Iam primum, qui solus et subvehere commeatus et
munire poterat a tergo, relictus Euphrates, dum
simulato transfugae cuidam Mazarae[3] Syro creditur.
7 Tum[4] in mediam camporum vastitatem eodem duce
ductus exercitus, ut undique hosti exponeretur.
8 Itaque vixdum venerat Carrhas, cum undique prae-
fecti regis Silaces et Surenas[5] ostendere signa auro
sericisque vexillis vibrantia. Tunc sine mora cir-
cumfusi undique equitatus in modum grandinis
atque nimborum densa pariter tela fuderunt. Sic
9 miserabili strage deletus exercitus. Ipse in con-
loquium sollicitatus, signo dato vivus hostium in
manus incidisset, nisi tribunis reluctantibus fugam
ducis barbari ferro occupassent. [Sic quoque rela-
tum caput ludibrio hostibus fuit.][6] Filium ducis

[1] hostilibus : hostibus *B*. [2] Orode : herode *B*.
[3] Mazarae : mazare *BL*.
[4] tum *om.* *B* : dum *L*.
[5] Surenas *Aldus* : sirenas *B* : syrenas *NL*.
[6] sic—fuit *secl.* *Iahnius*.

---

[1] The text adds: "Thus his head was carried back and treated with mockery by the enemy." These words are out of place here, and a similar statement occurs in its proper place a few lines further on.

and the loss of his own life. For Metellus, the tribune of the people, had called down terrible curses on the general as he was leaving Rome; and after the army had passed Zeugma, the Euphrates swallowed up the standards, which were swept away by its swirling eddies; and when Crassus had pitched his camp at Nicephorium, ambassadors arrived from King Orodes with a message bidding him remember the treaties made with Pompeius and Sulla. Crassus, who coveted the royal treasures, answered not a word that had any semblance of justice, but merely said that he would give his reply at Seleucia. The gods, therefore, who punish those who violate treaties, did not fail to support either the craft or the valour of our enemies. In the first place, Crassus deserted the Euphrates, which provided the sole means of transporting his supplies and protecting his rear, trusting to the advice of a pretended deserter, a certain Syrian named Mazaras. Next, again under the same guidance, the army was conducted into the midst of vast plains, to be exposed to enemy attacks from every side. And so he had scarcely reached Carrhae, when the king's generals, Silaces and Surenas, displayed all around him their standards fluttering with gold and silken pennons; then without delay the cavalry, pouring round on all sides, showered their weapons as thick as hail or rain upon them. Thus the army was destroyed in lamentable slaughter. The consul himself, invited to a parley, would on a given signal have fallen alive into the hands of the enemy, had not the barbarians, owing to the resistance of the tribunes, used their swords to prevent his escape.[1] The general's son they over-

paene in conspectu patris idem telis operuerunt. Reliquiae infelicis exercitus, quo[1] quemque rapuit fuga, in Armeniam, Ciliciam Syriamque distractae, vix nuntium cladis rettulerunt. Caput eius recisum cum dextera manu ad regem reportatum ludibrio fuit, neque indigno. Aurum enim liquidum in rictum oris infusum est, ut cuius animus arserat auri cupiditate, eius etiam mortuum et exsangue corpus auro ureretur.

XLVII. Anacephalaeosis

III, 12 Haec est illa tertia[2] aetas populi Romani transmarina, qua Italia progredi ausus orbe toto arma
2 circumtulit. Cuius aetatis superiores centum anni sancti, pii et, ut diximus, aurei, sine flagitio, sine scelere, dum sincera adhuc et innoxia pastoriae illius sectae integritas, dumque Poenorum hostium inminens metus disciplinam veterem continebat.
3 Posteri centum, quos a Carthaginis, Corinthi Numantiaeque excidiis et Attali regis Asiatica hereditate deduximus in Caesarem et Pompeium secutumque hos, de quo dicemus,[3] Augustum, ut claritate rerum bellicarum magnifici, ita domesticis cladibus
4 miseri et erubescendi. Quippe sicut Galliam, Thraciam, Ciliciam, Cappadociam, uberrimas vali-

[1] quo *om. B.*
[2] tertia *om. B.*
[3] dicemus *Voss. Palat.*: dicimus *cet.*

whelmed with missiles almost within his father's sight. The remnants of the unhappy army, scattered wherever their flight took them, through Armenia, Cilicia and Syria, scarcely even brought back the news of the disaster. The head of Crassus was cut off and with his right hand was taken back to the king and treated with mockery which was not undeserved; for molten gold was poured into his gaping mouth, so that the dead and bloodless flesh of one whose heart had burned with lust for gold was itself burnt with gold.

XLVII. Recapitulation

12. Such are the events overseas of the third period of the history of the Roman people, during which, having once ventured to advance outside Italy, they carried their arms over the whole world. The first hundred years of this period were pure and humane and, as we have said, a golden age, free from vice and crime, while the innocence of the old pastoral life was still untainted and uncorrupted, and the imminent threat of our Carthaginian foes kept alive the ancient discipline. The following hundred years, which we have traced from the destruction of Carthage, Corinth and Numantia and the inheritance of the Asiatic Kingdom of Attalus down to the time of Caesar and Pompeius and of their successor Augustus, with whose history we still have to deal, were as deplorable and shameful owing to internal calamities as they were illustrious for the glory of their military achievements. For, just as it was honourable and glorious to have won the rich and powerful provinces of Gaul, Thrace, Cilicia and

dissimasque provincias, Armenios etiam et Britannos,
ut non in usum, ita ad imperii speciem magna
5 nomina adquisisse pulchrum ac decorum: ita eodem
tempore dimicasse domi cum civibus, sociis, mancipiis,
gladiatoribus totoque inter se senatu turpe atque
6 miserandum. Ac nescio an satius[1] fuerit populo
Romano Sicilia et Africa contento fuisse, aut his
etiam ipsis carere[2] dominanti in Italia sua, quam
eo magnitudinis crescere, ut viribus suis conficeretur.
7 Quae enim res alia civiles furores peperit quam
nimiae felicitates? Syria prima nos victa corrupit,
8 mox Asiatica Pergameni regis hereditas. Illae opes
atque divitiae adflixere saeculi mores, mersamque
vitiis suis quasi sentina rem publicam pessum
dedere. Unde enim populus Romanus a tribunis
agros et cibaria flagitaret nisi per famem quam luxus
fecerat? Hinc ergo Gracchanae[3] prima et secunda
9 et illa tertia Apuleiana seditio. Unde iudiciariis
legibus divulsus ab[4] senatu eques nisi ex avaritia,
ut vectigalia rei publicae atque ipsa iudicia in
quaestu haberentur? Hinc Drusus et promissa
10 civitas Latio et per hoc arma sociorum. Quid
autem? Bella servilia unde nobis nisi ex abundantia familiarum? Unde gladiatorii adversum

[1] an satius: ac satis *B*. [2] carere: parcere *B*.
[3] Gracchanae *Iahnius*: gracchana et *L*: grachana et *B*.
[4] ab: at *B*.

Cappadocia as well as the territory of the Armenians and Britons, which, though they served no practical purpose, constituted important titles to imperial greatness; so it was disgraceful and deplorable at the same time to have fought at home with fellow-citizens and allies, with slaves and gladiators, and the whole senate divided against itself. Indeed I know not whether it would not have been better for the Roman people to have been content with Sicily and Africa, or even to have been without these and to have held dominion only over their own land of Italy, than to increase to such greatness that they were ruined by their own strength. For what else produced those outbursts of domestic strife but excessive prosperity? It was the conquest of Syria which first corrupted us, followed by the Asiatic inheritance bequeathed by the king of Pergamon. The resources and wealth thus acquired spoiled the morals of the age and ruined the State, which was engulfed in its own vices as in a common sewer. For what else caused the Roman people to demand from their tribunes land and food except the scarcity which luxury had produced? Hence arose the first and second Gracchan revolutions and the third raised by Apuleius. What was the cause of the violent division between the equestrian order and the senate on the subject of the judiciary laws except avarice, in order that the revenues of the State and the law-courts themselves might be exploited for profit? Hence arose the attempt of Drusus and the promise of citizenship to the Latins, which resulted in war with our allies. Again, what brought the servile wars upon us except the excessive size of our establishments? How else could those armies

dominos suos exercitus, nisi ad conciliandum plebis favorem effusa largitio, dum spectaculis indulget,
11 supplicia quondam hostium artem faceret?[1] Iam ut speciosiora vitia tangamus, nonne ambitus honorum
12 ab isdem divitiis concitatus? Atquin inde Mariana, inde Sullana tempestas. Aut magnificus apparatus conviviorum et sumptuosa largitio non ab opulentia
13 paritura mox egestatem? Haec Catilinam patriae suae inpegit. Denique illa ipsa principatus et dominandi cupido unde nisi ex nimiis opibus venit? Atquin haec Caesarem atque Pompeium furialibus
14 in exitium rei publicae facibus armavit. Hos igitur omnis domesticos motus separatos ab externis iustisque bellis ex ordine persequemur.

[1] artem faceret *Iahnius*: arte fecere *B*: artem facit *NL*.

of gladiators have arisen against their masters, save that a profuse expenditure, which aimed at conciliating the favour of the common people by indulging their love of shows, had turned what was originally a method of punishing enemies into a competition of skill? Again, to touch upon less ugly vices, was not ambition for office also stimulated by wealth? Why, it was from this the Marian and Sullan disturbances arose. Again, were not the sumptuous extravagance of banquets and the profuse largesses due to a wealth which was bound soon to produce want? It was this too that brought Catiline into collision with his country. Finally, whence did the lust for power and domination arise save from excessive wealth? It was this which armed Caesar and Pompeius with the fatal torches which kindled the flames that destroyed the State. We will, therefore, now describe in their order all these domestic disturbances as distinct from foreign wars properly so called.

L. ANNAEI FLORI

EPITOMAE DE TITO LIVIO BELLORVM OMNIVM ANNORVM DCC

Liber II

Capita Libri II

[1] Seditio Ti. Gracchi *add. Iahnius.*
[2] C. *add. Iahnius.*

LUCIUS ANNAEUS FLORUS

THE EPITOME, EXTRACTED FROM TITUS LIVIUS, OF ALL THE WARS OF SEVEN HUNDRED YEARS

THE SECOND BOOK

THE CHAPTERS OF BOOK II

[1] Called in the text "The State under Caesar Augustus"

I. De Legibvs Gracchanis

III, 13 Seditionum omnium causas tribunicia potestas excitavit, quae specie quidem plebis tuendae, cuius in auxilium comparata est, re autem dominationem sibi adquirens, studium populi ac favorem agrariis, frumentariis, iudiciariis legibus aucupabatur. Inerat
2 omnibus species aequitatis. Quid tam iustum enim quam recipere plebem sua a patribus, ne populus gentium victor orbisque possessor extorris aris ac
3 focis ageret? Quid tam aequum quam inopem
4 populum vivere ex aerario suo? Quid ad ius[1] libertatis aequandae magis efficax quam ut senatu regente provincias ordinis equestris auctoritas
5 saltem iudiciorum regno niteretur?[2] Sed haec ipsa in perniciem redibant, et misera res publica in
6 exitium[3] sui merces erat. Nam et a senatu in equitem translata iudiciorum potestas vectigalia, id

[1] quid ad ius: quid satius *B*: quid ius *L*.
[2] niteretur: uteretur *B*.
[3] in exitium: inexilium *B*.

I. On the Gracchan Laws

13. The original cause of all the revolutions was the tribunicial power, which, under the pretence of protecting the common people, for whose aid it was originally established, but in reality aiming at domination for itself, courted popular support and favour by legislation for the distribution of lands and corn and the disposal of judicial power. All these measures had some appearance of justice. For what could be fairer than that the commons should receive from the senate what was really their own, so that a people, who had been victorious over the nations and possessed the whole world, might not live banished from their own altars and hearths? What could be juster than that a people in want should be maintained from its own treasury? What could better conduce to secure equal liberty for all than that, while the senate controlled the provinces, the authority of the equestrian order should rest at least on the possession of judicial power? Yet these very measures resulted in the ruin of Rome, and the wretched State became, to its own destruction, an object of bargaining. For the transference of the judicial power from the senate to the equestrian order reduced the revenues, the ancestral wealth of the

7 est imperii patrimonium, subprimebat, et emptio
frumenti ipsos rei publicae nervos exhauriebat,
aerarium; et reduci plebs in agros unde poterat
sine possidentium eversione, qui ipsi pars populi
erant, et iam [1] relictas sibi a maioribus sedes aetate
quasi iure possidebant?

II. Seditio Tiberi Gracchi

III, 14 Primam certaminum facem Ti.[2] Gracchus accen-
2 dit, genere, forma, eloquentia facile princeps. Sed
hic, sive Mancinianae deditionis, quia [3] sponsor
foederis fuerat, contagium timens et inde popularis,
3 sive aequo et bono ductus, quia depulsam agris suis
plebem miseratus est, [ne populus gentium victor
orbisque possessor laribus ac focis suis exularet,] [4]
4 quacumque mente rem ausus ingentem est. Post-
quam [5] rogationis dies aderat, ingenti stipatus
agmine rostra conscendit, nec deerat obvia manu
5 tota inde nobilitas; et tribuni in partibus. Sed ubi
intercedentem legibus suis C. Octavium videt
Gracchus, contra fas collegii, ius [6] potestatis, iniecta

[1] et iam *Iahnius*: et tam *B*: et tamen *NL*.
[2] Ti. *add. Aldus.*
[3] deditionis, quia: seditionis qua *B*.
[4] ne populus—exularet *secl. Gruterus.*
[5] est. postquam *Halmius*: sed postquam *B*.
[6] ius: iuris *B*.

---

[1] See p. 153.
[2] These words occur in the previous chapter and should probably be omitted here.

empire, while the purchase of corn was a drain on the treasury, the very life-blood of the State; and how could the common people be restored to the land without dispossessing those who were in occupation of it, and who were themselves a part of the people and held estates bequeathed to them by their forefathers under the quasi-legal title of prescriptive right?

II. The Revolution of Tiberius Gracchus

14. The first flame of contention was kindled by Tiberius Gracchus, whose descent, personal attractions and eloquence made him undoubtedly the leading man of his time. Either because he was afraid of being involved in Mancinus' surrender[1] (for he had been a surety for the performance of the treaty) and therefore joined the popular party, or because he acted from motives of justice and right, pitying the commons who were deprived of their own lands [so that a people who had been victorious over the nations and possessed the whole world might not be exiled from their own hearths and homes],[2] whatever his motives, he ventured to take a very serious step. When the day for bringing forward the bill was at hand, he ascended the rostra surrounded by a large following; and the nobility were all there to resist him with their supporters, and the tribunes[3] were on their side. But when Gracchus saw that Gaius[4] Octavius was going to veto his proposals, he laid hands upon him, contrary to the rights of the tribunicial college and the privileges of

[3] *i.e.* the other tribunes of the people.

[4] He is called Marcus Octavius by Livy, Appian and Plutarch.

manu depulit rostris, adeoque praesenti metu mortis
6 exterruit, ut abdicare se magistratu cogeretur. Sic
triumvir creatus dividendis agris, cum ad perpetranda coepta die comitiorum prorogari sibi vellet imperium, obvia nobilitas manu eorum, quos agris
7 moverat. Caedes a foro coepit; inde cum in
Capitolium profugisset plebemque ad defensionem salutis suae manu caput tangens hortaretur, praebuit speciem regnum sibi et diadema poscentis, atque ita duce Scipione Nasica, concitato in arma populo, quasi iure oppressus est.

III. Seditio C. Gracchi

III, 15 Statim et mortis et legum fratris sui vindex non
2 minore impetu incaluit C. Gracchus. Qui cum
pari tumultu atque terrore plebem in avitos agros arcesseret, et recentem Attali hereditatem in ali-
3 menta populo polliceretur, iamque nimius et in-
potens[1] altero tribunatu secunda plebe volitaret,
4 obrogare[2] auso legibus suis Minucio tribuno, fretus

[1] inpotens *Heinsius*: potens *codd.*
[2] obrogare *Vinetus*: abrogare *codd.*

the office, and expelled him from the rostra, and so frightened him with the instant threat of death that he was forced to retire from his office. Having thus obtained his election as one of the three commissioners for distributing land, when, at the meeting of the comitia he demanded the prolongation of his term of office in order to carry out the work which he had begun, the nobility opposed him with the help of those whom he had expelled from their lands. The slaughter began in the forum; then when he had taken refuge in the Capitol and was urging the commons to come to the defence of his person, with the gesture of touching his head with his hand, he gave rise to the idea that he was demanding the kingship and a royal diadem. The people, therefore, under the leadership of Scipio Nasica, having been roused to take up arms, he was put to death with some show of legality.

III. The Revolution of Gaius Gracchus

15. Immediately after this Gaius Gracchus was fired with an equal zeal to avenge his brother's murder and to champion his proposals. By similar methods of disturbance and terrorism he incited the commons to seize the lands of their forefathers, and promised that the inheritance recently received from Attalus should be used to feed the people, and becoming headstrong and tyrannical on the strength of his second election to the tribunate, he was pursuing a successful course with the support of the common people. When, however, the tribune Minucius ventured to obstruct the passage of his proposals, relying on the help of his supporters he

comitum manu fatale familiae suae Capitolium
5 invasit. Inde proximorum caede depulsus cum se
in Aventinum recepisset, inde quoque obvia senatus
6 manu ab Opimio consule oppressus est. Insultatum
quoque mortis reliquiis, et illud sacrosanctum caput
tribuni plebis percussoribus auro repensatum.

IIII. SEDITIO APVLEIANA

III, 16 NIHILO minus Apuleius Saturninus Gracchanas
adserere leges non destitit. Tantum animorum
viro Marius dabat, [qui][1] nobilitati semper inimicus,
consulatu suo praeterea confisus. Occiso palam
comitiis A. Ninnio conpetitore tribunatus, subrogare
conatus est in eius locum C. Gracchum, hominem
sine tribu, sine notore, sine nomine; sed subdito
2 titulo in familiam ipse se adoptabat. Cum tot
tantisque ludibriis exultaret inpune, rogandis
Gracchorum legibus ita vehementer incubuit, ut
senatum quoque cogeret in verba iurare, cum
abnuentibus aqua et igni interdicturum minaretur.
3 Unus tamen extitit, qui mallet exilium. Igitur post
Metelli fugam omni nobilitate perculsa cum iam
tertium annum dominaretur, eo vesaniae progressus
est, ut consularia quoque comitia nova caede tur-
4 baret. Quippe ut satellitem furoris sui Glauciam

[1] qui *seclusi*.

[1] Consul in 121 B.C.
[2] The name is uncertain: Appian (*Bell. Civ.* 28) calls him Nonius, Valerius Maximus (IX. 7, 3) Nunnius.
[3] Of 100 B.C.

seized the Capitol which had already proved so fatal to his family. Being driven thence, after the loss of his adherents, he betook himself to the Aventine, where, being assailed by a body of senators, he was put to death by the consul Opimius.[1] Insults were also offered to his remains after his death, and a price was paid to his assassins for the sacred head of a tribune of the people.

IIII. The Revolution of Apuleius

16. Apuleius Saturninus continued nevertheless to promote the Gracchan proposals; so great was the encouragement given him by Marius, always a bitter opponent of the nobility and relying, moreover, on his position as consul. Aulus Ninnius,[2] his rival for the tribunate, having been openly murdered at the elections, Apuleius attempted to introduce in his place Gaius Gracchus, a man without a tribe, without anyone to vouch for him and without a name, who by a forged title tried to foist himself upon the Gracchan family. Revelling unchecked in all these outrageous acts of violence, Apuleius devoted himself so zealousy to passing the proposals of the Gracchi that he even compelled the senate to take an oath in their support by threatening that he would obtain a sentence of banishment against those who refused. There was one, however, who preferred exile, namely, Metellus. After his departure, when all the nobility were thoroughly cowed, Apuleius, now in the third year of his tyranny, became so utterly reckless that he even disturbed the consular elections[3] by a fresh murder. For in order to obtain the election as consul of Glaucia, a supporter of his

consulem faceret, C. Memmium[1] conpetitorem interfici iussit, et in eo tumultu regem se a satelliti-
5 bus[2] suis appellatum laetus accepit. Tum vero iam conspiratione senatus, ipso quoque iam Mario consule, quia tueri non poterat, adverso, directae
6 in foro acies; pulsus inde Capitolium invasit. Sed cum abruptis fistulis obsideretur senatuique per legatos paenitentiae fidem faceret, ab arce degressus cum ducibus factionis receptus in curiam est. Ibi eum facta inruptione populus fustibus saxisque opertum in ipsa quoque morte laceravit.

V. Seditio Drvsiana

III, 17 Postremo Livius Drusus non tribunatus modo viribus, sed ipsius etiam senatus auctoritate totiusque Italiae consensu easdem leges adserere
2 conatus, dum alium captat ex alio, tantum conflavit incendium, ut nec[3] primam illius flammam[4] posset sustinere et subita morte correptus hereditarium in
3 posteros suos bellum propagaret. Iudiciaria lege Gracchi diviserant populum Romanum et bicipitem ex una fecerant civitatem. Equites Romani tanta potestate subnixi, ut qui fata fortunasque principum

[1] C. Memmium: publium mummium *B*: c. menmium *L*: c. memmium *N*²: cf. *Liv. per.* 69, *Sall. Iug.* 27, 2.

[2] se a satellitibus *Halmius*: exatellitibus *B*.

[3] nec *Vinetus*: ne *codd.*

[4] primam illius flammam *Iahnius* prima illius flamma *codd.*

insane policy, he ordered the murder of his opponent Gaius Memmius, and in the confusion which followed, heard himself with pleasure hailed as king by his followers. Then at last the senators leagued themselves against him, and Marius himself, now consul, finding that he could no longer protect him, turned against him, and the two parties faced one another under arms in the forum. Driven from the forum Apuleius seized the Capitol. When he was besieged there and the water-supply had been cut off, he made the senate believe, through his representatives, that he repented of what he had done, and coming down from the citadel with the chief men of his party was received in the senate house. Here the people, bursting their way in, overwhelmed him with sticks and stones and tore him to pieces at the very moment of his death.

V. The Revolution of Drusus

17. Lastly, Livius Drusus, relying not only upon the powers of the tribunate but also upon the authority of the senate itself and the general agreement of all Italy, tried to carry out the same proposals, and by courting one party after another, kindled so violent a combustion that he could not withstand even its first outburst, and carried off by sudden death, left the struggle as an inheritance to his successors. The Gracchi by their judiciary law had created a cleavage in the Roman people and had destroyed the unity of the State by giving it two heads. The Roman knights, relying on the extraordinary powers,[1] which placed the fate and fortunes of the leading citizens

[1] *i.e.* the control of the law-courts.

haberent in manu, interceptis vectigalibus pecula-
bantur suo iure rem publicam; senatus[1] exilio
Metelli, damnatione Rutili debilitatus omne decus
4 maiestatis amiserat. In hoc statu rerum pares
opibus animis dignitate (unde et nata Livio Druso
aemulatio)[2] equitem[3] Servilius Caepio, senatum
5 Livius Drusus adserere. Signa, aquilae et vexilla
deerant: ceterum sic urbe in una quasi in binis
castris dissidebatur. Prior Caepio in senatum im-
petu facto reos ambitus Scaurum et Philippum
6 principes nobilitatis elegit. His ut motibus resis-
teret, Drusus plebem ad se Gracchanis legibus,
isdemque[4] socios ad plebem spe civitatis erexit.
Extat[5] vox ipsius, nihil se ad largitionem ulli
reliquisse, nisi si quis aut caenum dividere vellet
7 aut caelum. Aderat promulgandi dies, cum subito
tanta vis hominum undique apparuit, ut hostium
8 adventu obsessa civitas videretur. Ausus tamen
obrogare legibus consul Philippus, sed adprehensum
faucibus viator non ante dimisit quam sanguis in os
9 et oculos redundaret. Sic per vim latae iussaeque
leges. Et pretium rogationis statim socii flagitare,
cum inparem Drusum aegrumque rerum temere

[1] senatus *L Voss. Monac. Palat.*: pilatus *B*.
[2] unde et nata Livio Druso aemulatio *Graevius*: unde et natalium druso aemulatio accesserat *B*: unde et natalivio druso aemulatio accesserat *N*.
[3] equitem *Voss. Rehd.*: equitatem *B*: aequitum *NL*.
[4] isdemque: eisdem *NL*.
[5] extat *L*: exat *B*.

---

[1] P. Rutilius Rufus, the honest legatus of A. Scaevola in Asia, was unjustly condemned and exiled in 92 B.C.
[2] It is impossible to keep up in English the play upon the words *caenum* and *caelum*.

in their hands, were plundering the State at their pleasure by embezzling the revenues; the senate, crippled by the exile of Metellus and the condemnation of Rutilius,[1] had lost every appearance of dignity. In this state of affairs Servilius Caepio and Livius Drusus, men of equal wealth, spirit and dignity—and it was this which inspired the emulation of Livius Drusus—supported, the former the knights, the latter the senate. Standards, eagles and banners were, it is true, lacking; but the citizens of one and the same city were as sharply divided as if they formed two camps. First of all Caepio, attacking the senate, singled out Scaurus and Philippus, the chief men of the nobility, and prosecuted them for bribery. In order to counteract this move, Drusus rallied the commons to his support by the bait of the Gracchan laws, and used the same means to rally the allies to the support of the commons by the hope of receiving the citizenship. A saying of his has survived, that "he had left nothing for anyone else to distribute, unless he wished to share out the mire or the air."[2] The day for the promulgation of the bills was at hand, when on a sudden so vast a multitude appeared on all sides that the city seemed to be beset by a hostile force. Philippus the consul,[3] nevertheless, ventured to oppose the bills; but the tribune's attendant seized him by the throat and did not let go until blood poured into his mouth and eyes. Thus the bills were brought forward and passed by violence. Thereupon the allies immediately demanded the price of their support; but death carried off Drusus, who was unequal to the occasion and weary of the disturbance which he

[3] Consul in 91 B.C.

motarum matura, ut in tali discrimine, mors abstulit. Nec ideo [minus][1] socii promissa Drusi a populo Romano reposcere armis desierunt.

VI. Bellvm Adversvm Socios

iii, 18 Sociale bellum vocetur licet, ut extenuemus
invidiam, si verum tamen volumus, illud civile
bellum fuit. Quippe cum populus Romanus Etruscos,
Latinos Sabinosque sibi miscuerit et unum ex omni-
bus sanguinem ducat, corpus fecit ex membris et ex
2 omnibus unus est; nec minore flagitio socii intra
3 Italiam quam intra urbem cives rebellabant. Itaque
cum ius civitatis, quam viribus auxerant, socii
iustissime postularent, quam in spem eos cupidine
4 dominationis Drusus erexerat, postquam ille do-
mestico scelere oppressus est, eadem fax, quae illum
cremavit, socios in arma et expugnationem urbis
5 accendit. Quid hac clade tristius? Quid calamito-
sius? Cum omne Latium atque Picenum, Etruria
omnis atque Campania, postremo Italia contra
6 matrem suam ac parentem urbem consurgeret; cum
omne robur fortissimorum fidelissimorumque socio-
rum sub suis quisque signis haberent municipalia
illa prodigia, Poppaedius[2] Marsos et <Paelignos>[3],
Latinos Afranius,[4] Vmbros Plotius,[5] Egnatius Etrus-
7 cos,[6] Samnium Lucaniamque Telesinus; cum regum[7]

[1] minus *seclusit Perizonius.*

[2] Poppaedius (cf. *Liv. per.* 76, *C.I.L.* x. 220, 417, *Appian, Bell. Civ* I. 40, etc.): poppedius *BL*: poppedios *N*.

[3] Paelignos *add. Kellerbauerus.*

[4] Afranius: affranius *N*: afrienus *B*.

[5] Plotius *Tollius*: totos *B*: totus *NL*.

[6] Egnatius Etruscos *Lipsius*: senatos et consules *B*.

[7] regum: rerum *B*: regnum *L*.

had rashly aroused—a death opportune at such a crisis. But for all that the allies did not cease to demand from the Roman people by force of arms the privileges promised by Drusus.

VI. The War against the Allies

18. Though we call this war a war against allies, in order to lessen the odium of it, yet, if we are to tell the truth, it was a war against citizens. For since the Roman people united in itself the Etruscans, the Latins and the Sabines, and traces the same descent from all alike, it has formed a body made up of various members and is a single people composed of all these elements; and the allies, therefore, in raising a rebellion within the bounds of Italy, committed as great a crime as citizens who rebel within a city. So when the allies very justly demanded the rights of citizenship, for which Drusus, in his desire for power, had encouraged them to hope as members of a State which they had aggrandized by their exertions, the same brand which had consumed him kindled the allies, after he had fallen through the perfidy of his fellow-citizens, to take up arms and attack the city. What could be sadder, what more disastrous than this calamity? All Latium and Picenum, all Etruria and Campania, and finally all Italy rose against their mother and parent city. The flower of our bravest and most trusted allies were led, each under their several standards, by the most eminent leaders from the country towns, Poppaedius commanding the Marsians and Paeligni, Afranius the Latins, Plotius the Umbrians, Egnatius the Etruscans, and Telesinus the Samnites and

et gentium arbiter populus ipsum se regere non posset, et victrix Asiae et Europae a Corfinio Roma adpeteretur.

8 Primum fuit belli consilium, ut in Albano monte[1] festo die Latinarum Iulius Caesar et Marcius Philippus consules inter sacra et aras immolarentur.
9 Postquam id nefas proditione discussum est, Asculo furor omnis erupit,[2] in ipsa quidem ludorum frequentia trucidatis qui tunc aderant ab urbe legatis.
10 Hoc fuit inpii belli[3] sacramentum. Inde iam passim ab omni parte Italiae, duce et auctore belli discursante Poppaedio,[4] diversa per populos et urbes
11 signa cecinere. Nec Annibalis nec Pyrrhi fuit tanta vastatio. Ecce Ocriculum, ecce Grumentum, ecce Faesulae, ecce[5] Carseoli, Aesernia, Nuceria,[6] Picentia penitus[7] ferro et igne vastantur. Fusae Rutili
12 copiae, fusae Caepionis. Nam ipse Iulius Caesar, exercitu amisso, cum in urbem cruentus referretur, miserabili funere mediam per urbem viam fecit.[8]
13 Sed magna populi Romani fortuna, et semper in malis maior, totis denuo viribus consurrexit; adgressique singulos populos Cato discutit Etruscos, Gabinius Marsos, Carbo Lucanos, Sulla Samnites;
14 Pompeius vero Strabo[9] omnia flammis ferroque

[1] consilium, ut in Albano monte *Rossbachius*: in Albano monte consilium ut *B*.

[2] erupit: eripuit *B*. [3] inpii belli: imbellis *B*.

[4] Poppaedio: poppedio *NL*: pompeio *B*.

[5] Grumentum, ecce Faesulae, ecce: crumentum ecce pessulae et *B*.

[6] Aesernia, Nuceria *Iahnius*: reserat anuceria *B*: res erat nuceria *N*.

[7] Picentia penitus *Hauptius*: picenti moenibus *B*.

[8] mediam per urbem viam fecit *scripsi*: mediam urbem per viam fecit *codd.*

[9] Strabo *om. B*.

Lucanians. The people who had been the arbiters of the fates of kings and nations failed to rule themselves, and Rome, the conqueror of Asia and Europe, was attacked from Corfinium.

The first plan of campaign was to murder the consuls, Julius Caesar and Marcius Philippus [1] on the Alban Mount amid the sacrifices and altars at the celebration of the Latin Festival.[2] This crime having been defeated by betrayal, the full fury of the rising broke out at Asculum, where representatives who were present at the time from Rome were butchered amid the crowd which had gathered for the games. This act served as the oath which pledged them to civil war. Thereupon from all sides the various calls to arms rang out through the peoples and cities of every part of Italy, as Poppaedius, the leader and instigator of the war, hurried from place to place. The devastation wrought by Hannibal and Pyrrhus was less serious. Lo! Ocriculum, Grumentum, Faesulae, Carseoli, Aesernia, Nuceria and Picentia were utterly laid waste by fire and sword. The forces both of Rutilius and of Caepio were routed. Julius Caesar himself, after the loss of his army, being brought back still dripping with blood, was borne through the midst of the city with pitiable funeral rites. But the great good fortune of the Roman people, never so great as in the hour of misfortune, asserted itself afresh in all its vigour. Attacking the various peoples separately, Cato scattered the Etruscans, Gabinius the Marsians, Carbo the Lucanians, and Sulla the Samnites, while Pompeius Strabo wasted the whole country with

[1] Consuls in 91 B.C.

[2] sc. *feriarum*.

populatus non prius finem caedium fecit, quam Asculi eversione manibus tot exercituum, consulum direptarumque urbium dis litaretur utcumque.[1]

VII. Bellvm Servile

III, 19 Etsi cum sociis—nefas—cum liberis tamen et ingenuis dimicatum est: quis aequo animo ferat in
2 principe populo bella servorum? Primum servile bellum inter initia[2] urbis Herdonio duce Sabino in ipsa urbe temptatum est, cum occupata tribuniciis seditionibus civitate Capitolium obsessum est et a consule receptum; sed hic tumultus magis fuit quam bellum. Mox imperio per diversa terrarum occupato, quis crederet Siciliam multo cruentius
3 servili quam Punico bello esse vastatam? Terra frugum ferax et quodam modo suburbana provincia latifundiis civium Romanorum tenebatur. Hic ad cultum agri frequentia ergastula catenatique cultores
4 materiam bello praebuere. Syrus[3] quidam nomine Eunus[4]—magnitudo cladium[5] facit, ut meminerimus—fanatico furore simulato, dum Syriae deae comas iactat, ad libertatem et arma servos quasi

[1] utcumque *ab initio proximi capitis huc transposuit Lipsius*: id qualitercumque *B*.
[2] inter initia: in italia *B*.
[3] Syrus: sirus *B*.
[4] Eunus: conus *B*.
[5] cladium: gladium *BN*: claudium *L*.

fire and sword and did not make an end of slaughter until, by the destruction of Asculum, he made atonement in some measure to the shades of so many armies and consuls and to the gods of the devastated cities.

VII. The Servile War

19. Although we fought with allies—in itself an impious act—yet we fought with men who enjoyed liberty and were of free birth; but who could tolerate with equanimity wars waged by a sovereign people against slaves? The first attempt at war on the part of slaves took place in the city itself in the early days of its history under the leadership of Herdonius the Sabine. On this occasion, while the State was taken up with the troubles caused by the tribunes, the Capitol was besieged and afterwards rescued by the consul; but it was a local rising rather than a war. It is difficult to believe that, at a later date, while the forces of the empire were engaged in various parts of the world, Sicily was far more cruelly laid waste in a war against slaves than during the Punic War. This land, so rich in corn, a province lying, as it were, at our very doors, was occupied by large estates in the possession of Roman citizens. The numerous prisons for slaves employed in tilling the soil and gangs of cultivators who worked in chains provided the forces for the war. A certain Syrian named Eunus (the seriousness of our defeats causes his name to be remembered), counterfeiting an inspired frenzy and waving his dishevelled hair in honour of the Syrian goddess, incited the slaves to arms and liberty on the pretence

5 numinum imperio concitavit; idque ut divinitus
fieri probaret, in ore abdita nuce quam sulphure
et igni stipaverat, leniter inspirans flammam inter
6 verba fundebat. Hoc miraculum primo duo milia
ex obviis,[1] mox iure belli refractis ergastulis sexa-
ginta amplius milium fecit exercitum; regisque,
ne quid mali deesset, decoratus insignibus castella,
7 vicos, oppida miserabili direptione vastavit. Quin,[2]
illud quoque ultimum dedecus[3] belli, capta sunt
castra praetorum—nec nominare ipsos pudebit—
castra Manlii, Lentuli, Pisonis, Hypsaei.[4] Itaque
qui per fugitivarios abstrahi debuissent, praetorios
duces profugos proelio ipsi sequebantur. Tandem
Perperna imperatore supplicium de eis sumptum
8 est. Hic enim victos et apud Hennam[5] novissime
obsessos cum fame quasi pestilentia consumpsisset,
reliquias latronum compedibus, catenis crucibusque
punivit; fuitque de servis ovatione contentus, ne
dignitatem triumphi servili inscriptione violaret.
9 Vixdum respiraverat insula, cum statim Servilio
praetore a Syro[6] reditur ad Cilicem. Athenio
pastor interfecto domino familiam ergastulo liber-
10 atam sub signis ordinat. Ipse veste purpurea

[1] ex obviis *Rehd.*: exobulis *NL*, *om. B.*
[2] quin: quid *B.*
[3] dedecus: decus *B.*
[4] Hypsaei: hypsei *NL*: ipse *B.*
[5] Hennam: bennam *B.*
[6] Servilio praetore a Syro *Mommsenus*: servile et asyro *B*: servi. et a syro *NL.*

of a command from the gods. In order to prove that he was acting under divine inspiration, he secreted in his mouth a nut which he had filled with sulphur and fire, and, by breathing gently, sent forth a flame as he spoke. This miracle first of all collected 2,000 men from those whom he encountered, but presently, when the prisons had been broken open by force of arms, he formed an army of more than 60,000 men. Adorning himself—in order to fill up the cup of his wickedness—with the insignia of royalty, he laid waste fortresses, villages and towns with pitiable destruction. Nay, even the camps of the praetors were captured—the most disgraceful thing than can occur in war; nor will I shrink from mentioning the names of these commanders, who were Manlius, Lentulus, Piso and Hypsaeus. Thus those who ought to have been hauled away by the overseers, themselves pursued praetorian generals in flight from the battle-field. At last punishment was inflicted upon them under the leadership of Perperna, who, after defeating them and finally besieging them at Enna, reduced them by famine as effectually as by a plague and requited the surviving marauders with fetters, chains and the cross. He was content with an ovation for his victory over them, so that he might not sully the dignity of a triumph by the mention of slaves.

Scarcely had the island recovered itself, when, in the praetorship of Servilius, the command suddenly passed from the hands of a Syrian into those of a Cilician. A shepherd, Athenio, having murdered his master, released the slaves from their prison and formed them into an organized force. Himself arrayed in a purple robe, carrying a silver sceptre

argenteoque baculo et regium in morem fronte redimita non minorem quam ille fanaticus prior conflavit exercitum, acriusque multo, quasi et illum vindicaret, vicos, oppida, castella diripiens, in servos infestius quam in dominos[1] quasi in transfugas,
11 saeviebat. Ab hoc quoque praetorii exercitus fusi, capta Servili castra, capta Luculli. Sed Titus Aquilius Perpernae usus exemplo, interclusum hostem commeatibus ad extrema conpulit comminutasque copias fame armis facile delevit; dedidissentque se, nisi suppliciorum metu voluntariam
12 mortem praetulissent. Ac ne de duce quidem supplicium exigi potuit, quamvis vivus in manus venerit; quippe dum circa adprehendendum eum a multitudine contenditur, inter rixantium manus praeda lacerata est.

VIII. Bellvm Spartacivm

III, 20 Enimvero et servilium armorum dedecus feras; nam etsi per fortunam in omnia obnoxii, tamen quasi secundum hominum genus sunt et in bona libertatis nostrae adoptantur: bellum Spartaco duce
2 concitatum quo nomine appellem nescio; quippe cum servi[2] militaverint, gladiatores imperaverint, illi infimae sortis homines, hi pessumae auxere ludibriis calamitatem Romanam.
3 Spartacus, Crixus, Oenomaus effracto Lentuli

[1] in servos infestius quam in dominos *Rossbachius*: in dominos quam in servos infestius (quam *om. NL*) *codd.*
[2] servi: serviliberi *B*.

---

[1] Other authorities give his name as Manius Aquilius.
[2] *i.e.* by manumission.

and crowned like a king, he collected an army quite as large as that of his fanatical predecessor, and with even greater energy, on the pretext of avenging him, plundering villages, towns and fortresses, vented his fury with even greater violence upon the slaves than upon their masters, treating them as renegades. He too routed praetorian armies and captured the camps of Servilius and Lucullus. But Titus [1] Aquilius following the example of Perperna, reduced the enemy to extremities by cutting off their supplies and easily destroyed their forces in battle when they were reduced by starvation. They would have surrendered, had they not, in their fear of punishment, preferred voluntary death. The penalty could not be inflicted upon their leader, although he fell alive into their hands; for, while the crowd was quarrelling about his apprehension, the prey was torn to pieces in the hands of the disputants.

VIII. The War against Spartacus

20. One can tolerate, indeed, even the disgrace of a war against slaves; for although, by force of circumstances, they are liable to any kind of treatment, yet they form as it were a class (though an inferior class) of human beings and can be admitted [2] to the blessings of liberty which we enjoy. But I know not what name to give to the war which was stirred up at the instigation of Spartacus; for the common soldiers being slaves and their leaders being gladiators—the former men of the humblest, the latter men of the worse, class—added insult to the injury which they inflicted upon Rome.

Spartacus, Crixus and Oenomaus, breaking out of

ludo cum triginta aut amplius eiusdem fortunae
viris erupere Capua;[1] servisque ad vexillum[2]
vocatis cum statim decem milia amplius coissent,
homines modo effugisse contenti, iam et vindicari
4 volebant. Prima sedes velut rabidis beluis mons[3]
Vesuvius placuit. Ibi cum obsiderentur a Clodio
Glabro, per fauces cavi montis vitineis delapsi
vinculis[4] ad imas eius descendere radices et exitu
inviso[5] nihil tale opinantis ducis subito impetu
5 castra rapuerunt; inde alia castra, Vareniana,[6]
deinceps Thorani; totamque pervagantur Campa-
niam. Nec villarum atque vicorum vastatione con-
tenti Nolam atque Nuceriam, Thurios[7] atque
6 Metapontum terribili strage populantur. Adfluen-
tibus in diem copiis cum iam esset iustus exercitus,
e viminibus pecudumque tegumentis inconditos
sibi clipeos et ferro ergastulorum recocto gladios
7 ac tela fecerunt. Ac ne quod decus[8] iusto deesset
exercitui, domitis obviis etiam gregibus paratur
equitatus, captaque de praetoribus insignia et fasces
8 ad ducem detulere. Nec abnuit ille de stipendiario
Thrace miles, de milite desertor, inde latro,[9] deinde

[1] Capua: capuam *B*.

[2] ad vexillum: ad auxilium *B*: ad vexillum ad (et *L*) auxilium *NL*.

[3] velut rapidis beluis mons *Rossbachius*: velut bellus mons *B*: velut arauiris mons *NL*.

[4] delapsi vinculis: dilapsi ungulis *B*.

[5] inviso: indiviso *B*: inuno *NL*.

[6] castra *post* Vareniana *add.* *B*.

[7] Thurios: thauros *B*: turios *NL*.

[8] decus: dedecus *B*.

the gladiatorial school of Lentulus with thirty or rather more men of the same occupation, escaped from Capua. When, by summoning the slaves to their standard, they had quickly collected more than 10,000 adherents, these men, who had been originally content merely to have escaped, soon began to wish to take their revenge also. The first position which attracted them (a suitable one for such ravening monsters) was Mt. Vesuvius. Being besieged here by Clodius Glabrus, they slid by means of ropes made of vine-twigs through a passage in the hollow of the mountain down into its very depths, and issuing forth by a hidden exit, seized the camp of the general by a sudden attack which he never expected. They then attacked other camps, that of Varenius and afterwards that of Thoranus; and they ranged over the whole of Campania. Not content with the plundering of country houses and villages, they laid waste Nola, Nuceria, Thurii and Metapontum with terrible destruction. Becoming a regular army by the daily arrival of fresh forces, they made themselves rude shields of wicker-work and the skins of animals, and swords and other weapons by melting down the iron in the slave-prisons. That nothing might be lacking which was proper to a regular army, cavalry was procured by breaking in herds of horses which they encountered, and his men brought to their leader the insignia and fasces captured from the praetors, nor were they refused by the man who, from being a Thracian mercenary, had become a soldier, and from a soldier a deserter, then a highwayman, and

---

[9] inde latro *NL*: de latro *B*.

9 in honorem[1] virium gladiator. Quin[2] defunctorum
quoque proelio ducum funera imperatoriis[3] cele-
bravit exsequiis, captivosque circa rogum iussit
armis depugnare, quasi plane expiaturus omne
praeteritum dedecus, si de gladiatore munerarius
10 fuisset. Inde iam consulares[4] quoque adgressus
in Appenino Lentuli exercitum cecidit, apud
11 Mutinam Publi Crassi castra delevit. Quibus elatus
victoriis de invadenda urbe Romana—quod satis
12 est turpitudini nostrae—deliberavit. Tandem enim
totis imperii viribus contra myrmillonem consur-
gitur[5] pudoremque Romanum Licinius Crassus
adseruit; a quo pulsi fugatique—pudet dicere—
13 hostes in extrema Italiae refugerunt. Ibi circa
Brittium angulum clusi,[6] cum fugam in Siciliam
pararent neque navigia suppeterent, ratesque ex
trabibus et dolia conexa virgultis rapidissimo freto
frustra experirentur, tandem eruptione facta digna
14 viris obiere morte et, quod sub gladiatore duce
oportuit, sine missione pugnatum est. Spartacus
ipse in primo agmine fortissime dimicans quasi
imperator occisus est.

[1] honorem *Rehd.* : honore *cet.*
[2] quin *Freinshemius*: quia *B*: qui *NL.*
[3] imperatoriis: imperatorum *B.*
[4] consulares *NL*: consularem *cet.*
[5] consurgitur *NL*: consurgunt *cet.*

finally, thanks to his strength, a gladiator. He also celebrated the obsequies of his officers who had fallen in battle with funerals like those of Roman generals, and ordered his captives to fight at their pyres, just as though he wished to wipe out all his past dishonour by having become, instead of a gladiator, a giver of gladiatorial shows. Next, actually attacking generals of consular rank, he inflicted defeat on the army of Lentulus in the Apennines and destroyed the camp of Publius[1] Cassius at Mutina. Elated by these victories he entertained the project—in itself a sufficient disgrace to us—of attacking the city of Rome. At last a combined effort was made, supported by all the resources of the empire, against this gladiator, and Licinius Crassus vindicated the honour of Rome. Routed and put to flight by him, our enemies—I am ashamed to give them this title—took refuge in the furthest extremities of Italy. Here, being cut off in the angle of Bruttium and preparing to escape to Sicily, but being unable to obtain ships, they tried to launch rafts of beams and casks bound together with withies on the swift waters of the straits. Failing in this attempt, they finally made a sally and met a death worthy of men, fighting to the death[2] as became those who were commanded by a gladiator. Spartacus himself fell, as became a general, fighting most bravely in the front rank.

[1] The inferior MSS. read Gaius, which is supported by other authorities.

[2] *Sine missione* is a technical term from the gladiatorial contests.

---

[6] clusi: fusi *B*.

VIIII. Bellvm Civile Marianvm

III, 21 Hoc deerat unum populi Romani malis, ut iam ipse intra se parricidale telum domi stringeret, et in urbe media ac foro quasi harena cives cum
2 civibus suis gladiatorio more concurrerent. Aequiore animo utcumque ferrem, si plebei duces aut, si nobiles, mali saltem ducatum sceleri praebuissent. Tum vero—pro facinus—qui viri! qui imperatores! decora et ornamenta saeculi sui, Marius et Sulla, pessimo facinori suam etiam dignitatem praebuerunt.

3 Bellum civile Marianum sive Sullanum tribus, ut sic dixerim, sideribus agitatum est. Primum levi et modico tumultu magis[1] quam bello, intra ipsos
4 dumtaxat armorum duces subsistente saevitia; mox atrocius et cruentius, per ipsius viscera senatus
5 grassante victoria; ultimo non civicam modo, sed hostilem quoque rabiem supergressum est, cum armorum furor totius Italiae viribus niteretur, eo usque odiis saevientibus,[2] donec deessent qui occiderentur.

6 Initium et causa belli inexplebilis honorum Marii fames, dum decretam Sullae provinciam Sulpicia lege sollicitat. Sed inpatiens iniuriae statim Sulla legiones circumegit, dilatoque Mithridate Esquilina[3]

[1] magis *scripsi*: maiore *codd.*
[2] peractum est *post* saevientibus *add. B.*
[3] Mithridate Esquilina *Rehd.*: mithridates quilla *B*: mithridate escylia *N*.

---

[1] *i.e.* falls into three periods of stress and storm, the rise of certain constellations, such as Arcturus and the Pleiades, being proverbial for occasioning tempests.

VIIII. The Civil War of Marius

21. The only thing still wanting to complete the misfortunes of the Roman people was that they should draw the sword upon each other at home, and that citizens should fight against citizens in the midst of the city and in the forum like gladiators in the arena. It would be possible to bear the calamity with greater equanimity, if plebeian leaders, or leaders who, if noble, were yet bad men, had taken the chief part in such wickedness. On this occasion (alas for the crime of it!) what heroes, what generals they were—Marius and Sulla, the pride and glory of their age—who even gave the support of their high position to the very worst of misdeeds!

The Marian or Sullan civil war was waged under three different constellations,[1] if I may use the expression. In the first period the conflict was of the nature of a mild and unimportant rising rather than a war, the cruelty being confined to the leaders of the two parties; then it became a more bitter and cruel struggle, in which the victory struck at the very heart of the senate; finally, all the bounds of the rage, not merely of citizen against citizen, but of enemy against enemy, were exceeded, the fury of war being supported by all the resources of Italy, and hatred venting its cruelty till none remained to be slain.

The origin and cause of the war was Marius' insatiable desire for office, which led him to seek, by means of the law of Sulpicius, the province allotted to Sulla. The latter, unable to tolerate this injury, immediately wheeled round his legions, and postponing the war against Mithridates, poured his army

Collinaque porta geminum urbi agmen infudit.
7 Inde cum consules Sulpicius et Albinovanus obie-
cissent catervas suas, et saxa undique a moenibus
ac tela iacerentur, ipse quoque iaculatus incendia
viam fecit arcemque Capitolii, quae Poenos quoque,
quae[1] Gallos etiam Senonas evaserat, quasi cap-
8 tivam victor insedit. Tum[2] ex consulto senatus ad-
versariis hostibus iudicatis in praesentem tribunum
aliosque diversae factionis iure saevitum est;
Marium servilis fuga exemit, immo fortuna alteri
bello reservavit.

9 Cornelio Cinna Gnaeo Octavio consulibus male
obrutum resurrexit incendium, et quidem ab ip-
sorum discordia, quom[3] de revocandis quos senatus
10 hostes iudicaverat ad populum referretur; cincta
quidem gladiis contione, sed vincentibus quibus
pax et quies potior, profugus patria sua Cinna
confugit ad partes. Rediit ab Africa Marius clade
maior; si quidem carcer catenae, fuga exilium
11 horrificaverant dignitatem. Itaque ad nomen tanti
viri late concurritur, servitia—pro nefas—et ergas-
tula armantur, et facile invenit exercitum imperator.
12 Itaque vi patriam reposcens, unde vi fuerat ex-

[1] quae *add. Halmius.*
[2] tum *L. Voss. Palat.*: cum *BN.*
[3] quom: quam *B.*

---

[1] Neither Sulpicius nor Albinovanus were consuls; Sulpicius was tribune in 88 B.C.
[2] 87 B.C.

in two columns through the Esquiline and Colline Gates. When the consuls Sulpicius and Albinovanus [1] had thrown their troops in his way, and stones and weapons were being hurled on all sides from the walls, Sulla himself also forced a passage by hurling burning brands and occupied the citadel of the Capitol, which had escaped capture by the Carthaginians and Gallic Senones, like a victorious general in a captive city. Then after his adversaries had been declared enemies of the State by a decree of the senate, he took violent measures, under the form prescribed by law, against the tribune who was within reach and other members of the opposing faction. Marius saved himself by flight like that of a runaway slave, or rather fate preserved him to fight another day.

In the consulship of Cornelius Cinna and Gnaeus Octavius,[2] the flames, which had been imperfectly extinguished, burst forth afresh, owing, indeed, to a difference of opinion between the consuls themselves, when the question of recalling those whom the senate had declared enemies was referred to the people. The assembly met armed with swords, but when those prevailed who preferred peace and quiet, Cinna fled from his country and joined his confederates. Marius returned from Africa, all the greater for his misfortunes, since his imprisonment and chains, his flight and exile had added a certain awe to his high reputation. So at the name of so famous a general men flocked from far and near; recourse was had to the disgraceful expedient of arming slaves and convicts; and the general had no difficulty in finding an army. In thus seeking to return by violence to the country from which he had been

pulsus, poterat videri iure agere, nisi causam suam
saevitia corrumperet. Sed cum dis hominibusque
infestus rediret, statim primo impetu cliens et
alumna urbis Ostia[1] nefanda strage diripitur.
13 Mox in urbem quadruplici agmine intratur. Di-
visere copias Cinna, Marius, Carbo, Sertorius. Hic
postquam manus omnis Octavi depulsa Ianiculo
est, statim ad principum caedem signo dato ali-
quanto saevius quam vel in Punica urbe saevitur.
14 Octavi consulis caput pro rostris exponitur, Antonii
consularis in Mari ipsius mensis. Caesar et[2]
Fimbria in penatibus domuum[3] suarum trucidantur,
Crassi pater et filius in mutuo alter alterius aspectu.
Baebium atque Numitorium per medium forum
15 unci traxere carnificum. Catulus se ignis haustu
16 ludibrio hostium exemit. Merula flamen Dialis in
Capitolio Iovis ipsius oculos venarum cruore res-
persit. Ancharius ipso vidente Mario confossus
est, quia fatalem illam scilicet manum non por-
17 rexerat salutanti. Haec tot senatus funera intra
kalendas et idus Ianuarii mensis septima illa Marii
purpura dedit. Quid futurum fuit, si annum con-
sulatus implesset?

18 Scipione Norbanoque consulibus tertius ille turbo
civilis insaniae toto furore detonuit, quippe cum

[1] urbis Ostia: urbs urbis hostia *B*.
[2] Caesar et *NL*: caesare *B*.
[3] domuum *Iahnius*: domus *B*.

---

[1] *i.e.* Marius had told his followers to kill anyone whose salute he did not return.
[2] 86 B.C.
[3] 83 B.C.

driven by violence, Marius might seem to have acted justly, but that he disgraced his cause by cruelty. But returning at enmity with gods and men, he directed his first onslaught against Ostia, a city dependent upon Rome, and her foster-child, which he laid waste with impious destruction. Soon afterwards the city was entered by four detachments distributed under the command of Cinna, Marius, Carbo and Sertorius. When all Octavius' troops had been dislodged from the Janiculum, immediately, at a given signal, they wreaked their fury in the slaughter of the leading citizens with even greater cruelty than even in a Carthaginian city. The head of the consul Octavius was displayed on the *rostra*, that of Antonius, an ex-consul, on Marius' own table. Caesar and Fimbria were butchered at the household shrines of their own homes. The elder and younger Crassus were slain in the sight of one another. Baebius and Numitorius were dragged through the forum on the hooks of the executioners. Catulus saved himself from the insults of his enemies by swallowing fire. Merula, the priest of Jupiter in the Capitol, bespattered the visage of the god himself with the blood from his veins. Ancharius was stabbed in the presence of Marius himself, because, forsooth, when he saluted him, Marius had not stretched out to him the hand which was to decide his fate.[1] All these deaths of senators were the result of Marius' seventh consulship[2] between the 1st and the 9th of January. What would have happened if he had completed his full year of office?

In the consulship of Scipio and Norbanus,[3] the third storm of civil rage broke forth in all its fury.

hinc octo legiones,[1] quingentae cohortes starent in armis, inde ab Asia cum victore exercitu Sulla properaret. Et sane cum tam ferox in Sullanos Marius fuisset, quanta saevitia opus erat, ut Sulla de Mario vindicaretur? Primum apud Capuam sub amne Vulturno signa concurrunt, et statim omnis Norbani fusus exercitus, statim Scipionis copiae ostentata spe pacis oppressae. Tum Marius iuvenis et Carbo consules quasi desperata victoria, ne inulti perirent, in antecessum sanguine senatus sibi parentabant, obsessaque curia sic de senatu quasi de carcere qui iugularentur educti. Quantum[2] funerum in foro, in circo, in penitis[3] templis! nam Mucius Scaevola pontifex Vestalis amplexus aras tantum non eodem
22 igne sepelitur. Lamponius[4] atque Telesinus, Samnitum duces, atrocius Pyrrho et Annibale Campaniam Etruriamque populantur, et sub specie partium se
23 vindicant. Apud Sacriportum Collinamque portam debellatae omnes hostium copiae; ibi Marius, hic Telesinus oppressi. Nec idem tamen caedium qui belli finis fuit. Stricti enim et in pace gladii, animadversumque in eos, qui se sponte dediderant. Minus est, quod apud Sacriportum, apud Collinam septuaginta milia amplius Sulla concidit: bellum

[1] inde *post* legiones *add. BNL*, *del. Iahnius.*
[2] quantum *Iahnius*: quantum id *B*: quid *NL.*
[3] penitis *Rossbachius*: penitentibus *B*: patentibus *NL.*
[4] Lamponius (cp. Appian, *Bell. Civ.* I. 40; Plutarch, *Sulla*, 29): lucius amponius *B*: Iamponius *L.*

---

[1] Consuls in 82 B.C.

On the one side stood eight legions and 500 cohort in arms, while on the other side Sulla was hastening back from Asia with his victorious army. And, indeed, since Marius had acted so cruelly towards the supporters of Sulla, what cruelty was needed that Sulla might take vengeance upon Marius? Their forces first met at the River Vulturnus near Capua; the whole army of Norbanus was immediately routed and Scipio's forces were promptly overwhelmed after hopes of peace had been held out to them. Then the consuls, the younger Marius and Carbo,[1] as though despairing of victory and desirous of not perishing unavenged, offered sacrifice beforehand to their own shades with the blood of the senate; the senate-house was besieged and the senators were led out thence for execution as from a prison. What countless deaths took place in the forum, the circus and the innermost recesses of the temples! Mucius Scaevola, the priest of Vesta, clinging to the altar of the goddess, was almost buried in the flames which burnt upon it. Lamponius and Telesinus, the leaders of the Samnites, were laying waste Campania and Etruria with even more brutality than Pyrrhus or Hannibal, and were exacting vengeance on their own account under the pretence of helping their cause. But all the enemy's forces were defeated, those under Marius at Sacriportus, those under Telesinus at the Colline Gate. However, the end of the fighting was not also the end of the killing; for even after peace was made, swords were drawn and punishment was inflicted upon those who had surrendered voluntarily. The slaughter of more than 70,000 men by Sulla at Sacriportus and the Colline Gate was a lesser crime, for it was what one

erat. Quattuor milia deditorum inermium civium
25 in Villa Publica interfici iussit: isti tot in pace non
plures sunt? Quis autem illos potest conputare,
quos in urbe passim quisquis voluit occidit? Donec
admonente Fufidio[1] vivere aliquos debere, ut essent
quibus imperaret, proposita est ingens illa tabula,
et ex ipso equestris ordinis flore ac senatu duo milia
electi,[2] qui mori iuberentur: novi generis edictum.
26 Longum post haec referre ludibrio habita fata
Carbonis, fata[3] Sorani, Plaetorios atque Venuleios,[4]
Baebium sine ferro ritu ferarum inter manus lani-
atum, Marium, ducis ipsius fratrem, apud Catuli sepul-
crum oculis effossis, manibus cruribusque effractis
servatum aliquandiu, ut per singula membra more-
27 retur. Possis singulorum hominum ferre poenas:
municipia Italiae splendidissima sub hasta venie-
runt, Spoletium, Interamnium, Praeneste, Florentia.
28 Nam Sulmonem, vetus oppidum socium atque
amicum—facinus indignum—non expugnat aut
obsidet iure belli; sed quo modo morte damnati
duci iubentur, sic damnatam civitatem iussit Sulla
deleri.

[1] Fufidio *Dukerus*: forfidio *B*: furfidio *NL*.
[2] ac—electi *om. B*.
[3] fata . . . fata: facta . . . facta *B*.
[4] Plaetorios atque Venuleios: plaetorius atque venuleius *B*.

expects in war. But he ordered 4,000 unarmed citizens who had been surrendered to be slain in the Villa Publica.[1] Do not all these 4,000 slain in peace really outnumber those other 70,000? Who can compute the total of those whom anyone, who wished to do so, slew in various parts of the city? At last, when Fufidius advised that some men ought to be allowed to live in order that Sulla might have someone to whom to give orders, that vast proscription-list was put up, and from the flower of the equestrian order and the senate 2,000 men were chosen and condemned to death. It was an edict for which there was no precedent. It would be tedious after this to relate the insulting end of Carbo and Soranus, the deaths of Plaetorii and Venuleii; how Baebius was torn to pieces, not by the sword, but by men's hands, like a wild beast; and how Marius, the brother of the general, after his eyes had been gouged out at the tomb of Catulus, was kept alive for some time after his hands and legs had been broken off, so that he might die limb by limb. One could endure the punishment of individuals, but the most renowned towns of Italy were put up to auction—Spoletium, Interamnium, Praeneste, Florentia. As for Sulmo, an allied and friendly city of long standing, Sulla, instead of storming or besieging it according to the rules of warfare, committed an act of base injustice in condemning the city and ordering its destruction, even as those who are condemned to death are ordered to be led to execution.

[1] A building in the Campus Martius used for the entertainment of foreign ambassadors.

X. Bellvm Sertorianvm

II, 22 Bellum Sertorianum quid amplius quam Sullanae
proscriptionis hereditas fuit? Hostile potius an civile
dixerim nescio, quippe quod Lusitani Celtiberique
2 Romano gesserint duce. Exul et profugus feralis
illius tabulae, vir summae quidem sed calamitosae
virtutis malis suis maria terrasque permiscuit; et
iam Africae, iam Balearibus insulis fortunam ex-
pertus usque in Oceanum Fortunatasque Insulas
penetravit consiliis, tandem Hispaniam armavit.
3 Viro cum viris facile convenit. Nec alias magis
apparuit Hispani militis vigor quam Romano duce.
4 Quamquam ille non contentus Hispania ad Mithri-
datem quoque Ponticosque respexit[1] regemque
5 classe iuvit. Et quid futurum fuit satis tanto hosti,
cui uno imperatore resistere res Romana non
6 potuit? additus Metello Gnaeus Pompeius. Hi
copias adtrivere viri, prope tota Hispania per-
secuti. Diu et ancipiti semper acie pugnatum est;
nec tamen prius bello quam suorum scelere et
insidiis extinctus est.[2] Prima per legatos habita
certamina, cum hinc Domitius et Thorius, inde
7 Hirtulei proluderent; mox his apud Segoviam, illis
apud Anam flumen oppressis, ipsi duces comminus
invicem experti apud Lauronem atque Sucronem

[1] respexit: perrexit *B*.

[2] hi—extinctus est *Iahnius et Halmius*: hic copias adtriverant viri diu et ancipiti semper acie pugnatum est. Nec tamen prius bello quam suorum scelere et insidiis extinctus est. Copias eius prope tota hispania persequuti diu et varia semper acie domaverunt *B*: hi copias viri diu et ancipitis (ancipiti *L*) semper acie adtribuere (adtrivere *L*) nec tamen prius bello quam suorum scelere et insidiis extinctus copias eius prope tota (totas *L*) hispania persecuti diu et ancipiti semper acie donaverunt *NL*.

X. The War with Sertorius

22. What was the war with Sertorius except an inheritance from the Sullan proscription? I know not whether to call it a war against enemies or a civil war, for it was waged by the Lusitani and Celtiberi under a Roman leader. Sertorius, an exile and fugitive from that fatal proscription-list, a man of great, but ill-starred, valour, involved seas and lands in his personal misfortunes. Having tried his fortune at one time in Africa, at another time in the Balearic Islands, he extended his plans to include the Ocean and Fortunate Isles, and finally armed Spain. A brave man easily unites with other brave men; and the energy of the Spanish soldiers never appeared to better advantage than under a Roman leader. Yet Spain was not enough for him, and he turned his gaze towards Mithridates and the people of Pontus and helped the king with his fleet. Why should such a general have limited his ambitions, when the Roman State could not withstand him with one general only? Gnaeus Pompeius was therefore sent to help Metellus. They wore down his forces, pursuing him over almost the whole of Spain. The fighting continued for a long time, always with doubtful result; and his defeat was due not so much to operations in the field as to the crime and treachery of his own followers. The first engagements were fought by lieutenant-generals, Domitius and Thorius commencing operations on one side and the Hirtulei on the other. After the defeat of the latter at Segovia and of the former at the River Ana, the generals themselves tried their strength in combat and suffered equal disasters at Lauro and Sucro.

aequavere clades. Tum illis ad populationes agro-
8 rum,[1] his ad urbium excidia conversis, misera inter
Romanos duces Hispania discordiae poenas dabat;
9 donec oppresso domestica fraude Sertorio, victo
deditoque Perperna, ipsae quoque in Romanam
fidem venere urbes Osca, Termes,[2] Vlia, Valentia,
Auxuma et in fame nihil non experta Calagurris.
Sic recepta in pacem Hispania. Victores duces
externum id magis quam civile bellum videri
voluerunt, ut triumpharent.

XI. Bellvm Civile Svb Lepido

III, 23 Marco Lepido Quinto Catulo consulibus civile
bellum paene citius oppressum est quam inciperet:
sed quantulacumque fax illius motus ab ipso
2 Sullae rogo exarsit. Cupidus rerum novarum per
insolentiam Lepidus acta tanti viri rescindere
parabat; nec inmerito, si tamen posset sine magna
3 clade rei publicae. Nam cum iure belli Sulla
dictator proscripsisset inimicos, qui supererant
revocante Lepido quid aliud quam ad bellum
vocabantur? Cumque damnatorum civium bona
addicente Sulla quamvis male capta iure tamen
tenerentur,[3] repetitio eorum procul dubio labe-

[1] ad populationes agrorum: apopulatione sacrorum *B*: ad populationem agrorum *NL*.

[2] Termes, Vlia *Salmasius et Iahnius*: tergaest cum *B*: termestudia *NL*.

[3] tenerentur *add. Dukerus.*

Then one army devoting itself to laying waste the country and the other to the destruction of the cities, unhappy Spain was punished for Rome's quarrels at the hands of the Roman generals, until, after Sertorius had been brought low by treachery in his own camp and Perperna had been defeated and given up, the cities also of Osca, Termes, Ulia, Valentia, Auxuma and Calagurris (the last after suffering all the extremities of starvation) themselves entered in allegiance with Rome. Thus Spain was restored to peace. The victorious generals desired that the struggle should be considered a foreign rather than a civil war in order that they might celebrate a triumph.

XI. The Civil War under Lepidus

23. In the consulship of Marcus Lepidus and Quintus Catulus,[1] a civil war which arose was suppressed almost as soon as it began. Yet the spark which kindled this disturbance, however insignificant sprang from the funeral pyre of Sulla. Lepidus, desirous of change in affairs, presumptuously prepared to rescind the acts of that great man; and his action might have been justified, if only he could have carried it out without involving the State in a great disaster. For since Sulla in his dictatorship, on the strength of his victory, had proscribed his enemies, for what possible purpose, except for war, were the survivors recalled by Lepidus? And since the estates of the condemned citizens, assigned to others by Sulla, though wrongfully seized, were yet held under a form of law, the demand for their restoration un-

[1] 78 B.C.

4 factabat compositae civitatis statum. Expediebat
ergo quasi aegrae sauciaeque rei publicae quiescere
quomodocumque, ne[1] volnera curatione[2] ipsa re-
5 scinderentur. Ergo cum turbidis contionibus velut
classico civitatem terruisset, profectus in Etruriam
6 arma inde et exercitum urbi admovebat. Sed iam
Mulvium pontem collemque Ianiculum Lutatius[3]
Catulus Gnaeusque Pompeius, Sullanae dominationis
7 duces atque signiferi, alio exercitu insederant. A
quibus primo statim impetu retro pulsus hostisque
a senatu iudicatus incruenta fuga Etruriam, inde
Sardiniam recessit, ibique morbo et paenitentia
8 interiit. Victores quoque, quod non temere alias
in civilibus bellis, pace[4] contenti fuerunt.

XII. Bellvm Catilinae

IIII, 1 Catilinam luxuria primum, tum[5] hinc conflata
egestas rei familiaris, simul occasio, quod in extremis
finibus mundi arma Romana peregrinabantur, in
nefaria consilia opprimendae patriae suae con-
2 pulere.[6] Senatum confodere, consules trucidare,
distringere incendiis urbem, diripere aerarium,
totam denique rem publicam funditus tollere et
quidquid nec Annibal videretur optasse, quibus—

[1] ne *om.* *B.*
[2] curatione: cutio *B.*
[3] Lutatius: latius *B.*
[4] pace: pacis *B.*
[5] tum: cum *B*: tu *N.*
[6] conpulere: contulere *B.*

doubtedly tended to disturb the condition of the State now tranquillized. It was expedient, therefore, that the sick and wounded State should by some means or other be allowed to rest, lest its wounds should be torn open by the very attempt to heal them. Lepidus, therefore, having alarmed the State by his excited harangues, which seemed like a trumpet-call, set out for Etruria and thence directed his arms and troops against Rome. But Lutatius Catulus and Gnaeus Pompeius, who had been leaders and standard-bearers under Sulla's domination, had already occupied the Mulvian Bridge and the Hill of Janiculum with another army. Having been immediately driven back by these generals at his first onslaught and declared an enemy by the senate, he fled without further bloodshed to Etruria and thence to Sardinia, where he died of disease and remorse. The victors were content with restoring peace, a thing which has rarely happened in civil wars.

XII. The War against Catiline

1. It was, in the first place, his personal extravagance and then his consequent lack of means, combined with the favourable opportunity offered by the absence of the Roman armies in the uttermost quarters of the world, that induced Catiline to entertain the nefarious design of overthrowing his country. And what men were his associates (oh, the wickedness of it) in his attempt to murder the senate, to assassinate the consuls, to set fire to the city in various places, to plunder the treasury and, in a word, utterly to overturn the whole State and entertain every kind of design of which not even

3 o nefas—sociis adgressus est! Ipse patricius; sed
hoc minus est: Curii, Porcii, Sullae, Cethegi,
Autronii, Varguntei atque Longini, quae fami-
liae! quae senatus insignia! Lentulus quoque
tum cum maxime praetor. Hos omnis inmanissimi
4 facinoris satellites habuit. Additum est pignus
coniurationis sanguis humanus, quem circumlatum
pateris bibere: summum nefas, ni[1] amplius esset,
5 propter quod biberunt. Actum erat de pulcherrimo
imperio, nisi illa coniuratio in Ciceronem et
Antonium consules incidisset, quorum alter in-
6 dustria rem patefecit, alter manu oppressit. Tanti
sceleris indicium per Fulviam emersit, vilissimum
7 scortum, sed patriciis innocentius. Consul habito
senatu in praesentem reum peroravit; sed non
amplius profectum, quam ut hostis evaderet seque
tum[2] palam ac professe incendium suum restinc-
8 turum ruina minaretur. Et ille quidem ad prae-
paratum a Manlio in Etruria exercitum proficiscitur
signa inlaturus urbi. Lentulus, destinatum familiae
suae Sibyllinis versibus regnum sibi vaticinans, ad
praestitutum a Catilina diem urbe tota viros, faces,
9 tela disponit. Nec civili conspiratione contentus
legatos[3] Allobrogum, qui tum forte aderant, in

[1] ni: ne *B.* [2] tum: cum *B.*
[3] legatos *Halmius*: legatis *NL*: *om. B.*

Hannibal seems to have thought! He himself was a patrician, but that was a minor consideration. A Curius, a Porcius, a Sulla, a Cethegus, an Autronius, a Vargunteius and a Longinus—what men of family and high senatorial distinction!—and Lentulus, too, while actually holding the office of praetor, all these he had as accomplices in his atrocious crimes. Human blood, which they handed round in bowls and drank, was used as a pledge to bind the conspirators together—in itself an act of the utmost wickedness, were not the object for which they drank it still more wicked. There would have been an end of our glorious empire, had not the conspiracy happened to fall into the consulship of Cicero and Antonius, of whom the former by his diligence laid bare the plot, while the latter suppressed it by force of arms. Information about the outrageous crime came to light through Fulvia, a worthless prostitute, but less blameworthy than her patrician associates. The consul, having called the senate together, made a speech against the accused, who was present; but the only result of his action was that his enemy left Rome, and as he went, threatened openly and without disguise that he would extinguish the flames which he had kindled in general ruin. He set out for the army which Manlius had already prepared in Etruria, intending to march upon the city. Lentulus, prophesying for himself the kingship which the Sibylline verses foretold should belong to his family, disposed throughout the city men, torches and arms ready for the day prearranged by Catiline. Not content with a conspiracy in which only Romans were involved, he incited the representatives of the Allobroges, who happened to be in Rome at the

arma sollicitat. Isset[1] ultra Alpes furor, nisi altera proditione Volturci praetoris litterae tenerentur. Statim Ciceronis imperio iniecta est barbaris manus;
10 palam praetor in senatu convincitur. De supplicio agentibus, Caesar parcendum dignitati, Cato
11 animadvertendum pro scelere censebant. Quam sententiam secutis omnibus in carcere parricidae strangulantur. Quamvis parte coniurationis oppressa, tamen ab incepto Catilina non destitit; infestis ab Etruria signis patriam petens obvio
12 Antonii exercitu opprimitur. Quam atrociter dimicatum sit, exitus docuit. Nemo hostium bello superfuit; quem quis in pugnando ceperat locum, eum amissa anima corpore tegebat. Catilina longe a suis inter hostium cadavera repertus est, pulcherrima morte, si pro patria sic concidisset.

XIII. Bellvm Civile Caesaris et Pompei

IIII, 2 Iam toto orbe paene pacato maius erat imperium Romanum, quam ut ullis exteris viribus opprimi posset. Itaque invidens fortuna principi gentium
2 populo ipsum illum in exitium sui armavit. Ac

[1] sollicitat. Isset *Halmius*: sollicitatis. Sed *B*: sollicitatiset. Isset *N*: sollicitatis isset *L*.

---

[1] *i.e.* Lentulus.

time, to take up arms. The rage for conspiracy would have passed beyond the Alps had not a letter from the praetor[1] been intercepted by another betrayal, this time on the part of Volturcius. By Cicero's orders the barbarians were immediately arrested, and the praetor was openly proved guilty in the senate. When the question of punishment was discussed, Caesar expressed the opinion that the conspirators ought to be spared on account of their position; Cato thought that they ought to be punished in accordance with their crime. There was a general agreement in favour of the latter course, and the traitors were strangled in prison. Though part of the conspiracy was thus put down, Catiline did not abandon his designs; but, as he was marching against the city from Etruria with hostile intent, he was surprised by the army of Antonius. The result of the battle showed how desperate was the fighting; not a single one of the enemy survived, and each man's lifeless body covered the spot at which he had taken his post in the battle. Catiline was discovered far in front of his fellows amid the dead bodies of his foes, thus dying a death which would have been glorious if he had thus fallen fighting for his country.

XIII. The Civil War between Caesar and Pompeius

2. Almost the whole world having been now subjugated, the Roman Empire was too strong to be overcome by any foreign power. Fortune, therefore, envying a people that was sovereign of the world, armed it to its own destruction. The fury of

Mariana quidem Cinnanaque rabies iam intra urbem
praeluserat,[1] quasi si experiretur. Sullana tempestas
3 latius, intra Italiam tamen, detonuerat. Caesaris
furor atque Pompei urbem Italiam, gentes nationes,
totum denique qua patebat [2] imperium quodam
quasi diluvio et inflammatione corripuit, adeo ut non
4 recte tantum civile dicatur, ac ne sociale quidem,
sed nec externum, sed potius commune quoddam
5 ex omnibus et plus quam bellum. Quippe si duces
eius inspicias, totus senatus in partibus; si exercitus,
hinc undecim legiones, inde decem et octo, flos
omnis et robur Italici sanguinis; si auxilia sociorum,
hinc Gallici Germanique dilectus, inde Deiotarus,
Ariobarzanes, Tarcondimotus, Cotys et Rhascypolis,[3]
omne Thraciae, Cappadociae, Macedoniae, Ciliciae,
6 Graeciae totiusque robur orientis; si moram belli,
quattuor anni, sed [4] pro clade rerum breves; [5] si
locum et spatium,[6] commissum est intra Italiam,
inde se in Galliam Hispaniamque deflexit reversumque ab occasu totis viribus in Epiro Thessaliaque consedit; hinc in Aegyptum subito transiluit, inde respexit Asiam, Africae incubuit, postremo
7 in Hispaniam regyravit [7] et ibi aliquando defecit.
Sed non et odia partium finita cum bello. Non

[1] praeluserat *Graevius* : praecluserat *B* : precluxerat *L.*
[2] totum denique qua patebat : totumque potibat *B* : totum denique patebat *L.*
[3] Tarcondimotus, Cotys et Rhascypolis : tarcondi motus cotys et thascypolis *B.*
[4] anni, sed : annis sed *B* : anni et *L.*
[5] breves *Halmius* : breve *B* : breve tempus *NL.*
[6] ubi *post* spatium *del. Perizonius.*
[7] regyravit : regiravit *L* : regnavit *B.*

---

[1] Cp. Lucan, *Phars.* I. 1, *Bella per Emathios plus quam civilia campos.*

Marius and Cinna had, indeed, formed a prelude, and as it were a preliminary trial, within the city; the thunder of the storm raised by Sulla had rolled over a wider area, but within the confines of Italy. The rage of Caesar and Pompeius, like a flood or a fire, involved the city and Italy, and then tribes and nations, and finally the whole extent of the empire. It cannot, therefore, justly be called merely a civil war, nor a war between allies, nor yet a foreign war, but was rather a war with all these characteristics and something worse than a war.[1] If one looks at the leaders, the whole senate was ranged on one side or the other; if one considers the forces engaged, on one side were eleven legions, on the other eighteen, all the flower and strength of Italy's manhood; if one looks at the aid given by the allies, one finds on one side the levies of Gaul and Germany, on the other side Deiotarus, Ariobarzanes, Tarcondimotus, Cotys and Rhascypolis,[2] all the strength of Thrace, Cappadocia, Macedonia, Cilicia, Greece and the whole East. If one considers the duration of the war, it lasted for four years, a short period in view of the destruction which it wrought. If one looks at the ground and space which it covered, it began in Italy, it next directed its course into Gaul and Spain, and then, returning from the West, settled in full force upon Epirus and Thessaly; thence it suddenly leaped across into Egypt, whence it cast a backward glance upon Asia, brooded over Africa, and finally wheeled back into Spain, where at last it died out. But the close of the war did not see the end of party hatred, which

[2] For these names see Index.

enim prius quieverunt, quam in ipsa urbe medio senatu eorum, qui victi erant, odia victoris se caede satiarent.

8 Causa tantae calamitatis eadem quae[1] omnium, nimia felicitas. Si quidem Quinto Metello Lucio Afranio[2] consulibus cum Romana maiestas toto orbe polleret recentesque victorias, Ponticos et Armenios triumphos, in Pompeianis theatris Roma cantaret, nimia Pompei potentia apud otiosos, ut solet, cives
9 movit invidiam. Metellus ob inminutum Cretae triumphum, Cato adversus potentes semper obliquus detrectare Pompeio actisque eius obstrepere. Hic dolor transversum egit et ad praesidia dignitati
10 paranda inpulit. Forte tunc Crassus genere, divitiis, dignitate florebat, ut[3] vellet tamen auctioris opes; C. Caesar eloquentia et spiritu, ecce iam et consulatu adlevabatur; Pompeius tamen inter utrumque
11 eminebat. Sic igitur Caesare dignitatem conparare, Crasso augere, Pompeio retinere cupientibus, omnibusque pariter potentiae cupidis de invadenda re
12 publica facile convenit. Ergo cum mutuis viribus in suum quisque decus niterentur, Galliam Caesar invadit, Crassus Asiam, Pompeius Hispaniam: tres maximi exercitus, et in his orbis imperium societate

[1] eadem quae *Aldus*: eademque *codd.*
[2] Afranio: Africano *B.* [3] ut *add. Mommsenus.*

---

[1] 60 B.C.
[2] The leaders of his defeated enemies had, by Pompeius' orders, not been allowed to figure in Metellus' triumph.
[3] 59 B.C.

did not subside until the rancour of those who had been defeated sated itself with the murder of the victor in the city itself, in the midst of the senate.

The cause of this great calamity was the same which caused all our calamities, namely, excessive good fortune. In the consulship of Quintus Metellus and Lucius Afranius,[1] when the majesty of Rome held sway throughout the world and Rome was celebrating in the theatres of Pompeius her recent victories and her triumphs over the peoples of Pontus and Armenia, the excessive power enjoyed by Pompeius excited, as often happens, a feeling of envy among the ease-loving citizens. Metellus, because his triumph over Crete was shorn of its splendour,[2] and Cato, who always looked askance upon those in power, began to decry Pompeius and clamour against his measures. Annoyance at this drove Pompeius into opposition and induced him to seek support for his position. Crassus happened at this time to be at the height of a reputation due to his birth, wealth and the high offices which he had held, and yet he wished to increase his riches; Gaius Caesar's fame for eloquence and courage was now enhanced by his tenure of the consulship;[3] but Pompeius occupied a higher position than either of them. Caesar, therefore, being desirous of winning, Crassus of increasing, and Pompeius of retaining his position, and all alike being eager for power, readily came to an agreement to seize the government. So, each striving with the support of the others to win glory for himself, Caesar entered upon the government of Gaul, Crassus upon that of Asia, and Pompeius upon that of Spain. They possessed three great armies, and the rule of the whole world was vested in these by association

13 trium principum occupatur. Decem annos traxit
ista dominatio ex fide, quia mutuo metu tenebantur.
Crassi morte apud Parthos, morte Iuliae Caesaris
filiae, quae nupta Pompeio generi socerique con-
cordiam matrimonii foedere continebat, statim
14 aemulatio erupit. Iam Pompeio suspectae Caesaris
opes et Caesari Pompeiana dignitas gravis. Nec ille
ferebat parem, nec hic superiorem. Pro nefas! Sic
de principatu laborabant, tamquam duos tanti im-
15 perii fortuna non caperet. Ergo Lentulo Mar-
celloque consulibus rupta primum coniurationis
fides.[1] De successione Caesaris senatus, id est
Pompeius, agitabat, nec ille abnuebat, si ratio sui
16 proximis comitiis haberetur. Ut daretur consulatus
absenti, quem decem tribuni favente Pompeio nuper
decreverant, dissimulante eodem negabatur: veniret
17 et peteret more maiorum. Ille contra flagitare
decreta, ac, nisi fides permaneret, non remittere
exercitum. Ergo ut in hostem decernitur. His
Caesar agitatus statuit praemia armorum armis
defendere.

18 Prima civilis belli harena Italia fuit, cuius arces
levibus praesidiis Pompeius insederat; sed omnia

[1] primum coniurationis fides *Halmius*: prima coniurationis fide *codd.*

---

[1] 49 B.C.

of the three leaders. This domination lasted for ten years in accordance with their compact, because they were restrained by fear of one another. But when Crassus had fallen fighting against the Parthians, and Julia, who, as Caesar's daughter and the wife of Pompeius, by this bond of marriage maintained friendly relations between father-in-law and son-in-law, had died, rivalry immediately broke out. Caesar's power now inspired the envy of Pompeius, while Pompeius' eminence was offensive to Caesar; Pompeius could not brook an equal or Caesar a superior. Oh, the wickedness of it! They strove for the first place, as though the fortunes of a great empire could not find room for both of them. And so, in the consulship of Lentulus and Marcellus,[1] the bond of agreement was first broken. The senate—in other words, Pompeius—began to agitate for the appointment of a successor to Caesar, and he was not inclined to object provided that his name should be considered at the coming elections. The granting of the consulship to him in his absence, which the tribunes of the people had recently decreed with the support of Pompeius, was now refused through secret machinations on the part of Pompeius, and it was urged that he should come and stand as a candidate in accordance with ancient precedent. Caesar, on the other hand, demanded that the decree should be put into execution, and refused to disband his army unless the compact held good. A decree was, therefore, passed declaring him a public enemy. Caesar, exasperated at this, determined to defend by arms the prizes which he had won by arms.

The first arena of the civil war was Italy, the strongholds of which Pompeius had occupied with

19 subito Caesaris impetu oppressa sunt. Prima Ari-
mino signa cecinerunt. Tum pulsus Etruria Libo,
Vmbria Thermus, Domitius Corfinio. Et peractum
erat bellum sine sanguine, si Pompeium Brundisii
20 opprimere potuisset. Et ceperat; sed ille per
obsessi claustra portus nocturna fuga evasit. Turpe
dictu: modo princeps patrum, pacis bellique modera-
tor, per triumphatum a se mare lacera et paene
21 inermi nave fugiebat. Nec Pompei ab Italia quam
senatus ab urbe fuga turpior:[1] quam paene vacuam,
metu Caesar ingressus consulem se ipse fecit.
Aerarium quoque sanctum, quod quia tardius
aperiebant tribuni iussit effringi, censumque et
patrimonium populi Romani ante rapuit quam
imperium.

22 Pulso fugatoque Pompeio maluit prius ordinare
provincias quam ipsum sequi. Siciliam et Sardiniam,
23 annonae pignera, per legatos habet. Nihil hostile
erat in Gallia; pacem ipse fecerat. Sed ad His-
panienses Pompei exercitus transeunti per eam duci
portas claudere ausa Massilia est. Misera dum
cupit pacem, belli metu in bellum incidit; sed quia
tuta muris erat, vinci eam sibi iussit absenti.

[1] fuga turpior *Gruterus*: fugatur prior *BNL*.

---

[1] For the year 48 B.C.

light garrisons; but Caesar's sudden attack carried all before it. The first trumpet-call was sounded at Ariminum; Libo was driven out of Etruria, Thermus from Umbria, Domitius from Corfinium. The war would have terminated without bloodshed if Caesar could have surprised Pompeius at Brundisium; and he would have captured him, if he had not escaped by night through the entrance of the beleaguered harbour. A shameful tale, he who was but lately head of the senate and arbiter of peace and war fleeing, in a storm-beaten and almost dismantled vessel, over the sea which had been the scene of his triumphs. The flight of the senate from the city was as discreditable as that of Pompeius from Italy. Caesar on his entrance into Rome found it almost deserted owing to the fear which he inspired, and made himself consul.[1] When the tribunes showed themselves slow in unlocking the sacred treasury, he ordered it to be broken open, thus taking possession of the revenue and inheritance of the Roman people before he assumed the government.

Pompeius being routed and in flight, Caesar preferred to set the provinces in order before he pursued him. Sicily and Sardinia, which insure our corn supply, he secured by his lieutenant-generals. There was no hostility in Gaul, where he himself had established peace. Marseilles, however, as he was passing through on his way to attack Pompeius' armies in Spain, dared to close its gates to him; the luckless city, desirous of peace, became involved in war through its dread of war. But since it was protected by walls, he gave orders that it should be reduced for him in his absence. This, though only

24 Graecula civitas non pro mollitia nominis et vallum
rumpere et incendere machinas ausa, etiam congredi
25 navibus; sed Brutus, cui mandatum erat bellum,
victos terra marique perdomuit. Mox dedentibus
se omnia ablata praeter quam potiorem omnibus
habebant libertatem.

26 Anceps variumque sed incruentum in Hispania
bellum cum legatis Gnaei Pompei, Petreio et
Afranio, quos Ilerdae castra habentes apud Sicorim
amnem obsidere et ab oppido intercludere ad-
27 greditur. Interim abundatio verni fluminis com-
meatibus prohibebat: sic fame castra temptata sunt,
28 obsessorque ipse quasi obsidebatur. Sed ubi pax
fluminis redit, et[1] populationibus et pugnae[2]
campos aperuit, iterum ferox instat et cedentes ad
Celtiberiam consecutus aggere et vallo et per haec
29 siti ad deditionem conpulit.[3] Sic citerior Hispania
recepta est, nec ulterior moram fecit. Quid enim
una post quinque legiones? Itaque ultro cedente
Varrone Gades, fretum, Oceanus, omnia felicitatem
Caesaris sequebantur.

30 Aliquid tamen adversus absentem ducem ausa
Fortuna est circa Illyricum[4] et Africam,[5] quasi
31 de industria prospera eius adversis radiaret;[6] quippe
cum fauces Adriani maris iussi[7] occupare Dolabella

[1] et *add. Salmasius.* [2] pugnae: pugna *BL.*
[3] conpulit: contulit *B.*
[4] Illyricum: illirium *B*: illiricum *L.*
[5] moranti *post* Africam *add. B.*
[6] radiaret: radiarent *B*: radiarentur *NL.*
[7] iussi: iussit *B.*

a Greek city, failing to justify its reputation for effeminacy, had the courage to break through the enemy's circumvallations and to burn their engines of war and even to engage them at sea. But Brutus, to whom the operations had been entrusted, defeated and overcame them by land and sea. They quickly surrendered and were deprived of everything which they possessed except the most valued of all their possessions, their liberty.

In Spain an indecisive war with varying success, but without heavy bloodshed, was fought against Petreius and Afranius, the lieutenant-generals of Gnaeus Pompeius, whom, while they were encamped at Ilerda on the river Sicoris, Caesar attempted to besiege and cut off from the town. Meanwhile the flooding of the river in the spring prevented him from obtaining supplies; thus his camp was threatened with starvation, and the besieger was himself as it were besieged. When, however, the river resumed its tranquil course and opened the country to ravaging and fighting, he again fiercely attacked the enemy and, when they retreated into Celtiberia, followed them up and reduced them to surrender by ditch and rampart and consequent lack of water. Thus Hither Spain was recovered, nor did Further Spain delay Caesar long; for what could one legion do after five had been defeated? After the voluntary surrender of Varro, Gades, the Straits and the Ocean all obeyed Caesar's lucky star.

Fortune, however, ventured some opposition to the absent leader, namely, in Illyricum and Africa, as though on purpose to make his successes more glorious in contrast with failure elsewhere. For when Dolabella and Antonius, who had been ordered

et Antonius, ille Illyrico, hic Curictico[1] litore castra posuissent, iam maria late tenente Pompeio, repente legatus eius Octavius Libo ingentibus[2] copiis
32 classicorum utrumque circumvenit. Deditionem fames extorsit Antonio. Missae quoque a Basilo[3] in auxilium eius rates, quales inopia navium fecerat,[4] nova Pompeianorum arte Cilicum actis sub mari
33 funibus captae quasi per indaginem. Duas tamen aestus explicuit. Una, quae Opiterginos ferebat, in vadis haesit memorandumque posteris exemplum[5] dedit. Quippe vix mille iuvenum manus circumfusi undique exercitus per totum diem tela sustinuit, et cum exitum virtus non haberet, tandem,[6] ne in deditionem veniret, hortante tribuno Vulteio mutuis
34 ictibus inter se concurrit. In Africa quoque par et virtus et calamitas Curionis fuit, qui ad recipiendam provinciam missus, pulso fugatoque Varo[7] superbus, subitum Iubae regis adventum equitatumque Maurorum sustinere non potuit. Patebat victo fuga; sed pudor suasit, ut amissum sua temeritate exercitum morte[8] sequeretur.

35 Sed iam debitum par Fortuna flagitante sedem bello Pompeius Epiron elegerat; nec Caesar mora-
36 batur. Quippe ordinatis a tergo omnibus, quamvis

[1] Curictico: currictico *L*: syretico *B*.
[2] ingentibus: genibus *B*.
[3] a Basilo *Asulanus*: ablatio *B*: ablasio *NL*.
[4] fecerat: fecerant *B*.
[5] exemplum *Freinshemius*: exitum *codd.*
[6] tandem *Iahnius*: tamen *codd.*
[7] Varo: varro *B*.
[8] morte: mortis *B*.

to hold the entrance to the Adriatic, had encamped, the former on the Illyrian coast and the latter on the shore near Curicta, at a time when Pompeius enjoyed a wide command of the sea, the latter's lieutenant-general Octavius Libo suddenly surrounded both of them with large forces from the fleet. Famine compelled Antonius to surrender. Some rafts sent to his assistance by Basilus—as good a substitute as he could make for the lack of ships—were captured, as in a net, by means of ropes drawn along under the water, a new device on the part of some Cilicians in Pompeius' service. The tide, however, floated two of them off; but one of them, which carried troops from Opitergium, went aground on the shallows and provided an incident worthy of record in history. A band of barely 1,000 men withstood for a whole day the weapons of an army which had completely surrounded them, and when their valour procured no way of escape, at last, at the exhortation of the tribune Vulteius, in order that they might not be forced to surrender, they fell upon one another and died by the blows of their fellows. In Africa too Curio showed like bravery and met with a like disaster. Sent to recover that province and elated at having routed Varus and put him to flight, he was unable to resist a sudden attack of King Juba and the Moorish cavalry. A way of flight was open to the defeated general, but shame induced him to share the fate of an army which had been lost through his rashness.

But, Fortune now demanding that the destined pair of combatants should meet, Pompeius had chosen Epirus as the scene of operations, and Caesar was not slow to face him. Having set all things in

hiemps media prohiberet tempestate, ad bellum
37 navigavit; positisque ad Oricum castris, cum pars exercitus ob inopiam navium cum Antonio relicta Brundisii moram faceret, adeo inpatiens erat, ut ad arcessendos eos ardente ventis mari, nocte concubia, speculatorio navigio solus ire temptaverit. Extat ad trepidum tanto discrimine gubernatorem
38 vox ipsius, "Quid times? [1] Caesarem vehis." Contractis in unum undique omnibus copiis positisque comminus castris diversa erant ducum consilia. Caesar pro natura ferox et conficiendae rei cupidus
39 ostentare aciem, provocare, lacessere; nunc obsidione castrorum, quae sedecim milium vallo obduxerat—sed quid iis [2] obesset obsidio, qui patente mari
40 omnibus copiis abundarent?—nunc expugnatione Dyrrachi inrita, quippe quam vel [3] situs inexpugnabilem faceret; ad hoc adsiduis in eruptione[4] hostium proeliis, quo tempore egregia virtus Scaevolae centurionis emicuit, cuius in scuto centum atque
41 viginti tela sederunt; iam vero urbium direptione sociarum, cum Oricum et Gomphos et alia castella [5]
42 Thessaliae vastaret. Pompeius adversus haec nectere moras, tergiversari, sic hostem interclusum undique

[1] quid times *om.* *B.*
[2] iis: is *B.*
[3] vel: vis *B.*
[4] in eruptione: inruptione *B*: ineruptionem *L.*
[5] castella *om.* *B.*

order in his rear, although mid-winter impeded his passage with a storm, he sailed to war, and having pitched his camp at Oricum and finding that the absence of part of his army, which had been left behind at Brindusium with Antonius owing to lack of ships, was delaying operations, he was so impatient that, though a gale was raging at sea, he attempted to cross in the depth of the night alone in a light reconnoitring boat to keep them off. His remark to the master of the vessel, who was alarmed at the greatness of the risk, has come down to us: "Why are you afraid? You have Caesar on board." All their forces having been collected together from every side and their camps pitched close to one another, the plans of the two generals were very different. Caesar, naturally aggressive and eager to obtain a decision, displayed his troops in line of battle and provoked and challenged the enemy. At one time he blockaded Pompeius' camp, which he had surrounded with a rampart sixteen miles in circumference; but what harm could a siege do to an army which, from its command of the sea, could obtain supplies of every kind in abundance? At another time he made an attack on Dyrrhachium, but in vain, since its very site alone rendered it impregnable; and, further, he constantly encountered with the enemy whenever they made a sally—when extraordinary bravery was displayed by the centurion Scaevola, in whose shield a hundred and twenty weapons were lodged—and, finally, plundered the cities which had allied themselves with Pompeius, laying waste Oricum, Gomphi and other fortresses of Thessaly. Against these movements Pompeius contrived delays and subterfuges, and tried to wear down the enemy,

inopia commeatuum terere, usque dum ardentissimi
43 ducis consenesceret impetus. Nec diutius profuit
ducis salutare consilium. Miles otium, socii moram,
principes ambitum ducis increpabant. Sic praecipi-
tantibus fatis proelio sumpta Thessalia est, et
Philippicis campis urbis,[1] imperii, generis humani
44 fata commissa sunt. Numquam ullo loco tantum
virium populi Romani, tantum dignitatis Fortuna
respexit: trecenta amplius milia hinc vel illinc
45 praeter auxilia, reges et senatum. Numquam
inminentis ruinae manifestiora prodigia: fuga
victimarum, examina in signis, interdiu tenebrae.
Dux ipse in nocturna imagine plausu theatri sui in
modum[2] planctus circumsonatus et mane cum pullo
46 pallio—nefas—apud principia conspectus est. Num-
quam acrior neque alacrior exercitus Caesaris fuit;
inde classica prius, inde tela. Adnotatum quoque
committentis aciem Crastini pilum, qui mox adacto
in os gladio—sic inter cadavera repertus est—
libidinem ac rabiem qua pugnaverat ipsa novitate
47 volneris praeferebat. Sed nec minus admirabilior
illius[3] exitus belli. Quippe cum Pompeius adeo
equitum copia abundaret, ut facile circumventurus

[1] urbis: orbis *B*.
[2] plausu theatri sui in modum *Mommsenus*: plausum theatrisui audiens in modum *B*.
[3] illius: ullius *B*.

---

[1] Florus, like Virgil (*Georg.* I. 490), seems to imply that the battle of Pharsalia was fought on the same ground as the battle of Philippi. The confusion is doubtless due to the fact that these two decisive battles were both fought within the space of a few years in the Roman province of Macedonia.

who were hemmed in on all sides, by depriving them of their supplies, and waited for the moment when the zeal of the impetuous general should die down. But Pompeius' salutary plan did not avail him very long; the soldiers complained of his inactivity, the allies of the length of the war, the nobles of the ambition of their leader. The fates thus forcing on an issue, Thessaly was chosen as the scene of the battle, and the destiny of the city, the empire and the human race was entrusted for decision to the plains of Philippi.[1] Never did Fortune see so much of the might and dignity of the Roman people collected in one place; more than 300,000 men were assembled in the two armies as well as auxiliary troops, kings and senate. Never were the portents of impending disaster more clearly manifest, victims escaping from slaughter, bees swarming upon the standards, and darkness coming on in the daytime. Pompeius himself dreamed that he was surrounded in his own theatre by a clapping of hands which resembled the beating of breasts, and in the morning appeared at his head-quarters clad in a dark cloak—an omen of misfortune. Caesar's army was never more eager and alert, and it was from his side that the first trumpet-call was sounded and the first weapons were discharged. The javelin of Crastinus was noted as that of the man who started the battle, and the strangeness of the wound which he received—he was found among the dead with a sword thrust into his mouth—showed the zeal and rage with which he had fought. Nor was the issue of the campaign less wondrous; for although Pompeius had such a superiority in cavalry that he thought he could easily surround Caesar,

sibi Caesarem videretur, circumventus ipse est.
48 Nam cum diu aequo Marte contenderent, iussuque
Pompei fusus[1] a cornu erupisset equitatus, repente
hinc signo dato Germanorum cohortes tantum in
effusos equites fecere impetum, ut illi esse[2] pedites,
49 hi[3] venire in equis viderentur. Hanc stragem
fugientis equitatus levis armaturae ruina comitata
est; tunc terrore latius dato, turbantibus invicem
copiis, reliqua strages quasi una manu facta est;
nec ulla res magis exitio fuit quam ipsa exercitus
50 magnitudo. Multus in eo proelio Caesar fuit
mediusque inter imperatorem et militem. Voces
quoque obequitantis acceptae, altera cruenta, sed
docta et ad victoriam efficax "miles faciem feri!"
altera ad iactationem conposita "parce civibus!"
51 cum ipse sequeretur felicem utcumque in malis
Pompeium, si eadem ipsum quae[4] exercitum eius
fortuna traxisset. Superstes dignitatis suae vixit,
ut cum maiore dedecore per Thessalica Tempe equo
fugeret, ut una navicula Lesbon applicaret, ut[5]
Syedris[6] in deserto Ciliciae scopulo fugam in
52 Parthos, Africam vel Aegyptum agitaret, ut denique
Pelusio litore imperio vilissimi regis, consiliis spadonum et, ne quid malis desit, Septimii desertoris

[1] sui *post* fusus *add.* *B.*
[2] esse: essent *B.*
[3] hi: ulli *B.*
[4] ipsum quae: ipsumque *BL.*
[5] applicaret, ut *Rossbachius*: applicarentur et *B.*
[6] Syedris *Salmasius*: hedris *codd.*

he was himself surrounded. For when the fight had continued for a long time without advantage to either side and, by Pompeius' order, his cavalry had poured forth in an onslaught from the wing, suddenly at a given signal the German cohorts made so violent an attack from that quarter on the cavalry as they rushed out that the latter seemed but infantry, while their assailants seemed to be mounted on horseback. The slaughter of the retreating cavalry was accompanied by the destruction of the light infantry; then the panic extended further and, one body of troops spreading confusion to another, the slaughter of the rest was accomplished as though by one sweep of the hand, and the very size of the army contributed more than anything to its destruction. Caesar was everywhere in the battle and combined the functions of a general and of a common soldier. Some of his remarks too, made as he rode about, are preserved. One of them, "Soldiers, strike the foe in the face," was cruel but judicious and conducive to success. Another, "Spare your fellow-citizens," uttered when he was himself pursuing Pompeius (who would have been lucky in his misfortunes if the same fate which overtook his army had fallen upon himself), was intended merely as a boast. As it was, Pompeius survived his honours, only to suffer the still greater disgrace of escaping on horseback through the Thessalian Tempe; of reaching Lesbos with one small vessel; of meditating at Syedra, on a lonely rock in Cilicia, an escape to Parthia, Africa or Egypt; and finally of dying by murder in the sight of his wife and children on the shores of Pelusium, by order of the most contemptible of kings and by the advice of eunuchs, and, to complete the tale of his

sui gladio trucidatus sub oculis uxoris suae libero-
rumque moreretur.
53 Quis non peractum esse cum Pompeio crederet?
Atquin acrius multo atque vehementius Thessalici
54 incendii cineres recaluerunt. Et in Aegypto qui-
55 dem adversus Caesarem sine partibus bellum. Quippe
cum Ptolemaeus, rex Alexandriae, summum civilis
belli scelus peregisset et foedus amicitiae cum
Caesare medio Pompei capite sanxisset, ultionem
clarissimi viri manibus quaerente[1] Fortuna causa
56 non defuit. Cleopatra, regis soror, adfusa Caesaris
genibus partem regni reposcebat. Aderat puellae
forma, [et] quae duplicaretur ex illo, quod talis
passa videbatur iniuriam, <et>[2] odium ipsius regis,
57 qui Pompei caedem[3] partium fato, non Caesari
dederat, haud dubie idem[4] in ipsum ausurus, si
58 fuisset occasio.[5] Quam ubi Caesar restitui iussit
in regnum, statim ab isdem percussoribus Pompei
obsessus in regia quamvis exigua manu ingentis
59 exercitus molem mira virtute sustinuit. Ac primum
proximorum aedificiorum atque navalium[6] incendio
infestorum hostium tela summovit, mox in paenin-
sulam Pharon subitus evasit; inde depulsus in maria
mira felicitate ad proximam classem enatavit, relicto

[1] ultionem clarissimi viri manibus quaerente Fortuna: ultionem quaemanibus clarissimi viri omnibus quaerente fortunae *B*.

[2] et *post* forma *secl. et ante* odium *add. dubitanter Rossbachius.*

[3] Pompeii caedem: pompeium regem *B*: pompeio aedem *N*: pompeii cedem *L*.

[4] idem *om. B*. [5] fuisset occasio: ruisset hoccasio *B*.

[6] atque navalium *om. B*.

misfortunes, by the sword of Septimius, a deserter from his own army.

With the death of Pompeius, who could but suppose that the war was over? Yet the embers of the conflagration in Thessaly burst forth again in flames with far greater fury and violence. In Egypt, indeed, a war broke out against Caesar which had no connection with party faction. Since Ptolemaeus, king of Alexandria, had perpetrated the crowning atrocity of the civil war and had sealed a treaty of friendship with Caesar by means of Pompeius' murder, fate called for vengeance for the shade of so illustrious a victim; and an occasion soon presented itself. Cleopatra, the king's sister, threw herself at Caesar's feet and asked for the restoration of part of the kingdom. He was moved by the beauty of the damsel, which was enhanced by the fact that, being so fair, she seemed to have been wronged, and by hatred for the king himself, who had sacrificed Pompeius to the fortunes of a faction and not out of any consideration for Caesar, against whom he would certainly have made the same attempt if occasion had arisen. When Caesar ordered that Cleopatra should be restored to the throne, he was immediately surrounded in the palace by those who had assassinated Pompeius, but, though he had only a small body of troops, he resisted with wonderful bravery the pressure of a vast army. First of all, by setting fire to the neighbouring buildings and docks he kept the missiles of his assailants at a distance; then he made a sudden sally and occupied the peninsula of Pharos. Driven thence into the sea he succeeded, with wonderful good fortune, in swimming to the nearer vessels of the fleet, leaving

quidem in fluctibus paludamento seu fato seu
consilio, ut illud ingruentibus hostium telis saxisque
60 peteretur. Tunc receptus a classicis suis, undique
simul hostes adortus de inbelli ac perfida gente
iusta generi manibus dedit. Quippe et Theodotus
magister auctorque totius belli, et ne virilia quidem
portenta, Pothinus atque Ganymedes diversa per
mare et terras fuga morte consumpti. Regis ipsius
corpus obrutum limo repertum est in aureae loricae
honore.

61 In Asia quoque novus rerum motus a Ponto,
plane [1] quasi de industria captante fortuna hunc
Mithridatico regno exitum, ut a Pompeio pater, a
62 Caesare filius vinceretur. Rex Pharnaces magis
discordiae nostrae fiducia quam suae virtutis infesto
63 in Cappadociam agmine ruebat. Sed hunc Caesar
adgressus uno et, ut sic dixerim, non toto proelio
obtrivit, more fulminis, quod uno eodemque momento venit, percussit, abscessit. Nec vana [2] de se
praedicatio est Caesaris, ante hostem victum esse
quam visum.

64 Sic cum exteris; at in Africa cum civibus multo
atrocius quam in Pharsalia. Hic reliquias partium
naufragarum quidam fugae aestus expulerat; nec
65 reliquias diceres, sed integrum bellum. Sparsae

[1] plane *om. B.* [2] vana : una *B.*

his cloak behind him in the water, either through luck or by design, that it might be a target for the shower of missiles and stones thrown by the enemy. Having been taken on board by the sailors of the fleet, he attacked his foes on all sides at once and exacted vengeance for the shade of his son-in-law from that cowardly and treacherous people. Theodotus, the director and instigator of the whole war, and Pothinus and Ganymedes, monsters who were not even men, met their deaths after fleeing in different directions over sea and land. The body of the king himself was found buried in mud, distinguishable by his golden coat of mail.

In Asia too a fresh disturbance arose from Pontus, fortune as it were designedly seeking thus to make an end of the kingdom of Mithridates, in order that his son might be conquered by Caesar just as the father had been defeated by Pompeius. King Pharnaces, relying rather upon our internal feuds than upon his own valour, invaded Cappadocia with a hostile force. Caesar attacked him, and in a single battle—or, if I may use the expression, in part of a battle—crushed him like a thunderbolt which in one and the same moment has come, has struck and has departed. Caesar's boast was no vain one when he said that the enemy was defeated before he was seen.

So much for foreign enemies; in Africa Caesar had a much more bitter struggle against his fellow-countrymen than at Pharsalia. It was on the coast of Africa that the tide of flight had cast ashore the remnants of the shipwrecked faction—remnants, indeed, one can hardly call them, but rather material for a fresh war. Their forces had been scattered

magis quam oppressae vires erant; auxerat sacramentum ipsa clades imperatoris, nec degenerabat ducum successio. Quippe satis ample sonabant[1] in Pompeiani nominis locum Cato et Scipio. Accessit copiis Mauretaniae rex Iuba, videlicet ut
66 latius vinceret Caesar. Nihil ergo inter Pharsaliam et Thapson, nisi quod amplior; eoque acrior Caesareanorum impetus fuit, indignantium post Pompeium crevisse bellum; denique, quod alias numquam, ante imperium ducis sua sponte signa
67 cecinerunt. Strages[2] a Iuba coepit, cuius elephanti bellorum rudes et nuperi[3] a silva consternati subito clangore lituorum in suos sese circumegere. Statim exercitus in fugam, nec duces fortiores[4] quam ut effugerent. Non inconspicua tamen mors omnium.
68 Iam Scipio nave fugiebat; sed adsecutis hostibus gladium per viscera exegit et, ubi esset quodam requirente, respondit hoc ipsum, "Bene se habet
69 imperator." Iuba cum se recepisset in regiam, magnifice epulatus est postero die cum Petreio fugae comite superque mensas et pocula interficiendum se ei praebuit. Ille et regi suffecit et sibi, cum interim semesi in medio cibi et parentalia fercula

[1] sonabant: sonabat *B*: sanabant *L*.
[2] et primum *ante* strages *add. B*.
[3] nuperi *Heinsius*: nuper *codd.*
[4] fortiores *scripsi*: fortius *codd.*

---

[1] *i.e.* they had an additional obligation to avenge Pompeius' death.

rather than defeated, and the fate of their leader had in itself confirmed the obligation of their oath,[1] and they were no degenerate leaders who succeeded him; for the names of Cato and Scipio had a sufficiently imposing sound to take place of that of Pompeius. Juba, king of Mauretania, also joined their forces, apparently in order that Caesar might spread his conquests still more widely. There was no difference between Pharsalia and Thapsus, except that the latter was on a larger scale; also the attack of Caesar's troops was all the more vigorous because they were indignant that the war had assumed greater dimensions since Pompeius' death. Furthermore, the trumpeters gave the signal for the attack of their own accord before receiving the general's order—a thing which happened on no other occasion. The defeat began with Juba, whose elephants, unaccustomed to war and only recently brought from the woods, panic-stricken at the sudden noise of the trumpets, wheeled round and charged their own side. The army immediately turned to flight, nor were the generals too brave to flee; the deaths, however, of all of them were remarkable. Scipio was escaping on a ship, but, when the enemy came up with him, he thrust a sword right through his vitals; and when someone inquired where he was, he replied, "All is well with the general." Juba, having reached his palace, held a sumptuous banquet the following day with Petreius, the companion of his flight, and at the table, in the midst of his cups, offered himself to die at his hands. Petreius had courage enough for the king and himself, and the half-consumed meats, their funeral feast, on the table before them, were drenched with the blood of

70 regio[1] simul Romanoque sanguine madebant. Cato non interfuit bello. Positis apud Bagradam castris Vticam veluti altera Africae claustra servabat. Sed
71 accepta partium clade nihil cunctatus,[2] ut sapiente dignum erat, mortem sibi etiam laetus accivit. Nam postquam filium comitesque ab amplexu dimisit, in noctem lecto ad lucernam Platonis libro, qui inmortalitatem animae docet, paulum quieti dedit;
72 tunc circa primam vigiliam stricto gladio revelatum pectus semel iterumque percussit. Ausi post hoc virum medici violare fomentis. Ille passus, dum abscederent, rescidit plagas secutaque vi sanguinis moribundas manus in ipso volnere reliquit, quod ipse bis fecerat.

73 Quasi numquam esset dimicatum, sic arma rursus et partes, quantoque Africa supra Thessaliam fuit,
74 tanto Africam superabat Hispania. Plurimum quantum favoris partibus dabat fraternitas ducum et pro
75 uno duos stare Pompeios. Itaque nusquam atrocius nec tam ancipiti Marte concursum est. Primum in ipso ostio Oceani Varus[3] Didiusque legati conflixere. Sed acrius fuit cum ipso mari quam inter se navibus bellum, siquidem, quasi furorem civicum[4] castigaret,
76 Oceanus utramque classem naufragio cecidit. Quinam ille horror, cum eodem tempore fluctus,[5] procellae, viri, naves, armamenta[6] confligerent! Adde situs ipsius formidinem, vergentia[7] in unum hinc

[1] fercula regio: pericula quaeregio *B*.
[2] est *post* cunctatus *add B*.
[3] Varus: varius *B*.
[4] civicum: civium *B*: avicum *L*.
[5] fluctus: fluctibus *B*: fructus *NL*.
[6] armamenta: arma et armenta *B*.
[7] vergentia; urgentia *B*.

---

[1] The *Phaedo*.

the king and the Roman. Cato was not present at the fighting; having pitched his camp on the Bagradas, he was holding Utica as a second line for the defence of Africa. When, however, he received the news of the defeat of his party, he did not hesitate but cheerfully, as became a philosopher, called death to his aid. Having embraced and dismissed his son and the members of his staff, and having read far into the night by the light of a lamp the book of Plato which treats of the immortality of the soul,[1] he slept for a while and then, about the first watch, drew his sword and once and again struck his bared breast. After this the doctors with their fomentations must needs lay their vulgar hands upon this hero: he endured it until they departed, and then tore the wounds open and, a rush of blood ensuing, left his dying hands in the wound which he had twice dealt himself.

Just as though there had been no fighting hitherto, warfare and party spirit broke out afresh, and Spain outdid Africa, just as Africa surpassed Thessaly. The Pompeian party gained greatly in popularity from the fact that its leaders were brothers, and that two Pompeii took the place of one. Nowhere, therefore, were the encounters more bitter or the results so doubtful. First Varus and Didius, the lieutenant-generals, fought at the very mouth of the Ocean. But the ships had a harder struggle against the sea than against one another; for the Ocean, as though it were punishing the madness of civil war, destroyed both fleets by shipwreck. What a dread conflict was that in which waves, storms, men, ships and arms all strove together at the same time! Mark too the terrible nature of the battle-

Hispaniae, inde Mauritaniae litora, mare et intesti-
num et externum inminentesque Herculis speculas,
cum omnia undique simul proelio et tempestate
77 saevirent. Mox circa obsidionem urbium utrimque
discursum est, quae miserae inter hos atque illos
duces societatis Romanae[1] poenas dabant. Omnium
78 postrema certaminum Munda. Hic non pro cetera
felicitate, sed anceps et diu triste proelium, ut plane
79 videretur nescio quid deliberare[2] Fortuna. Sane
et ipse ante aciem maestior non ex more Caesar,
sive[3] respectu[4] fragilitatis humanae, sive nimiam
prosperorum suspectam habens continuationem, vel
eadem timens, postquam idem esse coeperat quod
Pompeius; et[5] in ipso proelio, quod nemo umquam
80 meminerat, cum diu pari Marte acies nihil amplius
quam occiderent, in medio ardore pugnantium subito
ingens inter utrosque silentium, quasi convenisset
81 et hic[6] omnium sensus esset, "quo usque illud?"
Novissime[7] inusitatum Caesaris oculis nefas: post
quattuordecim annos probata veteranorum manus
gradum retro dedit, quos, etsi nondum fugerant[8]
apparuit tamen pudore magis quam virtute resistere.
82 Itaque ille ablegato equo similis furenti primam in
aciem procurrit. Ibi prensare fugientis, confirmare

[1] Romanae: romae *B*.
[2] deliberare: liberare *B*.
[3] Caesar sive: caesaris sue *B*: cesar sui *L*.
[4] respectu: respectum *B*: respectus *NL*.
[5] et *Iahnius*: sed *codd.* [6] hic *NL*: in hic B.
[7] illud? novissime: illum novissime *B*: novissime illud *NL*.
[8] fugerant *Heinsius*: fugerat *codd.*

field—the shores of Spain closing in on one side and those of Mauretania on the other, an outer and an inner sea, and the Watch-towers of Hercules overhanging them, while all around was the rage of battle and of storm. Soon after this both sides scattered in different directions to besiege the unhappy cities, which, between the leaders on one side and the other, paid a heavy price for their alliance with Rome. The final struggle took place at Munda. On this occasion Caesar's usual good fortune was lacking, and the struggle was for a long time doubtful and anxious; so much so that Fortune seemed clearly to be deliberating some strange issue. Caesar himself too before the battle was unusually depressed, either from a consideration of human weakness, or because he felt doubtful whether his good luck, having lasted so long, would continue, or else because, having started on the same career as Pompeius, he feared that the same fate might befall him. In the battle itself too an incident occurred which was unparalleled in men's memory: when the two armies, being evenly matched, had long been simply cutting one another down, suddenly, at the height of the battle, silence fell upon both hosts, as though by mutual agreement and as if everyone was asking himself "What was to be the end of it all?" Finally, an unaccustomed disgrace presented itself to Caesar's eyes: his tried band of veterans, after fourteen years of service, gave ground, and though they had not gone so far as to flee, yet it was obvious that shame rather than valour made them resist. Sending away his horse, Caesar rushed forward like a madman to the forefront of the battle, where he seized hold of those who were fleeing, heartened the standard-bearers, uttered

signiferos, orare hortari increpare, per totum denique
83 agmen oculis manibus clamore volitare. Dicitur in
illa perturbatione et de extremis agitasse secum ma-
nifestoque voltu fuisse, quasi occupare mortem manu
vellet; nisi [1] cohortes hostium quinque per trans-
versam aciem actae, quas Labienus periclitantibus
castris praesidio miserat, speciem fugae praebuissent.
84 Hoc aut et [2] ipse credidit aut dux callidus arripuit
in occasionem, et quasi in fugientes et iam victos [3]
simul et suorum erexit animos et hostis perculit.
Nam et hi, dum se putant vincere, fortius sequi, et
Pompeiani, dum fugere credunt suos, fugere coepe-
85 runt. Quanta fuerit hostibus caedendis [4] ira rabies-
que victoribus, sic aestimare posses,[5] quod a proelio
profugi cum se Mundam recepissent, et Caesar
obsideri statim victos [6] imperasset, congestis cada-
veribus agger effectus est, quae pilis tragulisque [7]
confixa inter se tenebantur,—foedum etiam in
86 barbaros. Sed videlicet victoriam desperantibus
Pompei liberis, Gnaeum proelio profugum, crure
saucium,[8] deserta et avia petentem Caesonius apud
Lauronem oppidum consecutus, pugnantem—adeo
87 nondum desperabat—interfecit; Sextum fortuna in

[1] quod *post* nisi *add. codd. praeter Rehd.*
[2] aut et: autem et *B.*
[3] iam victos *Iahnius*: invictos *B.*
[4] caedendis B^1: caedentis *B.*
[5] posses *scripsi*: posset *B.*
[6] victos: victor *B.*
[7] pilis tragulisque *Rossbachius*: plaustri stragulisque *B*. pilis iaculisque *NL.*

prayers, exhortations and rebukes, and, in a word, dashed this way and that through the ranks with glances, gestures and shouts. In the turmoil he is even said to have meditated making an end of himself and to have shown clearly by his expression that he wished to take his own life; only, at that moment, five cohorts of the enemy, which had been sent by Labienus to protect the camp, which was in danger, crossed the battle-field and suggested an appearance of flight. Caesar either actually believed that the enemy was fleeing or else craftily made use of the incident and gave them heart against an enemy, who they thought was fleeing and already conquered, while he discouraged the foe. His men, thinking that they were winning the day, followed more boldly, while the Pompeians, thinking that their own side was in flight, began to flee. How great was the rage and fury of the victors in the slaughter of the enemy can be gathered from the fact that, when the fugitives had retreated to Munda, and Caesar immediately ordered that his conquered foes should be besieged, a rampart was constructed of corpses piled up and held together by the javelins and missiles which were thrust through them—an expedient which would have been horrible even if it had been used against barbarians. Pompeius' sons clearly had no longer any hope of victory; Gnaeus Pompeius, a fugitive from the battle-field and wounded in the leg, was overtaken, as he was seeking some solitary and inaccessible place of refuge, by Caesonius near the town of Lauro, and was killed, still showing enough spirit to resist; Fortune allowed Sextus Pompeius to remain hidden

[8] crure saucium: cruore avium *B*: crure saucio *NL*.

Celtiberia interim abscondit aliisque post Caesarem
bellis servavit.
88 Caesar in patriam victor invehitur, primum de
Gallia triumphum trahens: hic erat Rhenus et
Rhodanus et ex auro captivus Oceanus. Altera
laurus Aegyptia: tunc in ferculis Nilus, Arsinoe
89 et ad simulacrum ignium ardens Pharos. Tertius
de Pharnace currus et Ponto. Quartus Iubam et
Mauretaniam et bis subactam ostendebat Hispaniam.
Pharsalia[1] et Thapsos et Munda nusquam. Et
quanto maiora erant, de quibus non triumphabat!
90 Hic aliquando finis armis fuit; reliqua pax in-
cruenta pensatumque clementia bellum. Nemo
caesus imperio praeter Afranium (satis ignoverat
semel) et Faustum Sullam (docuerat generos timere
Pompeius) filiamque Pompei cum parvulis[2] ex
91 Sulla[3] (hic posteris cavebatur). Itaque non ingratis
civibus omnes in principem congesti honores: circa
templa imagines, in theatro distincta radiis corona,
suggestus in curia, fastigium in domo, mensis in
caelo, ad hoc pater ipse patriae perpetuusque dic-
tator, novissime, dubium an ipso volente,[4] oblata

[1] Pharsalia: pharsaliam *B*.
[2] cum parvulis *Perizonius*: et parvulus *B*: cum patruolis *N*: cum patruelis *L*.
[3] ex Sulla *N*: exylla *BL*.
[4] volente *om. B*.

---

[1] Arsinoe, sister of Cleopatra, actually figured in the procession (Dio Cass. XLIII, 19).

[2] Pompeius, having married Julia, was son-in-law of Caesar; but Faustus Sulla was no relative by marriage to Caesar, having married a daughter of Pompeius by another wife, Julia having been childless.

[3] Hirtius, *de bell. Afric.* 95, states that Caesar pardoned Pompeius' daughter and her children.

for the moment in Celtiberia and preserved him to fight again after Caesar's time.

Caesar returned home victorious and celebrated a triumph first over Gaul, in which figured the Rhine and the Rhone and the captive Ocean represented in gold. A second triumph was celebrated for the conquest of Egypt; on this occasion the Nile, Arsinoe,[1] and the Pharos lighted with a semblance of flames was displayed on moving platforms. A third procession celebrated the victory over Pharnaces of Pontus; a fourth set forth the defeat of Juba and Mauretania and the two conquests of Spain. Pharsalia, Thapsus and Munda made no appearance; yet how much greater were the victories for which he had no triumph!

At this point there was at last an end of fighting; the ensuing peace was free from bloodshed, and clemency made atonement for war. No one was put to death by Caesar's orders except Afranius (it was enough that Caesar had once pardoned him) and Faustus Sulla (for the example of Pompeius had taught Caesar to be afraid of sons-in-law),[2] and Pompeius' daughter and her children by Sulla,[3] as a precaution for posterity. His fellow-citizens were not ungrateful and heaped every kind of honour upon him as sole ruler. Statues of him were set up in the temples; in the theatre he wore a crown adorned with rays; he had a raised chair in the senate-house; a high gable was added to his house; a month in the calendar was named after him. In addition to this he was called Father of his Country and Perpetual Dictator. Finally—though it is doubtful whether it was by his own wish—he was offered the insignia of royalty in front of

92 pro rostris ab Antonio consule regni insignia. Quae
omnia velut infulae in destinatam morti victimam
congerebantur. Quippe clementiam principis vicit
invidia, gravisque erat liberis ipsa beneficiorum
93 potentia. Nec diutius lata[1] dominatio est, sed
Brutus et Cassius aliique patres consensere in caedem
94 principis. Quanta vis fati! Manaverat late coniu-
ratio, libellus etiam Caesari datus eodem die, nec
perlitare centum victimis potuerat. Venit in curiam
95 tamen expeditionem Parthicam meditans. Ibi in
curuli sedentem eum senatus invasit, tribusque et
viginti volneribus ad terram datus est. Sic ille, qui
terrarum orbem civili sanguine impleverat, tandem
ipse sanguine suo curiam implevit.

XIIII. Res svb Caesare Avgvsto

IIII, 3 Populus Romanus Caesare et Pompeio trucidatis
redisse in statum pristinum libertatis videbatur. Et
2 redierat, nisi aut Pompeius[2] liberos aut Caesar here-
dem reliquisset, vel, quod utroque perniciosius fuit,
si non collega quondam, mox aemulus Caesareanae
potentiae,[3] fax et turbo sequentis saeculi superfuisset
3 Antonius. Quippe dum Sextus paterna repetit,
trepidatum toto mari; dum Octavius mortem patris
4 ulciscitur, iterum fuit movenda Thessalia; dum

[1] lata: dilata *B*. [2] aut Pompeius: ad pompeii *B*.
[3] potentiae: potentiam *B*.

the *rostra* by the consul Antonius. But all these things were, as it were, decorations heaped upon a victim doomed to die; for the envy which he inspired influenced men more than his clemency, and his very power to confer favours was intolerable to free citizens. His rule was not long endured; Brutus and Cassius and other senators conspired together to kill their leader. How powerful is fate! The plot had become widely known; on the very day fixed for its execution, written information of it had been presented to Caesar, and, though he sacrificed a hundred victims, he had been unable to obtain favourable omens. Yet he came into the senate-house thinking of his campaign against Parthia. As he was seated there in his curule chair the senators attacked him, and he was borne to the ground wounded in twenty-three places. Thus he who had filled the whole world with the blood of his fellow-citizens at last filled the senate-house with his own.

XIIII. The State under Caesar Augustus

3. The Roman people, after the murders of Caesar and Pompeius, seemed to have returned to their former state of liberty; and they would have done so if either Pompeius had left no children or Caesar no heir, or, what was still more fatal than either of these circumstances, if Antonius, once Caesar's colleague and afterwards his rival in power, had not survived to cause fire and storm in the succeeding age. For Sextus Pompeius sought to recover his father's inheritance, with the result that there was alarm over the whole sea; Octavius sought to avenge his father's death, and Thessaly was again to be

Antonius vario ingenio aut successorem Caesaris
indignatur Octavium aut amore Cleopatrae desciscit
in regem[1] *** . Nam aliter salvus esse non potuit,
5 nisi confugisset ad servitutem. Gratulandum tamen
ut in tanta perturbatione est, quod potissimum ad
Octavium Caesarem Augustum summa rerum redit,
qui sapientia sua atque sollertia perculsum undique
6 ac perturbatum ordinavit imperii corpus, quod haud
dubie numquam coire et consentire potuisset, nisi
unius praesidis nutu quasi anima et mente regeretur.
7 Marco Antonio Publio Dolabella consulibus imperium
Romanum iam ad Caesarem transferente fortuna
varius et multiplex motus civitatis fuit. Quodque
in annua caeli conversione[2] fieri solet, ut mota
8 sidera tonent ac suos flexus tempestate significent,
sic tum Romanae dominationis, id est humani
generis, conversione penitus intremuit omnique
genere discriminum, civilibus, externis, servilibus
terrestribus ac navalibus bellis omne imperii corpus
agitatum est.

XV. Bellvm Mvtinense

IIII, 4 Prima civilium motuum causa testamentum Caesaris fuit, cuius secundus heres Antonius, praelatum sibi Octavium furens, inexpiabile contra adoptionem

[1] *post* regem *spatium vacuum octo circiter litterarum B.*
[2] conversione : conversatione *B.*

disquieted; Antonius, fickle as ever, either refused to tolerate Octavius as the successor of Caesar, or else, for love of Cleopatra, degenerated into a king, and . . .[1] For the Roman people could find no salvation except by taking refuge in subservience. It was, however, a ground for congratulation that, in that great upheaval, the chief power passed into the hands of none other than Octavius Caesar Augustus, who by his wisdom and skill restored order in the body of the empire, everywhere paralyzed and confused, which certainly would never have been able to achieve coherence and harmony unless it had been controlled by the will of a single ruler which formed, as it were, its soul and mind. In the consulship of Marcus Antonius and Publius Dolabella,[2] while fortune was already transferring the Roman Empire to Caesar, diverse and manifold confusion afflicted the State. Just as, in the annual revolutions of the heavens, the constellations by their movements cause thunder and make known their changes of position by storms, so, in the change which came over the Roman dominion, that is, the whole world, the body of the empire trembled through and through and was disturbed by every kind of peril, by wars, civil, foreign, and against slaves, by land and by sea.

XV. The War round Mutina

4. The first cause of civil dissension was Caesar's will; for his second heir, Antonius, furious because Octavius had been preferred to himself, had engaged in an implacable war to prevent the adoption of

[1] There is a lacuna in the best MS. at this point.
[2] 44 B.C.

2 acerrimi iuvenis susceperat bellum. Quippe cum
intra octavum decimum annum tenerum et obnox-
ium et opportunum iniuriae iuvenem videret, se
plenae[1] ex commilitio Caesaris dignitatis, lacerare
furtis[2] hereditatem,[3] ipsum insectari probris, cunctis
3 artibus cooptationem Iuliae gentis inhibere, denique
ad opprimendum iuvenem palam arma moliri, et iam
parato exercitu in Cisalpina Gallia resistentem moti-
4 bus suis Decimum Brutum obsidere. At[4] Octavius
Caesar, et aetate et iniuria favorabilis et nominis
maiestate quod sibi induerat, revocatis ad arma
veteranis, privatus—quis crederet?[5]—consulem ad-
5 greditur, obsidione Mutinae liberat Brutum, Anto-
nium exuit castris. Tunc quidem etiam manu
pulcher apparuit. Nam cruentus et saucius aquilam
a moriente signifero traditam suis umeris in castra
referebat.

XVI. Bellvm Pervsinvm

IIII, 5 Alterum bellum concitavit agrorum divisio, quod
2 Caesar veteranis patris pretium militiae persolvebat.
Semper alias Antonii pessimum ingenium Fulvia
tum[6] gladio cincta virilis militiae uxor agitabat.
Ergo depulsos agris colonos incitando iterum arma

[1] se plenae *scripsi*: is plenae *B*: ·se· plene *L*.
[2] furtis: viri fortis *B*: fortis (o *in* u *mut.*) *L*.
[3] et heredem *ante* hereditatem *add.* *B*.
[4] obsidere. At *Iahnius*: obsiderat *B*: obsidebat *NL*.
[5] crederet: credere *B*.
[6] tum *Mommsenus*: ut *B*.

that high-spirited youth. Looking upon Octavius, who was under eighteen years of age, as a lad of tender years and a fit and easy victim of injustice, and upon himself as enjoying all the prestige of his long service with Caesar, Antonius proceeded to destroy his inheritance by embezzlement, to pursue him with personal insults, and to hinder his adoption into the Julian family by every device in his power; finally, he took up arms openly with the object of crushing his youthful rival and, having formed an army, besieged Decimus Brutus, who, in Cisalpine Gaul, was opposing his movements. Octavius Caesar, however, winning popularity from his youth, his wrongs, and the dignity of the name which he had assumed, recalled the veterans to arms, and—what is scarcely credible—though he was holding no office, attacked the consul, released Brutus by relieving Mutina, and captured Antonius' camp. On this occasion indeed he also showed his gallantry by an act of personal courage; for, though bleeding and wounded, he took an eagle from the hands of a dying standard-bearer and bore it back upon his shoulder to the camp.

XVI. The War round Perusia

5. The distribution of lands to the soldiers was the cause of another war; for Caesar assigned land to his father's veterans as a reward for their services. Though the nature of Antonius was always evil, on this occasion his wife Fulvia, girding herself with the sword of her husband's service, egged him on yet more. He had, therefore, stirred up further hostilities by rousing the farmers who had been dis-

3 cierat.[1] Hic vero iam non [2] privatis, sed totius senatus suffragiis iudicatum hostem Caesar adgressus intra Perusiae muros redegit [3] conpulitque ad extrema deditionis turpi et nihil non experta fame.

Trivmviratvs

IIII, 6 Cum solus etiam gravis paci,[4] gravis rei publicae esset Antonius, quasi ignis incendio Lepidus accessit. Quid [5] contra duos consules, duos exercitus? Necesse fuit venire in cruentissimi foederis societatem. Diversa omnium vota, ut ingenia.
2 Lepidum divitiarum cupido, quarum spes erat ex perturbatione rei publicae, Antonium ultionis [6] de his qui se hostem iudicassent, Caesarem inultus pater et manibus eius graves Cassius et Brutus
3 agitabant. In hoc velut foedus pax inter tres duces conponitur. Apud Confluentes inter Perusiam et Bononiam iungunt manus, et exercitus consalutant. Nullo bono more triumviratus invaditur, oppressaque armis re publica redit Sullana proscriptio, cuius atrocitas nihil insignius [7] habet quam numerum centum
4 et quadraginta senatorum. Exitus foedi, truces, miserabiles toto terrarum orbe fugientium. Quis pro indignitate ingemescat, cum Antonius Lucium

[1] arma cierat *Hauptius*: in arma revocaverat *B*: in arma ierat *NL*.

[2] non *om. B.*

[3] redegit *L*: redigit *B.*

[4] gravis paci *om. B.*

[5] quid *Graevius*: cui *B.*

[6] ultionis: ultionem *B.*

[7] insignius *Mommsenus*: in se minus *codd.*

---

[1] *i.e.* that of the previous triumvirate of Julius Caesar, Pompeius and Crassus.

possessed of their lands. He was thereupon declared a public enemy not merely in the judgment of private citizens but by the votes of the whole senate, and Caesar, attacking him, drove him within the walls of Perusia, and by the humiliating device of starvation, against which he tried every expedient, finally reduced him to surrender.

The Triumvirate

6. Although Antonius by himself was a sufficient menace to peace and to the State, Lepidus joined him and thus, as it were, added fire to fire. What could be done against two consuls and two armies? Caesar was forced to become a party to a horrible compact. The three leaders were as different in their aims as in their characters. Lepidus was actuated by a desire for wealth, which he might expect to gain from confusion in the State; Antonius desired vengeance upon those who had declared him an enemy; Caesar was spurred on by the thought that his father's death was still unpunished and that the survival of Cassius and Brutus was an insult to his departed spirit. Under a compact for these objects peace was concluded between the three leaders. At Confluentes between Perusia and Bononia they joined hands, and the armies saluted one another. The formation of the triumvirate followed a bad precedent,[1] and with the overthrow of the constitution by arms, the Sullan proscription came back. Its most remarkable act of atrocity was the murder of as many as a hundred and forty senators. Shocking, brutal and pitiable deaths in every part of the world awaited those who escaped. What lamentation can do justice to the disgrace involved in the

Caesarem avunculum suum, Lepidus Lucium Paulum
5 fratrem suum proscripserint? Romae[1] capita caesorum proponere in rostris iam usitatum erat; verum sic quoque civitas lacrimas tenere non potuit, cum recisum Ciceronis caput in illis suis rostris videret, nec aliter ad videndum eum, quam solebat ad
6 audiendum, concurreretur. Haec scelera in Antonii Lepidique tabulis: Caesar percussoribus patris contentus fuit, ideo ne, si inulta fuisset, etiam iusta eius caedes haberetur.

XVII. Bellvm Cassi et Brvti

IIII, 7 Brutus et Cassius sic Caesarem quasi Tarquinium regem depulisse[2] regno videbantur,[3] sed libertatem, quam maxime restitutam voluerunt, illo ipso parri-
2 cidio perdiderunt. Igitur caede perfecta cum veteranos Caesaris, nec inmerito, timerent, statim e curia in Capitolium confugerant. Nec illis ad ultionem deerat animus, sed ducem nondum habe-
3 bant. Igitur cum appareret, quae strages rei publicae inmineret, displicuit ultio, cum caedes inprobaretur.
4 Igitur Ciceronis consiliis abolitione decreta, ne tamen publici doloris oculos ferirent, in provincias ab illo ipso quem occiderant Caesare datas, Syriam

[1] Romae: romanae *B.* [2] depulisse: depulisset *B.* [3] videbantur: videbatur *B.*

proscription by Antonius of his uncle Lucius Caesar, and of his brother Lucius Paulus by Lepidus? It had long been customary to expose on the *rostra* at Rome the heads of those who had been executed; but, even so, the citizens could not restrain their tears when they saw the severed head of Cicero on those very *rostra* which he had made his own, and men rushed to gaze upon him as once they were wont to crowd to listen to him. These crimes were the result of the proscription-lists of Antonius and Lepidus; Caesar contented himself with proscribing his father's murderers, for fear lest his death might be considered to have been deserved if it had remained unavenged.

XVII. The War against Cassius and Brutus

7. Brutus and Cassius seemed to have cast forth Caesar from the throne like another King Tarquin; yet by that very act of murder they destroyed that liberty, the restoration of which was their dearest wish. After the deed had been committed, being, not without reason, afraid of Caesar's veterans, they had immediately left the senate-house and taken refuge in the Capitol. They were not without the courage to avenge Caesar, but they were as yet without a leader. So, since it was manifest what a calamity was threatening the State, the idea of vengeance was rejected, though the murder met with disapprobation. Therefore although on the advice of Cicero an amnesty was passed, yet, to avoid offending the gaze of the sorrowful populace, the murderers had withdrawn to Syria and Macedonia, the provinces which had been assigned to them by Caesar, the

et Macedoniam concesserant. Sic vindicta Caesaris
dilata potius quam oppressa est.
5 Igitur iam ordinata magis ut poterat quam ut
debebat inter triumviros re publica, relicto ad urbis
praesidium Lepido, Caesar cum Antonio in Cassium
6 Brutumque succingitur. Illi comparatis ingentibus
copiis eandem illam, quae fatalis Gnaeo Pompeio
fuit, harenam insederant. Sed nec tum [1] inminentia
7 cladis destinatae signa latuerunt.[2] Nam et signis
insedit examen et adsuetae cadaverum pabulo volu-
cres castra [3] quasi iam sua circumvolabant, et in
8 aciem prodeuntibus obvius Aethiops [4] nimis aperte
ferale signum fuit. Ipsique Bruto per noctem, cum
inlato lumine ex more aliqua secum agitaret, atra
quaedam imago se obtulit et, quae esset interrogata,
"Tuus" inquit "malus genius," ac [5] sub oculis
9 mirantis evanuit. Pari in meliora praesagio in
Caesaris castris omnia aves victimaeque promiserant.
Sed nihil illo praestantius, quod Caesaris medicus
somnio admonitus est,[6] ut Caesar castris excederet,
10 quibus capi inminebat; ut factum est. Acie namque
commissa cum pari ardore aliquandiu dimicatum
foret, et [7] quamvis duces inde praesentes adessent,
hinc alterum corporis aegritudo, illum metus et
ignavia subduxissent, stabat [8] tamen pro partibus

[1] tum: tot *B*.
[2] inminentia cladis destinatae signa latuerunt *N*: imminentia destinate cladis latuerunt *B*.
[3] castra *om. B*. [4] Aethiops: aethiope *B*.
[5] ac: hoc *B*. [6] est *om. BN*. [7] et *om. BN*.
[8] stabat *Salmasius*: staret *B*: starent *NL*.

---

[1] See note on p. 280. [2] Augustus.
[3] Antonius. Plutarch (*vit. Ant.* 28) merely observes, "According to some, Antonius was absent from the battle

very man whom they had murdered. Thus revenge for Caesar was delayed rather than stifled.

The governing power having been distributed between the triumvirs rather as it could be than it should be, Caesar and Antonius prepared to make war on Cassius and Brutus, while Lepidus remained behind to guard the capital. Brutus and Cassius, having collected vast forces, had occupied the same ground as had been fatal to Gnaeus Pompeius.[1] On this occasion too threatening signs of impending disaster were not lacking. A swarm of bees settled on the standards; the birds which usually feed upon corpses flew round the camp, as though it were already their prey; and an Ethiopian who met the troops as they were marching to battle was only too clearly an omen of disaster. Also, while Brutus himself was meditating at night, according to his custom, with a lamp at his side, a gloomy phantom presented itself, and on being asked who it was replied, "I am your evil genius," and then vanished from his wondering sight. In Caesar's camp birds and victims had with equal clearness given every promise of better fortune. The most striking incident was that Caesar's physician was warned in a dream that Caesar should quit his camp, which was on the point of being captured. And this actually happened; for when the battle had begun and both sides had been fighting for some time with equal ardour and, though on one side both generals were present, on the other side one[2] had been kept away by illness, the other[3] by fear and cowardice, yet the

and did not reach the field until his men were already in pursuit of the enemy."

invicta fortuna et ultoris et qui vindicabatur, ut[1]
exitus proelii docuit. Primum adeo anceps fuit,
11 ut—par utrimque[2] discrimen—capta sint[3] hinc
Caesaris castra, inde Cassi.[4] Sed quanto efficacior est
fortuna, quam virtus! Et quam verum est, quod
moriens ⟨Brutus⟩[5] efflavit, non in re, sed in verbo
tantum esse virtutem! Victoriam illi proelio error[6]
12 dedit. Cassius, inclinato cornu suorum, cum captis
Caesaris castris rapido impetu recipientes se equites
13 videret, fugere arbitratus evadit in tumulum. Inde
pulvere et strepitu, etiam nocte vicina eximentibus
gestae rei sensum, cum speculator quoque in id
missus tardius nuntiaret, transactum de partibus
ratus uni ex proximis auferendum praebuit caput.
14 Brutus cum in Cassio etiam suum animum perdi-
disset, ne quid ex constituti fide resignaret, (ita
enim non superesse[7] bello convenerat) ipse quoque
uni comitum suorum confodiendum praebuit latus.
15 Quis sapientissimos ac fortissimos viros non miretur
ad ultimum non suis manibus usos? Nisi hoc quoque
ex persuasione[8] sectae fuit, ne violarent manus, sed
in amolitione fortissimarum piissimarumque animarum
iudicio suo, scelere alieno uterentur.

[1] ut *om. B.*
[2] utrimque *Palat. Rehd.* : utrumque *BN.*
[3] sint *Spengelius* : sunt *codd.*
[4] Cassi : classi *B* : cassii *N* : cassias *L.*
[5] Brutus *add. Tollius* : *cf. Dio Cass.* XLVII, 49.
[6] error : errore *B.*
[7] superesse : superesset *B.*
[8] persuasione *N* : suasione *B.*

---

[1] This quotation is singularly inept, since *virtus* was used by Brutus in the sense of moral virtue, whereas Florus interprets it in the sense of military valour.

invincible good fortune both of the avenger and of him who was being avenged supported their cause, as the result of the battle proved. At first the issue was so doubtful that, danger threatening both sides alike, the camp of Caesar was captured on the one hand and that of Cassius on the other. But how much more powerful is fortune than valour, and how true it is, as the dying Brutus said with his last breath, that virtue exists not in reality but in name only![1] A mistake decided the victory in this battle. Cassius, at a moment when the wing of his army had given way, on seeing the cavalry returning at full speed after the capture of Caesar's camp, thought that they were in flight and made his way to some higher ground. Here, when the dust and confusion and the approaching darkness prevented him from seeing what had happened, and a scout whom he had sent out to obtain news was slow in bringing it, thinking that his cause was lost, he made one of those who were standing by cut off his head. Brutus, having lost his second self by the death of Cassius, in order that he might not fail in carrying out every detail of their compact (for it had been agreed that neither of them should survive the battle), presented his side to one of his companions that he might plunge his sword into it. Who can but wonder that these wise and brave men did not die by their own hands? But it was perhaps a further example of their adherence to their philosophic principles, that they should not stain their hands with blood, but that, for the destruction of their brave and pious lives, though the decision to die was their own, they should employ the hands of others to execute the crime.

XVIII. Bellvm cvm Sexto Pompeio

IIII, 8 Sublatis percussoribus Caesaris supererat Pompei domus. Alter iuvenum in Hispania occiderat, alter fuga evaserat contractisque infelicis belli reliquiis, cum insuper ergastula armasset, Siciliam Sardiniamque habebat; iam et classe medium mare insederat.
2 O quam diversus a patre! Ille Cilicas extinxerat, hic se piratica tuebatur. Puteolos,[1] Formias, Vulturnum, totam denique Campaniam, Pontias et Aenariam,[2] ipsa Tiberini fluminis ora populatus est. Subinde congressus[3] Caesaris naves et incendit et demersit;[4] nec ipse tantum, sed Menas[5] et Menecrates, foeda servitia, quos classi praefecerat, prae-
3 dabundi[6] per litora cuncta volitabant. Ob haec tot prospera centum bubus auratis Peloro litavit spirantemque equum cum auro in fretum misit, dona Neptuno,[7] ut se maris rector in suo mari regnare pateretur. Eo denique discriminum ventum est, ut foedus et[8] pax cum hoste—si modo hostis Pompei
4 filius—tamen feriretur. Quantum id, sed breve gaudium fuit, cum in Baiani litoris mole de reditu eius et bonorum restitutione convenit, cumque invitante ipso in navem discubitum est, et ille sortem suam increpitans "hae sunt" inquit "carinae

[1] tuebatur. Puteolos *Bezzenbergerus*: turbatur per (= *pn* = *proprium nomen*) puteolos *B.*
[2] Aenariam: tenariam *B.*
[3] congressus: congressas *B.*
[4] demersit: emersit *B.*
[5] Menas: mensas *B.*
[6] praedabundi *Halmius*: praedendi *B.*
[7] hoc putabant *post* Neptuno *add. B, del Hauptius.*
[8] et: ut *B.*

---

[1] *Medium mare* seems to mean the sea in the middle of the Roman Empire, *i.e.* in the neighbourhood of Italy.

XVIII. The War against Sextus Pompeius

8. Though Caesar's assassins had been thus removed, Pompeius' family still survived. One of his young sons had fallen in Spain, but the other had escaped by flight, and after collecting the survivors of their unsuccessful war and also arming the slave-prisons, was holding Sicily and Sardinia. He had also already occupied the central sea [1] with his fleet. But how great the difference between him and his father! The latter had exterminated the Cilician pirates, his son protected himself by piracy. He ravaged Puteoli, Formiae, Vulturnum, in a word, the whole coast of Campania, the Pontine marshes, Aenaria and even the mouth of the river Tiber. Then, meeting with Caesar's fleet, he burnt and sank it; and not only Pompeius himself, but also Menas and Menecrates, base slaves whom he had put in command of his fleet, made sudden raids in search of plunder along all the coasts. In return for all these successes he made a sacrifice of a hundred bulls with gilded horns at Pelorum and flung a living horse with an offering of gold into the straits as gifts to Neptune, in order to induce the ruler of the sea to allow him to reign in his domain. At last the danger became so great that a treaty of peace was concluded with the enemy—if a son of Pompeius can be called an enemy. How great was the joy (though it was short-lived), when an agreement was made on the embankment on the shores of Baiae permitting his return and the restitution of his property, and when, at his invitation, they dined on board his ship, and railing against his fate, he said, "There are keels (*carinae*) where I live"— a

meae"; haud incomiter, quod, cum in celeberrima parte urbis Carinis pater eius habitasset, ipsius
5 domus et penates in navi penderent. Sed inportunitate[1] Antonii, et Pompeianorum bonorum, quorum sector ille fuerat, praeda devorata, possessio manere non poterat; detrectare coepit foederis pactum. Itaque itum[2] ad arma rursus, et iam totis[3] imperii viribus classis in iuvenem conparata est, cuius molitio
6 ipsa magnifica. Quippe interciso Herculanae viae limite refossisque litoribus Lucrinus lacus mutatus in portum eique interrupto medio additus est Avernus, ut in illa aquarum[4] quiete classis exercita
7 imaginem belli navalis agitaret. Tanta mole belli petitus in Siculo freto iuvenis oppressus est, magnique famam ducis ad inferos secum tulisset, si nihil temptasset ulterius; nisi quod magnae indolis signum
8 est sperare semper. Perditis enim rebus profugit Asiamque velis petit, venturus[5] ibi in manus hostium et catenas et, quod miserrimum est fortibus viris, ad
9 hostium arbitrium sub percussore moriturus. Non

[1] inportunitate *Iahnius*: inportu *B.*
[2] itum *Halmius*: inille *B.*
[3] et iam totis *Halmius*: et intotis *B.*
[4] illa aquarum: illae quarum *B.*
[5] venturus: ventus *B.*

---

[1] It is impossible to keep up the play upon the word *carinae* (keels), which was also the name of a district of Rome.

witty remark,[1] seeing that his father had lived in Carinae, the most fashionable quarter of the capital, while his own home and his household gods tossed in a ship. But owing to the incivility of Antonius and because the spoil from Pompeius' property, of which Antonius had been the purchaser, had been squandered, the entry of Sextus into possession of his estates could not be sustained; thus Pompeius began to back out of the pact of agreement. So recourse was had to arms again, and a fleet was now equipped with all the resources of the Empire against the young leader. Preparations for it were made on a magnificent scale; for by cutting through the track of the Herculean Way and digging up the shore,[2] the Lucrine Lake was turned into a harbour and the Lake of Avernus added to it by cutting away the ground between, in order that manœuvring on these quiet waters the fleet might practise a semblance of naval warfare. The young commander was brought to action by this superior force and defeated in the Sicilian straits, and would have carried with him to the grave the reputation of a great leader if he had attempted nothing further; but it is a characteristic of genius never to lose hope. When his position became desperate, he fled away and made sail for Asia, only to fall there into the hands of the enemy and to suffer imprisonment and undergo the most wretched fate which can befall a brave man, namely, death by the sword of the executioner at the bidding of his foes. There had been no such pitiable

[2] *i.e.* by removing the narrow strip of land which separated the Lucrine Lake from the sea and carried the road (Via Herculea) between Baiae and Puteoli.

alia post Xerxen miserabilior fuga. Quippe modo trecentarum quinquaginta navium dominus cum sex septemve fugiebat extincto praetoriae[1] navis lumine, anulis in mare abiectis, pavens atque respectans, et tamen non timens nisi ne periret.

XVIIII. Bellvm Parthicvm svb Ventidio

iiii, 9 Quamvis in Cassio et Bruto partes sustulisset, in Pompeio totum partium nomen abolevisset, nondum tamen ad pacis stabilitatem profecerat Caesar, cum scopulus et nodus et mora publicae securitatis
2 superesset Antonius. Nec ille defuit vitiis quin periret, immo omnia expertus ambitu[2] et luxuria primum hostes, deinde cives, tandem etiam saeculum terrore[3] liberavit.
3 Parthi clade Crassiana altius animos erexerant civilesque populi Romani[4] discordias laeti acceperant.[5] Itaque ut prima adfulsit occasio, non du-
4 bitaverunt erumpere, ultro quidem invitante Labieno, qui missus a Cassio Brutoque—qui furor scelerum—sollicitaverat hostes in auxilium. Et illi Pacoro duce, regio iuvene, dispulerant Antoniana

[1] praetoriae: portitoriae *B*: praetorio *NL*.
[2] ambitu: ambitus *B*.
[3] saeculum terrore *Halmius*: terrore saeculum *B*.
[4] populi Romani: populus romanus *B*.
[5] regi *post* acceperant *add. B*.

---

[1] The meaning appears to be that Sextus Pompeius threw away his rings so that he might not be recognized by them if he were captured. Some commentators think that the reference is to the fetters worn by the rowers (*anulus*

flight since that of Xerxes; for he who had been but lately lord of three hundred and fifty ships fled with six or seven and with the lights extinguished on his flagship, after throwing his rings[1] into the sea, casting anxious looks behind him, though his only fear was lest he should fail to meet with death.

XVIIII. The Parthian War under Ventidius

9. Although, by the defeat of Cassius and Brutus, Caesar had demolished the republican faction and, by conquering Pompeius, had completely wiped out its very name, still he had not achieved a stable peace, as long as Antonius still survived, a rock in his path, an unsolved problem, an obstacle[2] to public security, However, owing to his vices, he did not fail to work his own destruction; nay more, by trying every expedient to which his ambition and luxury prompted him, he freed first his enemies, then his fellow-citizens, and finally the age in which he lived, from any fear which he had inspired.

The disaster of Crassus had further increased the confidence of the Parthians, and they had heard with joy of the internal discords of the Roman people. So, as soon as there was a gleam of hope, they did not hesitate to break out, being actually invited to do so by Labienus, who had been sent to Parthia by Cassius and Brutus, and—such was their mad fury—had urged the enemies of Rome to assist them. Under the leadership of Pacorus, a young prince, they had driven out the garrisons of An-

is used by Martial xiv. 169, in this sense), which were removed that they might make no noise.

[2] *Nodus et mora* is clearly a reminiscence of Vergil, *Aen.* x. 428, *pugnae nodumque moramque.*

praesidia; Saxa legatus ne veniret in potestatem
5 gladio[1] impetravit. Denique ablata Syria emanabat latius malum, hostibus sub auxilii specie sibi vincentibus, nisi Ventidius, et hic legatus Antonii, incredibili felicitate et Labieni copias ipsumque Pacorum et omnem Parthicum equitatum toto[2] inter
6 Oronten et Euphraten sinu late cecidisset. Viginti amplius milium fuit. Nec sine consilio ducis, qui simulato metu adeo passus est hostem castris succedere, donec absumpto iactus spatio adimeret usum
7 sagittarum. Rex fortissime dimicans cecidit. Mox circumlato eius per urbes, quae desciverant, capite Syria sine bello recepta. Sic Crassianam cladem Pacori caede pensavimus.

XX. Bellvm Parthicvm svb Antonio

IIII, 10 Expertis invicem Parthis atque Romanis, cum Crassus et Pacorus utrimque virium mutuarum documenta fecissent, pari rursus reverentia integrata amicitia, et quidem ab ipso foedus Antonio cum
2 rege percussum. Sed—inmensa vanitas hominis—dum titulorum cupidine Araxen et Euphraten sub imaginibus suis legi concupiscit, neque causa neque

[1] gladio *Vossius*: claudio *B*: aclaudio *NL*.
[2] equitatum toto: et que tantum totum *B*.

tonius, and the latter's lieutenant-general Saxa owed it to his sword that he did not fall into their hands. At length Syria was snatched from us, and the trouble was like to spread more widely—the enemy making conquests for themselves on the pretence of helping others—had not Ventidius, another lieutenant-general of Antonius, with marvellous good luck severely defeated the forces of Labienus and Pacorus himself and all the Parthian cavalry over the whole area between the Euphrates and the Orontes. The defeated force numbered more than 20,000. The defeat was not inflicted without a stratagem on the part of the general, who, under a pretence of panic, allowed the enemy to approach so close to the camp that he prevented them from making use of their arrows by depriving them of room to shoot. The king died fighting with great gallantry. After his head had been carried round the cities which had revolted, Syria was recovered without further fighting. Thus we obtained compensation for the disaster of Crassus by the slaughter of Pacorus.

XX. The Parthian War under Antonius

10. Now that the Parthians and Romans had made trial of one another, and Crassus and Pacorus had given proof of the strength of either side, friendship was renewed on the basis of mutual respect, and a treaty actually concluded with the king by Antonius himself. But such was the exceeding vanity of the man that, in his desire for fresh titles of honour, he longed to have the Araxes and Euphrates inscribed beneath his statues, and, without any pretext or design and without even

consilio ac ne imaginaria quidem belli indictione,
quasi hoc quoque ex arte ducis esset obrepere,
3 relicta repente Syria in Parthos impetum facit.
Gens praeter armorum fiduciam callida simulat
trepidationem et in campos fugam. Et hic statim
quasi victor sequebatur, cum subito nec magna
manus ex inproviso et iam in[1] fessos via sub vespere
velut nimbus erupit. Missis undique sagittis duas[2]
4 legiones operuerunt. Nihil acciderat in compara-
tionem cladis, quae in posterum diem inminebat,
nisi intervenisset deum miseratio. Unus ex clade
Crassiana Parthico habitu castris adequitat et salute
Latine data, cum fidem ipso sermone fecisset, quid
5 inmineret edocuit; iam adfuturum cum omnibus
copiis regem; irent retro peterentque montis: sic
quoque hostem fortasse non defore. Atque ita
secuta est minor vis hostium quam inminebat;
6 adfuit tamen. Deletae reliquae copiae forent, nisi
urguentibus telis in modum grandinis quidam forte
quasi docti procubuissent in genua milites, et elatis
supra capita scutis caesorum speciem[3] praebuissent.
7 Tunc Parthus arcus inhibuit. Dein rursus cum se

[1] in *om. B.* [2] duas: suas *B.*
[3] speciem: specie *B.*

a pretended declaration of war, just as if it were part of the art of generalship to attack by stealth, he left Syria and made a sudden attack upon the Parthians. The Parthians, who were crafty as well as confident in their arms, pretended to be panic-stricken and to fly across the plains. Antonius immediately followed them, thinking that he had already won the day, when suddenly a not very large force of the enemy unexpectedly burst forth, like a storm of rain, upon his troops in the evening when they were weary of marching, and overwhelmed two legions with showers of arrows from all sides. No disaster had ever occurred comparable with that which threatened the Romans on the following day, if the gods in pity had not intervened. A survivor from the disaster of Crassus dressed in Parthian costume rode up to the camp, and having uttered a salutation in Latin and thus inspired trust by speaking their language, informed them of the danger that was threatening them. The king, he said, would soon be upon them with all his forces; they ought, therefore, to retreat and make for the mountains, though, even so, they would probably have no lack of enemies to face. The result was that a smaller body of the enemy than was anticipated came up with them. However, it did come up with them, and the rest of their forces would have been destroyed, had not some of the soldiers, as though they had been drilled to it, by chance kneeled down, when the missiles fell like hail upon them, and raising their shields above their heads presented the appearance of dead men; whereupon the Parthians refrained from further use of their bows. Then, when the Romans rose up again,

Romani extulissent, adeo res miraculo fuit, ut unus
ex barbaris miserit vocem "Ite et bene valete,
Romani! Merito vos victores fama gentium loqui-
tur, qui Parthorum tela fugistis." Non minor [1] ex
8 via postea quam ab hostibus accepta clades. Infesta
primum siti regio, tum quibusdam salmacidae
infestiores,[2] novissime quae iam ab invalidis et
9 avide hauriebantur [3] noxiae etiam dulces fuere.
Mox et ardores per Armeniam et nives per Cappa-
dociam et utriusque caeli subita mutatio pro pesti-
10 lentia fuit. Sic vix tertia parte de sedecim legioni-
bus reliqua, cum argentum eius passim dolabris
concideretur, et [4] subinde inter moras mortem ab
gladiatore suo flagitasset egregius imperator, tandem
perfugit in Syriam, ubi incredibili quadam mentis
vaecordia ferocior aliquanto factus est, quasi vicisset,
quia evaserat.

XXI. Bellvm cvm Antonio et Cleopatra

IIII, 11 Furor Antonii quatenus per ambitum non poterat
interire, luxu et libidine extinctus est. Quippe cum
post Parthos exosus arma in otio ageret, captus
amore Cleopatrae quasi bene gestis rebus in regio
2 se sinu reficiebat. Hinc mulier Aegyptia ab ebrio
imperatore pretium libidinum Romanum imperium [5]

[1] minor: minora *B*.
[2] salmacidae infestiores *Halmius*: salmacidae fluvius in *B*: salmacidis fluvius infestior *M*.
[3] hauriebantur: hauriebat *B*: hauriebatur *NL*.
[4] et *om.* *B*.
[5] pretium—imperium *om.* *B*.

it seemed so like a miracle that one of the barbarians cried out, "Depart, Romans, and farewell; rumour deservedly calls you victorious over the nations, since you have escaped the weapons of the Parthians." The subsequent losses of the Romans on the march were quite as heavy as those inflicted by the enemy. In the first place the lack of water in the district was fatal, but still more fatal to some was the brackish water which they drank; and, finally, even fresh water was harmful when drunk with avidity by the soldiers in their already debilitated condition. Afterwards the heat in Armenia and the snows of Cappadocia and the sudden change from one climate to another were as destructive as a plague. Thus, when scarcely a third part of the sixteen legions was left, and his silver plate had been cut up with hatchets and distributed, and the famous general had on several occasions begged his sword-bearer to put him to death, he at last reached Syria in flight, where, by an extraordinary perversion of mind, he grew even more self-confident, for all the world as if, by escaping, he had won the day.

XXI. The War against Antonius and Cleopatra

11. The madness of Antonius, since it could not be laid to rest by the satisfaction of his ambition, was brought to an end by his luxury and licentiousness. After the Parthian expedition he acquired a loathing for war and lived a life of ease, and a slave to his love for Cleopatra, rested in her royal arms as though all had gone well with him. The Egyptian woman demanded the Roman Empire from the drunken general as the price of her favours; and

petit; et promisit Antonius, quasi facilior[1] esset
3 Partho Romanus. Igitur coepit non sibi domina-
tionem parare nec tacite, sed patriae, nominis, to-
gae, fascium oblitus totus in monstrum illud ut
mente, ita amictu[2] quoque cultuque desciverat.
Aureum in manu baculum, in latere acinaces,
purpurea vestis ingentibus obstricta gemmis: dia-
4 dema deerat, ut regina rex et ipse frueretur. Ad
primam novorum motuum famam Caesar a Brundisio
traiecerat, ut venienti bello occurreret, positisque
castris in Epiro omne litus Actiacum, Leucada[3]
insulam montemque Leucaten et Ambracii sinus
5 cornua infesta classe succinxerat. Nobis quadrin-
gentae amplius naves, ducentae[4] minus hostium;
sed numerum magnitudo pensabat. Quippe a senis[5]
in novenos remorum ordines, ad hoc turribus atque
tabulatis adlevatae castellorum vel urbium specie,
non sine gemitu maris et labore ventorum fere-
6 bantur; quae quidem ipsa moles exitio fuit. Cae-
saris naves a binis remigum in senos nec amplius
ordines creverant; itaque habiles in omnia quae
usus posceret, ad impetus et recursus flexusque
capiendos, illas graves et ad omnia praepeditas
singulas plures adortae missilibus, simul rostris, ad
7 hoc ignibus iactis ad arbitrium[6] dissipavere. Nec
ulla re[7] magis hostilium copiarum apparuit magni-

[1] facilior: felicior *B.*
[2] amictu *Freinshemius*: animo *codd.*
[3] Leucada *Rossbachius*: leucadam *B.*
[4] non *post* ducentae *codd.*, *del. Titzius.*
[5] a senis: adenis *B.* [6] ad arbitrium *om. B.*
[7] re: res *B.*

this Antonius promised her, as though the Romans were more easily conquered than the Parthians. He, therefore, began to aim at sovereignty—though not for himself—and that in no secret manner; but, forgetful of his country, his name, his toga and the emblems of his office, he soon completely degenerated into the monster which he became, in feeling as well as in garb and dress. In his hand was a golden sceptre, at his side a scimitar; he wore a purple robe studded with huge gems; a crown only was lacking to make him a king dallying with a queen. At the first rumour of his latest proceedings Caesar had crossed over from Brundisium to meet the approach of war, and, pitching his camp in Epirus, had surrounded all the shore of Actium, the island of Leucas, Mount Leucate and the promontories enclosing the Ambracian Gulf with a formidable fleet. We had more than four hundred ships, the enemy less than two hundred; but their size compensated for their numerical inferiority. For having from six to nine banks of oars and also rising high out of the water with towers and platforms so as to resemble castles or cities, they made the sea groan and the wind labour as they moved along. Their very size, indeed, was fatal to them. Caesar's ships had from two to six banks of oars and no more; being, therefore, easily handled for any manœuvre that might be required, whether for attacking, backing water or tacking, they scattered at their will the opposing vessels, which were clumsy and in every respect unwieldy, several of them attacking a single ship with missiles and with their beaks, and also with firebrands hurled into them. The vastness of the enemy's forces was never more

tudo quam post victoriam. Quippe inmensae classis
naufragium bello factum toto mari fluitabat, Ara-
bumque et Sabaeorum et mille Asiae gentium
spolia purpura auroque inlita adsidue mota ventis
8 maria revomebant.[1] Prima dux fugae regina cum
aurea puppe veloque purpureo in altum dedit. Mox
9 secutus Antonius, sed instare vestigiis Caesar.
Itaque nec praeparata in Oceanum fuga nec munita
praesidiis utraque Aegypti cornua, Paraetonium
atque Pelusium, profuere; prope manu tenebantur.
Prior ferrum occupavit Antonius, regina ad pedes
Caesaris provoluta temptavit oculos ducis. Frustra
quidem; nam pulchritudo infra[2] pudicitiam princi-
10 pis fuit. Nec illa de vita, quae offerebatur, sed de
parte regni laborabat. Quod ubi desperavit a
principe servarique se triumpho vidit, incautiorem
nancta custodiam in mausoleum se (sepulchra re-
11 gum[3] sic[4] vocant) recepit.[5] Ibi maximos, ut
solebat, induta cultus in referto odoribus solio
iuxta suum se conlocavit Antonium, admotisque
ad venas serpentibus sic morte quasi somno soluta[6]
est.

IIII, 12 Hic finis armorum civilium: reliqua adversus
exteras gentes, quae districto circa mala sua[7]
2 imperio diversis orbis emicabant. Nova quippe pax,

[1] revomebant: removebant *B.*
[2] infra *Aldus*: intra *codd.*
[3] regum: regem *B.* [4] sic *om. B.*
[5] recepit: recipit *BNL.*
[6] soluta: resoluta *cod. Iordanis Polling.*: victa *B.*
[7] districto circa mala sua: destricto circa asa sua *B.*

[1] Plutarch (*vit. Ant.* 89) tells us that a project was discussed of dragging the Egyptian fleet over the Isthmus of Suez into the Red Sea and escaping to found a new kingdom.

apparent than after the victory; for, as a result of the battle, the wreckage of the huge fleet floated all over the sea, and the waves, stirred by the winds, continually yielded up the purple and gold-bespangled spoils of the Arabians and Sabaeans and a thousand other Asiatic peoples. The queen led the retreat, putting out into the open sea in her golden vessel with purple sails. Antonius soon followed her, but Caesar was hard upon his tracks. And so neither their preparations for flight into the Ocean,[1] nor their occupation of the two promontories of Egypt, Paraetonium and Pelusium, with garrisons availed them aught; they were almost within Caesar's grasp. Antonius was the first to seize the sword of a suicide; the queen, casting herself at Caesar's feet, tried to attract his glances, but in vain, for her beauty was unable to prevail over his self-control. Her efforts were aimed not at saving her life, which was freely offered to her, but at obtaining a portion of her kingdom. Despairing of winning this from Caesar and perceiving that she was being reserved to figure in his triumph, profiting by the carelessness of her guard, she betook herself to the Mausoleum, as the royal sepulchre is called. There, having put on the elaborate raiment which she was wont to wear, she placed herself by the side of her beloved Antonius in a coffin filled with rich perfumes, and applying serpents to her veins thus passed into death as into a sleep.

12. Thus the civil wars came to an end; the other wars were waged against foreign nations and broke out in different quarters of the world while the empire was distracted by its own troubles. Peace was a new state of affairs, and the proud and

necdum adsuetae frenis servitutis tumidae gentium inflataeque cervices ab inposito nuper iugo resilie-
3 bant. Ad septentrionem conversa ferme plaga ferocius agebat, Norici, Illyrii, Pannonii, Delmatae, Moesi,[1] Thraces et Daci,[2] Sarmatae atque Germani.

XXII. Bellvm Noricvm

4 Noricis animos Alpes dabant, quasi in rupes et nives bellum non posset ascendere; sed omnes illius cardinis populos, Breunos, Vcennos[3] atque Vindelicos, per privignum suum Claudium Drusum pacavit.
5 Quae fuerit Alpinarum gentium feritas, facile est vel per mulieres ostendere, quae deficientibus telis infantes suos adflictos humi[4] in ora militum adversa miserunt.

XXIII. Bellvm Illyricvm

6 Illyrii quoque sub Alpibus agunt imasque valles earum et quaedam quasi claustra custodiunt abruptis torrentibus inplicata. In hos expeditionem ipse
7 sumpsit fierique pontes imperavit. Hic et aquis et hoste turbantibus, cunctanti ad ascensum militi scutum de manu rapuit et viam primus ingressus est. Tum agmine secuto cum subrutus multitudine pons succidisset, saucius[5] manibus et cruribus,

[1] Moesi: misi *B.* [2] Daci: claci *B.*
[3] Breunos, Vcennos *Rossbachius*: brennos, cennos *B.*
[4] humi I, *om. B.*
[5] saucius *Aldus*: sauciis *BI.*

haughty necks of the nations, not yet accustomed to the reins of servitude, revolted against the yoke recently imposed upon them. It was in particular the northern region, where dwelt the Noricans, the Illyrians, the Pannonians, the Dalmatians, the Moesians, the Thracians and Dacians, the Sarmatians and Germans, that showed the most spirit.

XXII. The Norican War

The Alps gave confidence to the Noricans, who imagined that war could not reach their rocks and snows; but Caesar, by the hand of his stepson Claudius Drusus, subdued all the nations in that quarter, the Breuni, the Ucenni and the Vindelici. How savage these Alpine peoples were is proved by the action of their women, who, when missiles failed, dashed out the brains of their own children against the ground and hurled them in the faces of the soldiers.

XXIII. The Illyrian War

The Illyrians also live at the foot of the Alps and keep watch over the depths of their valleys and the barriers formed there by the windings of precipitous torrents. Caesar himself undertook an expedition against them and gave orders for the building of bridges. It was here that, in the confusion caused by the water and the enemy, he snatched a shield from the hand of a soldier who was hesitating to mount the bridge, and was the first to cross. When the army followed him and the bridge had collapsed, broken down by the number of persons upon it, Caesar, wounded in the hands and legs, his comeli-

speciosior[1] sanguine et ipso periculo augustior[2] terga hostium percecidit.

XXIIII. Bellvm Pannonicvm

8 Pannonii duobus acribus fluviis, Dravo Savoque vallantur. Populati proximos intra ripas se recipiebant. In hos domandos Vinnium misit. Caesi
9 sunt in utrisque fluminibus. Arma victorum non ex more belli cremata, sed rupta[3] sunt et in profluentem[4] data, ut Caesaris nomen eis qui resistebant sic nuntiaretur.

XXV. Bellvm Delmaticvm

10 Delmatae plerumque sub silvis agebant; unde in
11 latrocinia promptissimi. Hos iam pridem Marcius consul incensa urbe Delminio[5] quasi detruncaverat, postea Asinius Pollio gregibus, armis, agris multaverat—hic secundus orator—sed Augustus perdo-
12 mandos Vibio mandat, qui efferum genus fodere terras coegit aurumque venis repurgare; quod alioquin gens omnium stupidissima[6] eo studio, ea diligentia anquirit,[7] ut illud in usus suos eruere videantur.

[1] speciosior: specior *B*: speciosiore *N*.
[2] augustior: auctior *BI*.
[3] rupta *Rossbachius*: capta *codd.*
[4] profluentem: profluente *B*: profluentes *NL*.
[5] Delminio: deiminio *B*.
[6] stupidissima *Graevius*: cupidissima *codd.*
[7] anquirit *Vinetus*: adquirit *codd.*

ness enhanced by his blood and his dignity by his very danger, dealt the enemy a heavy blow in the rear.

XXIIII. The Pannonian War

The Pannonians are protected by two swiftly-flowing rivers, the Drave and the Save; after ravaging the territory of their neighbours, they used to withdraw behind the banks of these streams. Caesar sent Vinnius to subdue them, and they were defeated on both rivers. The arms of the conquered enemy were not burnt, as was the usual custom in war, but broken to pieces and hurled into the current, that the fame of Caesar might thus be announced to those who were still resisting.

XXV. The Dalmatian War

The Dalmations for the most part lived in the forests, whence they frequently made predatory raids. Marcius the consul had already[1] crippled them by burning Delminium, their capital; afterwards Asinius Pollio—the second greatest of Roman orators[2]—had deprived them of their flocks, arms and territory; Augustus entrusted the task of completely subjugating them to Vibius, who forced this savage people to dig the earth and to melt from its veins the gold, which this otherwise most stupid of peoples seeks with such zeal and diligence that you would think they were extracting it for their own purposes.

[1] In 156 B.C.

[2] *i.e.* second only to Cicero, with whom he is compared by Quintilian, x. 1, 113. Some commentators regard *hic secundus orator* as a gloss.

XXVI. Bellvm Moesicvm[1]

13 Moesi[2] quam feri, quam truces fuerint, quam
ipsorum etiam barbari barbarorum horribile dictu
14 est. Unus ducum ante aciem postulato silentio
"qui vos estis?" inquit. Responsum invicem
15 "Romani gentium domini." Et ille "ita" inquit
"fiet, si nos viceritis." Accepit omen Marcus[3]
Crassus. Illi statim ante aciem inmolato equo
concepere votum, ut caesorum extis[4] ducum et
16 litarent et vescerentur. Deos audisse crediderim:
nec tubas sustinere potuerunt. Non minimum
terroris incussit barbaris Cornidius[5] centurio satis
barbarae, efficacis tamen apud tales homines stolidi-
tatis, qui foculum gerens super cassidem, agitatum
motu corporis, flammam velut ardenti capite fundi-
tabat.

XXVII. Bellvm Thracicvm

17 Thraces antea saepe, tum maxime Rhoemetalce[6]
rege desciverant. Ille barbaros et signis militaribus
et disciplina, armis etiam Romanis adsueverat; sed
a Pisone perdomiti in ipsa captivitate rabiem osten-
dere. Quippe cum catenas morsibus temptarent,
feritatem suam ipsi puniebant.

[1] Moesicum: Mysicum *B*.
[2] Moesi N^2I: mysi *BN*.
[3] Marcus *Monach.*: marcius *BN*: martius *L*.
[4] extis: exitus *B*.
[5] Cornidius: chornidius *B*: Comidius *Mommsenus*.
[6] Rhoemetalce: rhemetalce *B*.

XXVI. The Moesian War

It is a repulsive task to describe the savagery and cruelty of the Moesians and their barbarity surpassing that of all other barbarians. One of their leaders, after calling for silence, exclaimed in front of the host, "Who are you?" And when the reply was given, "We are Romans, lords of the world," "So you will be," was the answer, "if you conquer us." Marcus Crassus accepted the omen. The Moesians immediately sacrificed a horse in front of the army and made a vow that they would offer up and feed upon the vitals of the slaughtered leaders of their enemies. I can well believe that the gods heard their boast, for they would not even endure the sound of our trumpets. No little terror was inspired in the barbarians by the centurion Cornidius, a man of rather barbarous stupidity, which, however, was not without effect upon men of similar character; carrying on the top of his helmet a pan of coals which were fanned by the movement of his body, he scattered flame from his head, which had the appearance of being on fire.

XXVII. The Thracian War

Though the Thracians had often revolted before, their most serious rising had taken place now under King Rhoemetalcis. He had accustomed the barbarians to the use of military standards and discipline and even of Roman weapons. Thoroughly subdued by Piso, they showed their mad rage even in captivity; for they punished their own savagery by trying to bite through their fetters.

XXVIII. Bellvm Dacicvm

18 Daci montibus inhaerent. Inde Cotisonis[1] regis
imperio, quotiens concretus gelu Danuvius iunxerat
19 ripas, decurrere solebant et vicina populari. Visum
est Caesari Augusto gentem aditu difficillimam summovere. Misso igitur Lentulo ultra ulteriorem perpulit ripam; citra praesidia constituta. Sic tum Dacia non victa, sed summota atque dilata[2] est.

XXVIIII. Bellvm Sarmaticvm

20 Sarmatae patentibus[3] campis inequitant. Et hos per eundem Lentulum prohibere Danuvio satis fuit. Nihil praeter nives pruinasque et silvas habent. Tanta barbaria est, ut nec intellegant pacem.

XXX. Bellvm Germanicvm

21 Germaniam quoque utinam vincere tanti non putasset! Magis turpiter amissa est quam gloriose
22 adquisita. Sed quatenus sciebat patrem[4] suum C.
Caesarem bis transvectum ponte Rhenum quaesisse bellum, in illius honorem concupierat facere provinciam; et factum erat, si barbari tam[5] vitia nostra quam imperia[6] ferre potuissent.

[1] Cotisonis: gotisoni *B.*
[2] dilata: deleta *B*: dilatata *L.*
[3] patentibus: iacentibus *B.*
[4] patrem: patroni *B.*
[5] barbari tam: barbaricam *B.*
[6] quam imperia *om. B.*

XXVIII. The Dacian War

The Dacians cling close to the mountains, whence, whenever the Danube froze and bridged itself, under the command of their King Cotiso, they used to make descents and ravage the neighbouring districts. Though they were most difficult to approach, Caesar resolved to drive back this people. He, therefore, sent Lentulus and pushed them beyond the further bank of the river; and garrisons were posted on the nearer bank. On this occasion then Dacia was not subdued, but its inhabitants were moved on and reserved for future conquest.

XXVIIII. The Sarmatian War

The Sarmatians range on horseback over wide-spreading plains. Them too it was deemed sufficient to debar from access to the Danube, and Lentulus was entrusted with this task also. Their territory consists entirely of snow, ice and forest. So barbarous are they that they do not even understand what peace is.

XXX. The German War

It could be wished that Caesar had not set such store on conquering Germany also. Its loss was a disgrace which far outweighed the glory of its acquisition. But since he was well aware that his father, Gaius Caesar, had twice crossed the Rhine by bridging it and sought hostilities against Germany, he had conceived the desire of making it into a province to do him honour. His object would have been achieved if the barbarians could have tolerated our vices as well as they tolerated our rule.

23 Missus in eam provinciam Drusus primos domuit Vsipetes, inde Tencteros[1] percurrit et Catthos. Nam Marcomannorum spoliis et insignibus quendam
24 editum tumulum in tropaei modum excoluit. Inde validissimas nationes Cheruscos Suebosque et Sicambros pariter adgressus est, qui viginti centurionibus in crucem actis hoc velut sacramento sumpserant bellum, adeo certa[2] victoriae spe, ut praedam in anticessum pactione[3] diviserint.[4] Cherusci equos,
25 Suebi aurum et argentum, Sicambri captivos elegerant; sed omnia retrorsum. Victor namque Drusus equos, pecora, torques eorum ipsosque
26 praedam divisit et vendidit; et praeterea in tutelam provinciae praesidia atque custodias ubique disposuit per Mosam flumen, per Albin, per Visurgin. In Rheni quidem ripa quinquaginta amplius castella direxit. Bormam et Gesoriacum[5] pontibus iunxit
27 classibusque firmavit. Invisum atque inaccessum in id tempus Hercynium saltum patefecit. Ea denique in Germania pax erat, ut mutati homines, alia terra, caelum ipsum mitius molliusque solito
28 videretur. Denique non per adulationem, sed ex meritis, defuncto ibi fortissimo iuvene, ipse,[6] quod numquam alias, senatus cognomen ex provincia dedit.

[1] Tencteros: cenceros *B*.

[2] certa: certae *B*.

[3] in anticessum pactione: ante pactionem *B*: inanticessum *L*.

[4] diviserint: diviserunt *B*: dividerent *L*.

[5] Gesoriacum: caesoria cum *B*: gesogiam cum *N*: genoso niam cum *L*.

Drusus was sent into the province and conquered the Usipetes first, and then overran the territory of the Tencturi and Catthi. He erected, by way of a trophy, a high mound adorned with the spoils and decorations of the Marcomanni. Next he attacked simultaneously those powerful tribes, the Cherusci, Suebi and Sicambri, who had begun hostilities after crucifying twenty of our centurions, an act which served as an oath binding them together, and with such confidence of victory that they made an agreement in anticipation for dividing the spoils. The Cherusci had chosen the horses, the Suebi the gold and silver, the Sicambri the captives. Everything, however, turned out contrariwise; for Drusus, after defeating them, divided up their horses, their herds, their necklets and their own persons as spoil and sold them. Furthermore, to secure the province he posted garrisons and guard-posts all along the Meuse, Elbe and Weser. Along the banks of the Rhine he disposed more than five hundred forts. He built bridges at Borma and Gesoriacum, and left fleets to protect them. He opened a way through the Hercynian forest, which had never before been visited or traversed. In a word, there was such peace in Germany that the inhabitants seemed changed, the face of the country transformed, and the very climate milder and softer than it used to be. Lastly, when the gallant young general had died there, the senate itself, not from flattery but as an acknowledgment of his merit, did him the unparalleled honour of bestowing upon him a surname derived from the name of a province.

---

[6] ipse *Perizonius*: ipsi *codd.*

29 Sed difficilius est provincias obtinere quam facere;
30 viribus parantur, iure retinentur. Igitur breve id
gaudium. Quippe Germani victi magis quam
domiti erant, moresque nostros magis quam arma
31 sub imperatore Druso suspiciebant; postquam ille
defunctus est, Vari Quintilli libidinem ac superbiam
haud secus quam saevitiam odisse coeperunt. Ausus
ille agere conventum, et in Catthos[1] edixerat, quasi
violentiam[2] barbarorum lictoris virgis et praeconis
32 voce posset inhibere. At illi, qui iam pridem ro-
bigine obsitos[3] enses inertesque maererent equos,
ut primum togas et saeviora armis iura viderunt,
33 duce Armenio[4] arma corripiunt; cum interim tanta
erat Varo pacis fiducia, ut ne prodita quidem[5] per
Segestem[6] unum[7] principum coniuratione com-
34 moveretur. Itaque inprovidum et nihil tale me-
tuentem ex inproviso adorti, cum ille—o securitas—ad
tribunal citaret, undique invadunt; castra rapiuntur,
35 tres legiones opprimuntur. Varus perditas res[8]
eodem quo Cannensem diem Paulus et fato est et[9]
36 animo secutus. Nihil illa caede per paludes perque
silvas cruentius, nihil insultatione barbarorum
intolerabilius, praecipue tamen in causarum patro-

[1] in Catthos (*vel* Chaucos) edixerat *Rossbachius*: incauto sedixerat *B*: incastos sedi rexerat *N*: incastris se direxerat *L*: incautius edixerat *Halmius*.

[2] violentiam: vinolentia *B*.

[3] obsitos *Rehd.*: oblitos *BN*.

[4] Armenio *NL*: ar meno *B*.

[5] prodita quidem *Iahnius*: perdita quidem aut prodita *B*.

[6] Segestem *L*: segentem *B*.

[7] unum: unius *B*.

[8] perditas res *N*: perdi castra *B*.

But it is more difficult to retain than to create provinces; they are won by force, they are secured by justice. Therefore our joy was short-lived; for the Germans had been defeated rather than subdued, and under the rule of Drusus they respected our moral qualities rather than our arms. After his death they began to detest the licentiousness and pride not less than the cruelty of Quintillius Varus. He had the temerity to hold an assembly and had issued an edict against the Catthi, just as though he could restrain the violence of barbarians by the rod of a lictor and the proclamation of a herald. But the Germans who had long been regretting that their swords were rusted and their horses idle, as soon as they saw the toga and experienced laws more cruel than arms, snatched up their weapons under the leadership of Armenius. Meanwhile Varus was so confident of peace that he was quite unperturbed even when the conspiracy was betrayed to him by Segestes, one of the chiefs. And so when he was unprepared and had no fear of any such thing, at a moment when (such was his confidence) he was actually summoning them to appear before his tribunal, they rose and attacked him from all sides. His camp was seized, and three legions were overwhelmed. Varus met disaster by the same fate and with the same courage as Paulus on the fatal day of Cannae. Never was there slaughter more cruel than took place there in the marshes and woods, never were more intolerable insults inflicted by barbarians, especially those directed

[9] Paulus et fato est et *NL*: diem potuisse fassus est ex *B*.

37 nos. Aliis oculos, aliis manus amputabant, uni os
obsutum, recisa prius lingua, quam in manu tenens
barbarus "tandem" ait "vipera sibilare desisti."
38 Ipsius quoque consulis corpus, quod militum pietas
humi abdiderat, effossum. Signa et aquilas duas
adhuc barbari possident, tertiam signifer, prius quam
in manus hostium veniret, evolsit mersamque intra
baltei sui latebras gerens in cruenta palude sic
latuit. Hac clade factum, ut imperium, quod in
39 litore Oceani non steterat,[1] in ripa Rheni fluminis
staret.

XXXI. Bellvm Gaetvlicvm

40 Haec ad septentrionem: sub meridiano tumultuatum magis quam bellatum est. Musulamos atque Gaetulos, accolas Syrtium, Cosso duce compescuit; unde illi Gaetulici nomen latius quam ipsa victoria.
41 Marmaridas atque Garamantes Quirinio[2] subigendos
dedit. Potuit et ille redire Marmaricus, sed
modestior in aestimanda victoria fuit.

XXXII. Bellvm Armenicvm

42 Ad orientem plus negotii cum Armeniis. Huc alterum ex Caesaribus, nepotibus suis, misit. Ambo

[1] non steterat *Baehrensius*: constiterat *codd.*

[2] Quirinio: quirjnio *N om. B*: curinio *L Voss. Monac. Palat.*

against the legal pleaders. They put out the eyes of some of them and cut off the hands of others; they sewed up the mouth of one of them after first cutting out his tongue, which one of the barbarians held in his hand, exclaiming, "At last, you viper, you have ceased to hiss." The body too of the consul himself, which the dutiful affection of the soldiers had buried, was disinterred. As for the standards and eagles, the barbarians possess two to this day; the third eagle was wrenched from its pole, before it could fall into the hands of the enemy, by the standard-bearer, who, carrying it concealed in the folds round his belt, secreted himself in the blood-stained marsh. The result of this disaster was that the empire, which had not stopped on the shores of the Ocean, was checked on the banks of the Rhine.

XXXI. The Gaetulian War

Such were the operations in the north; in the south there were risings rather than wars. Augustus put down the Musulami and Gaetulians who dwell near the Syrtes, through the agency of Cossus, who thus gained the name of Gaetulicus, a title more extensive than his actual victory warranted. He entrusted the subjugation of the Marmarides and Garamantes to Quirinius, who likewise might have returned with the title of Marmaricus, had he not been too modest in estimating his victory.

XXXII. The Armenian War

In the east the Armenians caused more trouble. Hither Caesar sent one of the Caesars, his grandsons.

fato breves, sed alter inglorius. Massiliae quippe
morbo Lucius solvitur, in Syria Gaius ex volnere
occubuit, cum Armeniam[1] ad Parthos se subtra-
43 hentem in ius[2] recepit. Armenios victo rege
Tigrane[3] in hoc unum servitutis genus Pompeius
adsueverat, ut rectores a nobis acciperent. Inter-
missum ergo ius per hunc recuperatum non in-
44 cruento, nec multo[4] tamen certamine. Quippe
Dones, quem rex Artageris[5] praefecerat, simulata
proditione adortus virum intentum libello, quem ut
thensaurorum rationes continentem ipse porrexerat,
stricto repente ferro subiit. Et tunc quidem Caesar
45 recreatus[6] est ex volnere in tempus, sed * * *.[7]
Ceterum barbarus undique infesto exercitu oppressus
gladio et pyra, in quam se percussus[8] inmisit,[9] super-
stiti etiam nunc Caesari satisfecit.

XXXIII. Bellvm Cantabricvm et Astvricvm

46 Sub occasu pacata erat fere omnis Hispania, nisi
quam Pyrenaei desinentis scopulis inhaerentem
citerior adluebat[10] Oceanus. Hic duae validissimae

[1] Armeniam: armenia *B*.
[2] in ius *Iahnius*: ipsos *B*.
[3] victo rege Tigrane: victor gentis Tigranen *B*.
[4] multo: ulto *B*: multa *L*.
[5] Artageris *G. Vossius*: artaxer ser par this *B*: artaxatis *N*: artasatis *L*.
[6] recreatus—profundo (60, 6) *scripsit* B^1.
[7] *lacunam indicavit Iahnius.*
[8] percussus: percussu* B^1.
[9] inmisit: summisit B^1: immisit *L*.
[10] adluebat: abluebat B^1: alluebat *L*.

Both were cut off in early life, one without having distinguished himself; for Lucius died of disease at Marseilles, while Gaius perished in Syria by a wound received while recovering Armenia, which was transferring its allegiance to Parthia. Pompeius, after defeating Tigranes, had accustomed the Armenians to a state of bondage which merely obliged them to accept rulers appointed by Rome. The exercise of this right, which had been interrupted, was re-established by Gaius Caesar after a struggle which, though not serious, involved some loss of life. For Dones, whom the king had appointed governor of Artagerae,[1] pretending to betray his master, attacked the general while he was engaged in examining a document, which he had himself handed to him as containing a list of the treasures, and suddenly struck him with his drawn sword. Caesar recovered from the wound for the time being but . . .[2] His barbarian assailant, beset on all sides by the angry soldiers, made atonement to the still surviving Caesar; for he fell by the sword, and was burnt upon the pyre on which he hurled himself after he was stabbed.

XXXIII. The War against the Cantabrians and Asturians

In the west almost all Spain had been subjugated, except that part which adjoins the cliffs where the Pyrenees end and is washed by the nearer waters of the Ocean.[3] Here two powerful nations,

[1] The Artageira of Strabo XI, p. 529.

[2] There is a lacuna in the text at this point.

[3] The Ocean being regarded as a broad stream, the Atlantic shores of Spain form its nearer bank.

gentes, Cantabri et Astures, inmunes imperii agitabant.
47 Cantabrorum et prior et acrior et magis pertinax in
rebellando animus fuit, qui non contenti libertatem
suam defendere proximis etiam imperitare tempta-
bant Vaccaeosque et Turmogos et Autrigonas[1]
48 crebris incursionibus fatigabant. In hos igitur,
quia[2] vehementius agere nuntiabatur, non est
mandata expeditio, sed sumpta. Ipse venit Segi-
samam, castra posuit, inde tripertito exercitu totam
Cantabriam amplexus efferam gentem ritu ferarum
49 quasi quadam cogebat indagine. Nec ab Oceano
quies, cum infesta classe ipsa quoque terga hostium
caederentur. Primum adversus Cantabros sub
moenibus Bergidae proeliatum. Hinc statim fuga
in eminentissimum Vindium[3] montem, quo maria
prius Oceani quam arma Romana ascensura esse
50 crediderant. Tertio Aracelium oppidum magna
vi repugnat;[4] captum tamen. Postremo fuit Medulli
montis obsidio, quem perpetua decem et octo milium
fossa conprehensum undique simul adeunte Romano
postquam extrema barbari vident, certatim igne,
ferro inter epulas[5] venenoque, quod ibi volgo taxo[6]
exprimitur, praecepere[7] mortem, seque pars maior
a[8] captivitate, quae morte gravior ad id tempus
51 indomitis videbatur, vindicaverunt. Haec per

[1] Autrigonas *Salmasius*: aurigantes B^1: aurigonas *NL*.
[2] quia: qua B^1.
[3] Vindium: vinnium B^1.
[4] repugnat: oppugnat B^1.
[5] inter epulas *om.* B^1.
[6] taxo *scripsi*: taxeo B^1.
[7] praecipere *N*: praecoepere B^1.
[8] maior a: magis (*om.* a) B^1.

the Cantabrians and the Asturians, lived in freedom from the rule of Rome. The Cantabrians rose first and were more energetic and obstinate in their rebellion; not content with defending their liberty, they tried also to dominate their neighbours and harassed the Vaccaei, the Turmogi and the Autrigones by frequent raids. The news of their unusual activity induced Caesar himself to undertake an expedition instead of entrusting it to another. He came personally to Segisama, where he pitched his camp, and then, dividing his army into three parts, enveloped the whole of Cantabria and enclosed its fierce people like wild beasts in a net. Nor did he give them any peace on the side of the Ocean; for they were also assailed in the rear by the attacks of his fleet. The first battle against the Cantabrians was fought under the walls of Bergida. From here they fled to the lofty peak of Mount Vindius, to which they had thought the Roman army was less likely to ascend than the waters of the Ocean. Next the town of Aracelium offered a stout resistance, but was eventually taken. The last incident was the siege of Mount Medullus. When it had been surrounded by a continuous earthwork extending over eighteen miles and the Romans were closing in upon it on every side, the barbarians, seeing that their last hour had come, vied with one another in hastening on their own deaths in the midst of a banquet by fire and the sword and a poison which is there commonly extracted from the yew-tree. Thus most of them saved themselves from a captivity which was deemed more grievous than death itself by men who had hitherto never been conquered. Caesar received the news of these operations, which

Antistium[1] Furniumque[2] legatos et Agrippam
hibernans in Tarraconis[3] maritimis Caesar accepit.
52 Mox ipse praesens hos deduxit montibus, hos
obsidibus astrinxit, hos sub corona iure belli venun-
53 dedit. Digna res lauro, digna curru[4] senatui
visa est; sed iam tantus erat Caesar, ut triumpho
54 augeri contemneret. Astures per id tempus ingenti
agmine a montibus niveis descenderant. Nec
temere sumptus barbaris videbatur hic impetus;
sed positis castris apud Asturam[5] flumen trifariam
diviso agmine tria simul Romanorum adgredi
55 parant castra. Fuissetque anceps et cruentum et
utinam mutua clade certamen cum tam fortibus,
56 tam[6] subito, tam cum consilio venientibus, nisi
Brigaecini[7] prodidissent,[8] a quibus praemonitus
Carisius cum exercitu advenit. Pro victoria fuit
oppressisse consilia, sic[9] quoque non incruento
57 certamine. Reliquias fusi exercitus validissima
civitas Lancea excipit, ubi cum locis adeo certatum
est, ut, cum in captam urbem faces poscerentur, aegre
58 dux impetraverit veniam, ut victoriae Romanae
stans potius esset quam incensa monumentum.

[1] Antistium: antatium B^1: antestium *L.*
[2] Furniumque: firmumque B^1.
[3] in Tarraconis: in terra tonis B^1: intarrachonis *N*: interraconis *L.*
[4] digna curru: dignas currus B^1.
[5] Asturam: astaram B^1: scuram *NL.*
[6] tam *L Voss. Rehd.*: quam B^1.
[7] Brigaecini: dri caecini B^1: drigaecini *N*: drigenici *L.*
[8] prodidissent: providissent B^1.
[9] tamen *post* sic *add.* B^1N: *om. Iahnius.*

---

[1] This is the only sense which can be extracted from the words *utinam mutua clade* which is read by all MSS.; but *utinam* is possibly corrupt.

were carried out by Antistius and Furnius, his lieutenant-generals, and Agrippa, while he was wintering on the coast at Tarraco. Himself arriving quickly on the scene, he brought some of the inhabitants down from the mountains, secured the fidelity of others by taking hostages, and sold others, by right of conquest, into slavery. His success was considered by the senate to be worthy of a laurel crown and a triumphal chariot; but Caesar was now so mighty that he despised any glory that a triumph could bestow. The Asturians meanwhile had come down from the snow-clad mountains in a vast host. This attack seems not to have been undertaken without consideration by the barbarians; but they pitched their camp at the river Astura and, dividing their forces into three parts, prepared a simultaneous attack on the three camps of the Romans. With such brave enemies attacking suddenly and with so well-conceived a plan the struggle would have been doubtful and bloody—and I would I could think that the losses on both sides would have been equal [1] —had not the Brigaecini acted as traitors and had not Carisius arrived with his army as a result of their warnings. To have frustrated the enemy's designs meant victory, though, even so, the struggle was a bloody one. The well-fortified city of Lancea opened its gates to the remains of the defeated army; here such efforts were needed to counteract the natural advantage of the place, that when firebrands were demanded to burn the captured city, it was only with difficulty that the general won mercy for it from the soldiers, on the plea that it would form a better monument of the Roman victory if it were left standing than if it were burnt.

59 Hic finis Augusto bellicorum certaminum[1] fuit,
idem rebellandi finis Hispaniae. Certa mox fides
et aeterna pax, cum ipsorum ingenio in pacis artes[2]
promptiore, tum consilio Caesaris, qui fiduciam
montium timens in quos se recipiebant, castra sua,
60 quia in plano erant, habitare et incolere iussit; ibi
gentis esse concilium, illud observari[3] caput. Fave-
bat consilio natura regionis; circa enim omnis
aurifera[4] est et chrysocollae[5] miniique et aliorum
colorum ferax. Itaque exerceri solum iussit. Sic
Astures[6] nitentes in profundo opes suas atque
divitias, dum aliis quaerunt, nosse coeperunt.

XXXIIII. Pax Parthorvm et Consecratio Avgvsti

61 Omnibus ad occasum et meridiem pacatis gentibus,
ad septentrionem quoque, dum taxat intra Rhenum
atque Danuvium, item ad orientem intra Cyrum[7]
et Euphraten, illi quoque reliqui, qui inmunes
imperii erant, sentiebant tamen magnitudinem et
victorem[8] gentium populum Romanum[9] revere-
62 bantur. Nam et Scythae misere legatos et Sarmatae
amicitiam petentes. Seres etiam habitantesque sub
ipso sole Indi, cum gemmis et margaritis elephantos
quoque inter munera trahentes, nihil magis quam

[1] bellicorum certaminum: belli civilium certamin B^1.
[2] artes: arte B^1: partes *NL*.
[3] observari: observare B^1.
[4] aurifera: auriferae B^1.
[5] chrysocollae: chriso calle B^1.
[6] Astures N^2: astare B^1.
[7] Cyrum: ecyrum *N*: circum *L*.
[8] victorem *Aldus*: victoriam *codd.*
[9] populum Romanum *Aldus*: populi Romani *codd.*

This was the end of Augustus' campaigns as well as of the rebellion in Spain. After this we were able to rely on the loyalty of the Spaniards, and uninterrupted peace ensued as a result both of their natural disposition for the arts of peace and also of the wise measures taken by Caesar, who, dreading the confidence inspired by the mountains into which they were wont to retire, ordered them to occupy and cultivate the district in the plain where his camp had been; he urged that the council of the nation should be held there and the place regarded as the capital. The natural advantages of the place favoured his plan; for the whole district bears gold and is rich in *chrysocolla*,[1] vermilion and other pigments; he, therefore, ordered that the soil should be tilled. Thus the Astures, digging deep into the ground in search of riches for others, gained their first knowledge of their own resources and wealth.

XXXIIII. The Peace with Parthia and the Deification of Augustus

Now that all the races of the west and south were subjugated, and also the races of the north, those at least between the Rhine and the Danube, and of the east between the Cyrus and Euphrates, the other nations too, who were not under the rule of the empire, yet felt the greatness of Rome and revered its people as the conqueror of the world. For the Scythians and the Sarmatians sent ambassadors seeking friendship; the Seres[2] too and the Indians, who live immediately beneath the sun, though they

[1] A green pigment. [2] Chinese.

longinquitatem viae inputabant—quadriennium in-
pleverant; et iam[1] ipse hominum color ab alio
63 venire caelo fatebatur. Parthi quoque, quasi vic-
toriae paeniteret,[2] rapta clade Crassiana signa ultro
64 rettulere. Sic ubique certa[3] atque continua totius
generis humani aut pax fuit aut pactio,[4] aususque
tandem Caesar Augustus septingentesimo ab urbe
condita anno Ianum geminum cludere, bis ante se
clusum sub Numa rege et victa primum Carthagine.
65 Hinc conversus ad pacem pronum in omnia mala
et in luxuriam fluens saeculum gravibus severisque
legibus multis coercuit, ob haec tot facta ingentia
66 dictus imperator perpetuus et pater patriae. Trac-
tatum etiam in senatu, an, quia condidisset imperium,
Romulus vocaretur; sed sanctius et reverentius
visum est nomen Augusti, ut scilicet iam tum, dum
colit terras, ipso nomine et titulo consecraretur.

[1] iam *Mommsenus*: tamen *codd.*
[2] paeniteret *Rehd.*: pertineret *N*: permaneret *L Monac.*
[3] certa *Freinshemius*: cuncta *codd.*
[4] pactio *L Palat.*: paccio *Voss. Monac. Rehd.*: factio *N.*

---

[1] Strictly speaking the year of the closing of the temple of Janus (29 B.C.) was A.U.C. 725.

brought elephants amongst their gifts as well as precious stones and pearls, regarded their long journey, in the accomplishment of which they had spent four years, as the greatest tribute which they rendered; and indeed their complexion proved that they came from beneath another sky. The Parthians too, as though they repented of their victory, voluntarily returned the standards which they had won at the time of Crassus' defeat. Thus everywhere throughout the inhabited world there was firmly-established and uninterrupted peace or truce, and Caesar Augustus ventured at last, in the seven hundredth year since the foundation of the city,[1] to close the double doors of the temple of Janus, which had previously been shut on two occasions only, in the reign of Numa and after the first defeat of Carthage. Next, devoting himself to securing tranquillity, by many strict and severe enactments he restrained an age which was prone to every vice and readily led into luxury. For all these great achievements he was named Perpetual Imperator and Father of his Country. It was also discussed in the senate whether he should not be called Romulus, because he had established the empire; but the name of Augustus was deemed more holy and venerable, in order that, while he still dwelt upon earth, he might be given a name and title which raised him to the rank of a deity.

INDEX

OF PROPER NAMES

INDEX OF PROPER NAMES

INDEX OF PROPER NAMES

INDEX OF PROPER NAMES

INDEX OF PROPER NAMES

INDEX OF PROPER NAMES

INDEX OF PROPER NAMES

INDEX OF PROPER NAMES

INDEX OF PROPER NAMES

INDEX OF PROPER NAMES

INDEX OF PROPER NAMES

INDEX OF PROPER NAMES

INDEX OF PROPER NAMES

INDEX OF PROPER NAMES

INDEX OF PROPER NAMES

INDEX OF PROPER NAMES

INDEX OF PROPER NAMES

INDEX OF PROPER NAMES